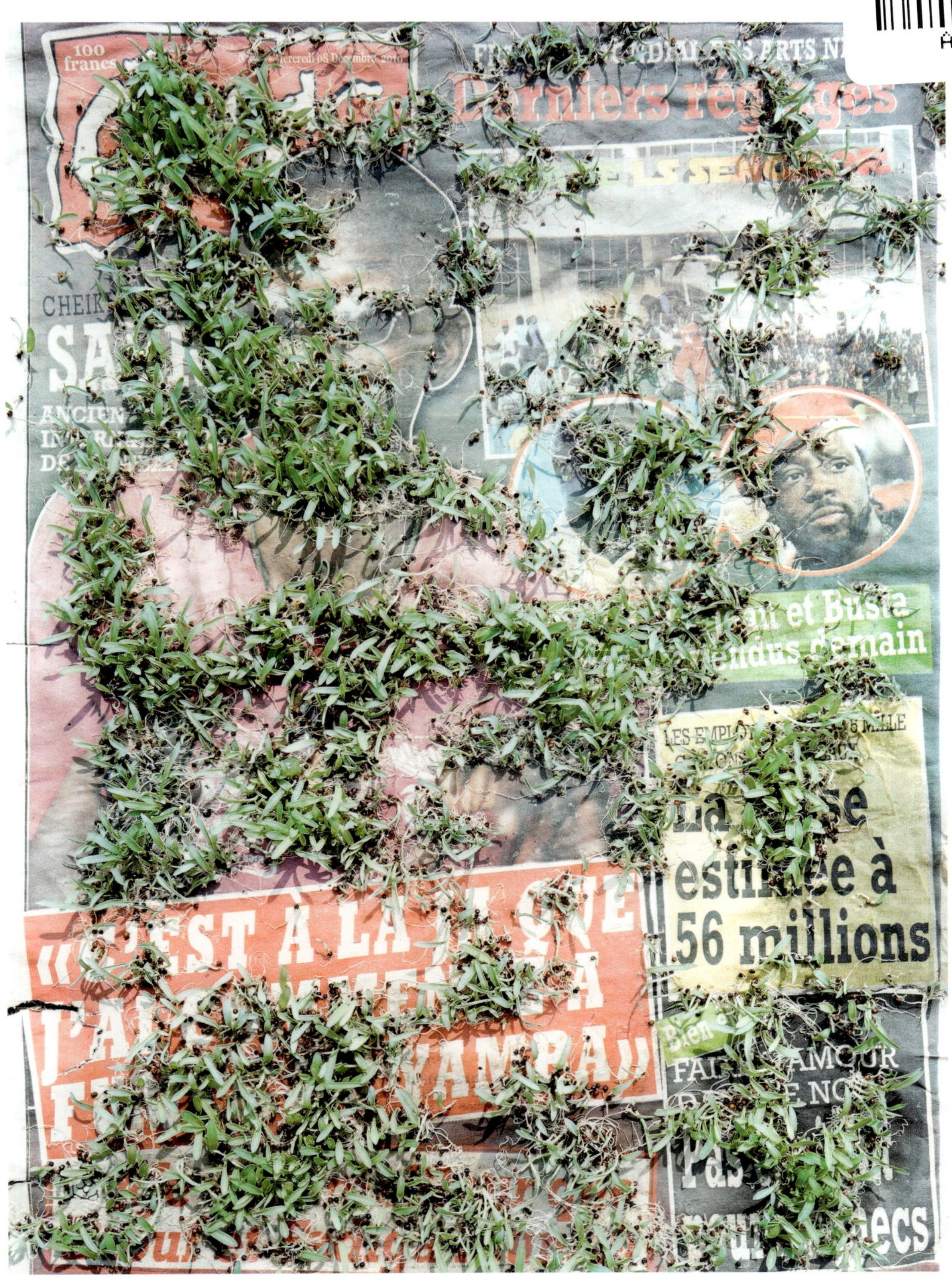
100 francs
Derniers réglages
CHEIK
SA
et Busta
endus demain
LES EMPLOI
estimée à
56 millions
«C'EST À LA
WAMPA»

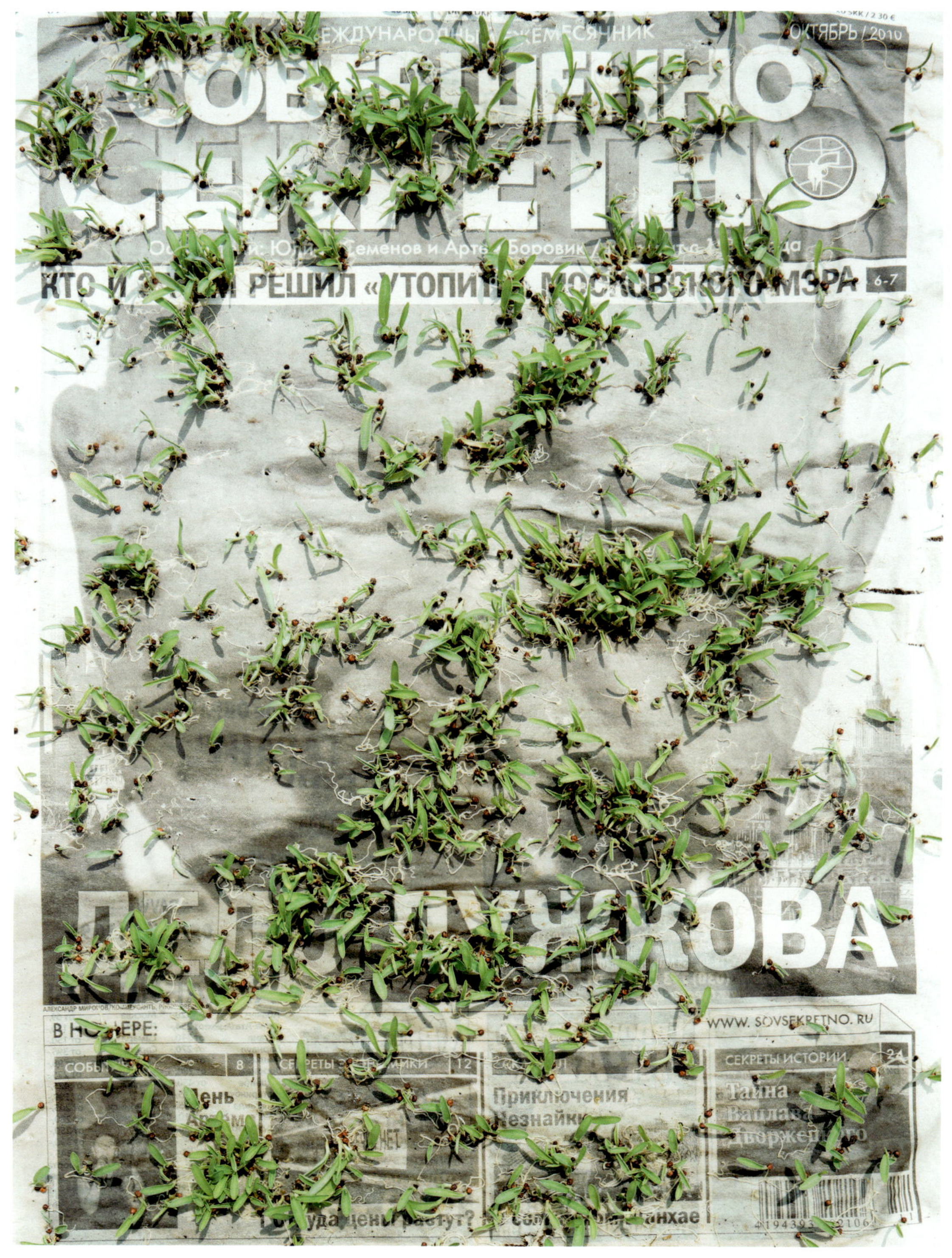
МЕЖДУНАРОДНЫЙ ЕЖЕМЕСЯЧНИК
ОКТЯБРЬ / 2010
СОВЕРШЕННО СЕКРЕТНО
КТО И ЗАЧЕМ РЕШИЛ «УТОПИТЬ» МОСКОВСКОГО МЭРА 6-7
ЛУЖКОВА
WWW.SOVSEKRETNO.RU
В НОМЕРЕ:
СЕКРЕТЫ ИСТОРИИ 24
Приключения Незнайки
Тайна Вацлава Дворжецкого

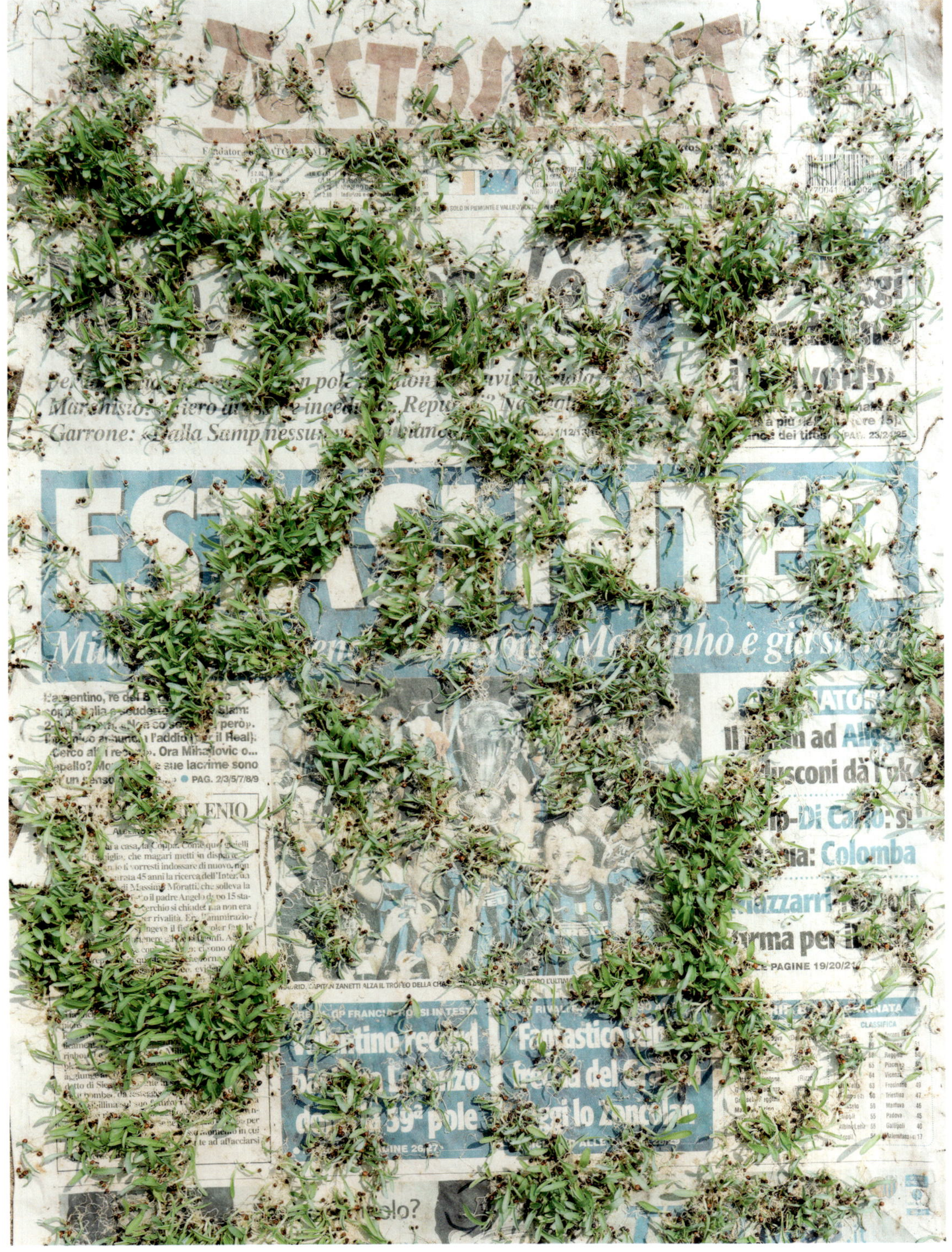

A HISTORY OF ACCUMULATION
VIVAN SUNDARAM
introduced by his gallerist
Devika Daulet-Singh

When asked about the artists represented by Photoink, I often have to explain how Vivan Sundaram fits into a program, inherently meant for either younger or forgotten photographers. Born in 1943, Vivan Sundaram's art practice has over the last forty years embraced many mediums and challenged the status quo. He abandoned canvas and paper in the late 80s and was amongst the first in his generation of artists to use sculpture, installation, photography and video in his works. He belongs to a family of artists – the legacy of his grandfather, Umrao Singh Sher-Gil, today acknowledged as the flag bearer of modernism in Indian photography and aunt, Amrita Sher-Gil, a pioneering figure in the annals of pictorial modernism, has undoubtedly shaped his art practice. In the role of an archivist-artist, Vivan exhumed photographs from family albums and shoeboxes and digitally reconstructed real and imagined narratives in photomontages collectively titled, *Re-take of Amrita* (2001-2006). It was this work that presented an extraordinary opportunity to work closely with him to resurrect the vintage archive of his grandfather, Umrao Singh Sher-Gil for Les Rencontres d'Arles 2007 photography festival in France.

In a departure from the personal, Vivan Sundaram's fascination for found objects and second hand goods has imposed itself in installations and sculptural works that he has made since 1997. The photographs presented in the following pages, titled *Trash*, re-imagines a city constructed entirely with garbage and recycled objects and revisits the growing global concern with consumption and waste. In a role recalling grand city planners, Vivan worked with rag pickers and constructed an enormous cityscape in his studio, which was then photographed from several vantage points. Master Plan offers an aerial view of the garbage city and Prospect the only real perspective view. The other photographs are a composite of views, which serve to disorient, confound and delight the onlooker. This city of entropy offers a visual confrontation with urban detritus that would have otherwise been hidden from public view and unbearable to be around.

Vivan's preoccupation with accumulation, both the personal and the discarded and the way he has refashioned one's interaction with it, makes him one of the most stimulating and lively personalities in the Indian art world.

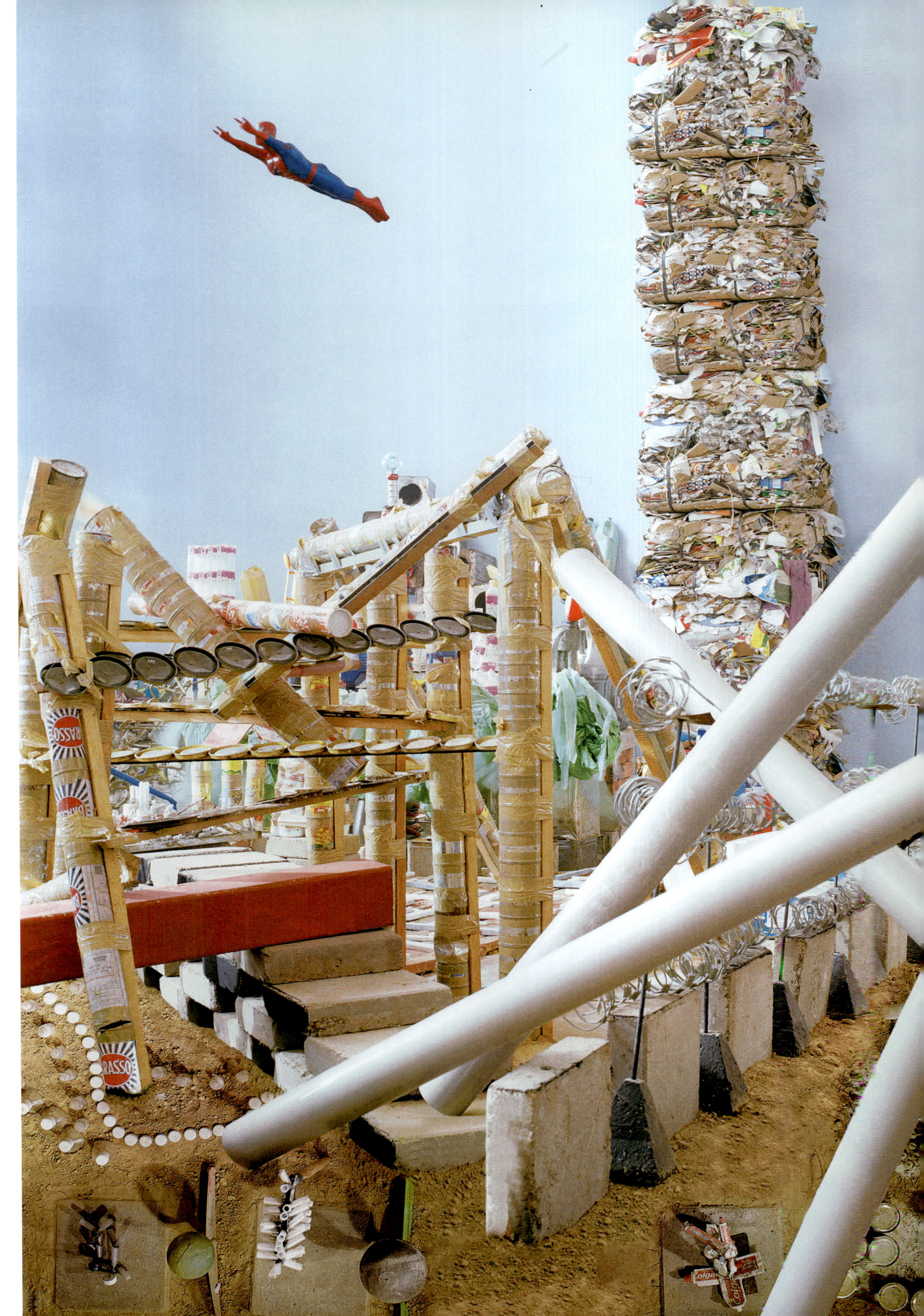

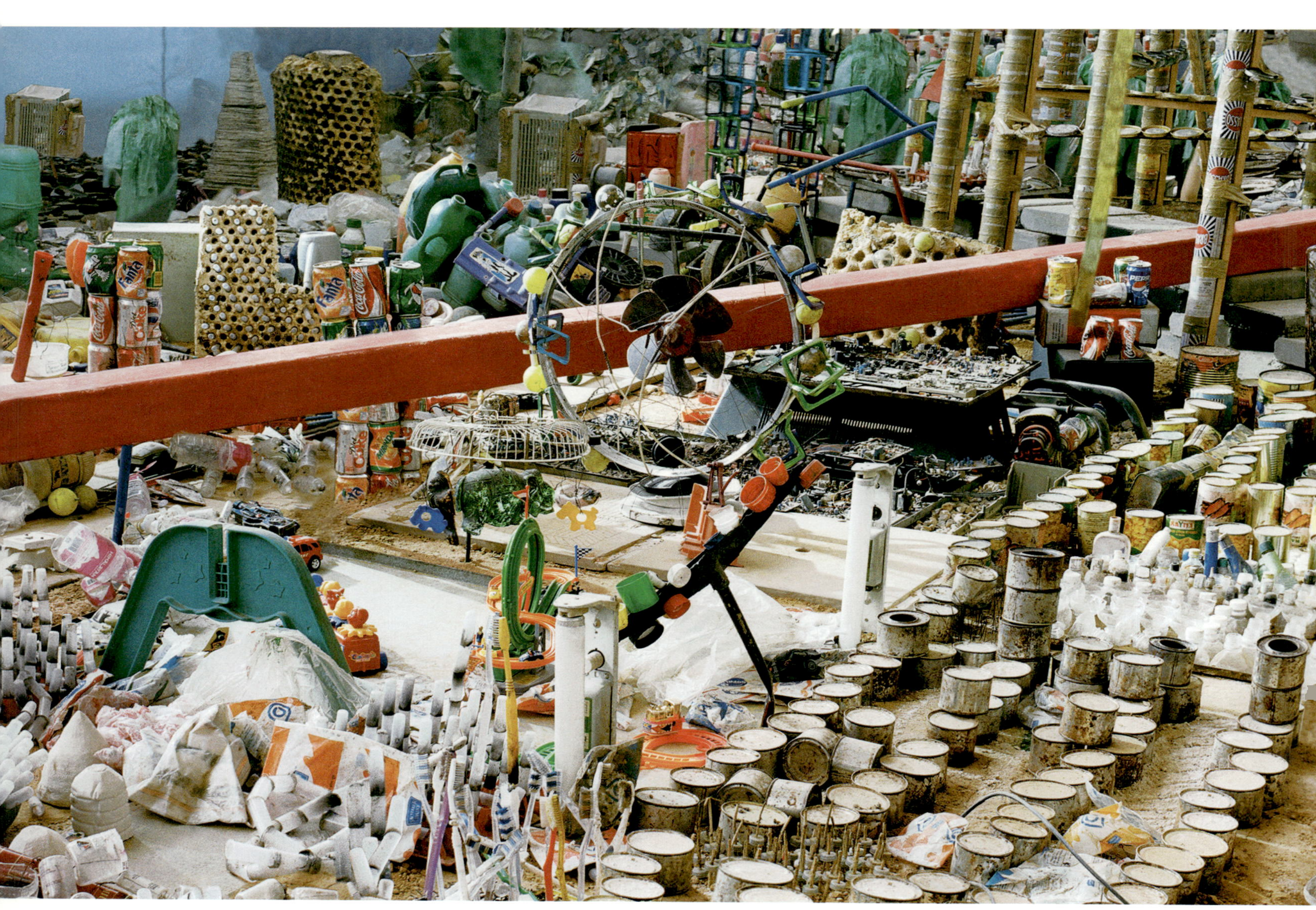

Previous page Fly, 2008, cm 152.5 x 100. *Above* Barricade (with red beam), 2008, cm 100 x 254

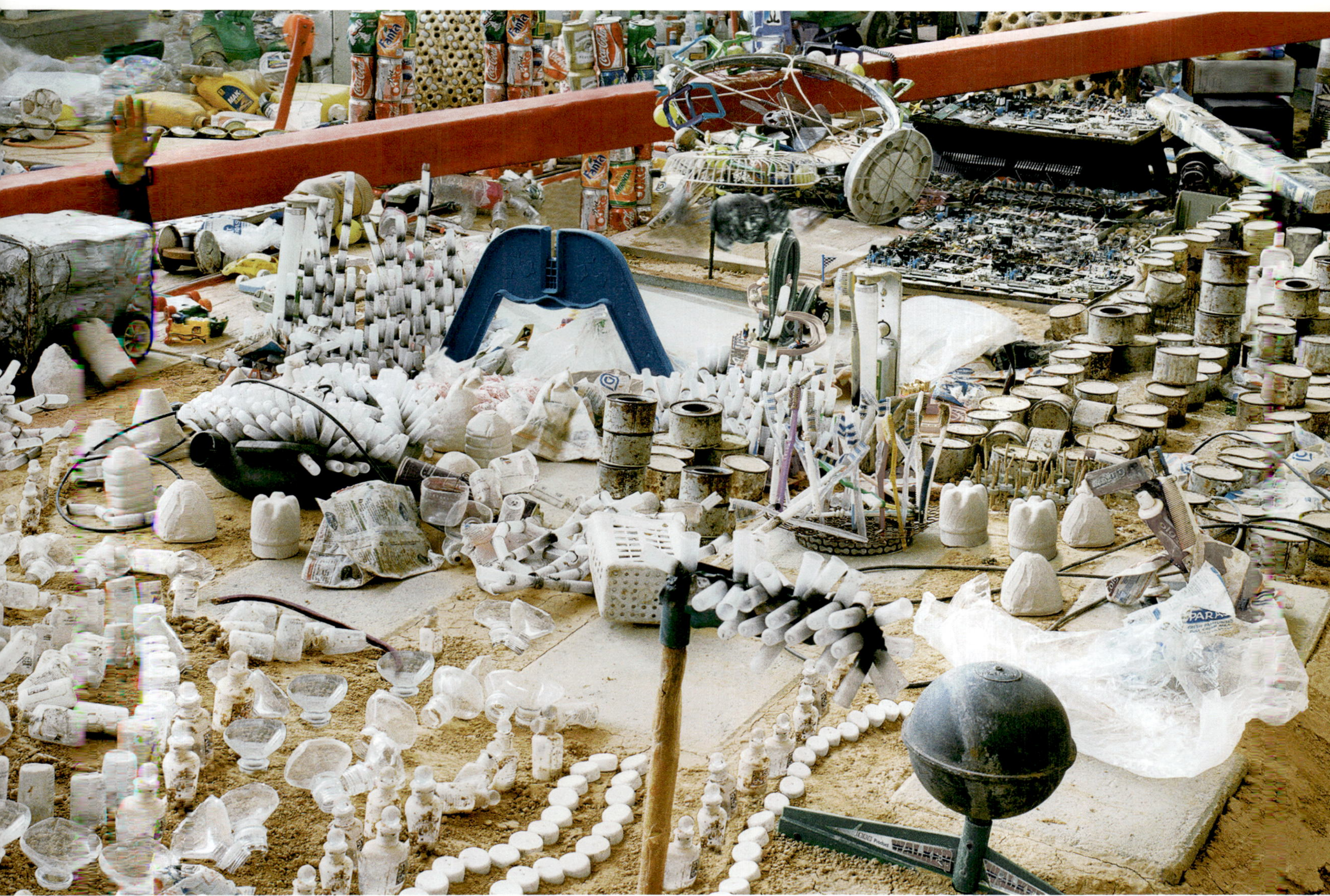

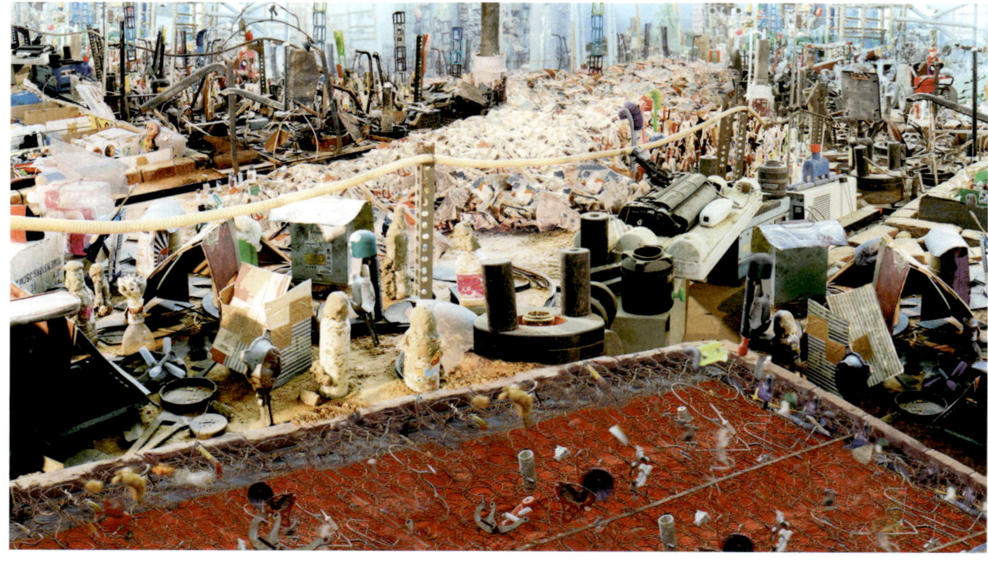

Above Barricade (with mattress), 2008, cm 98.5 x 170. *Right* Two Towers, 2008, cm 152.5 x 96.5. *Following spread* Master Plan, 2005-2008, cm 143.5 x 503. *All images archival pigment print © and courtesy the artist and Photoink, New Delhi*

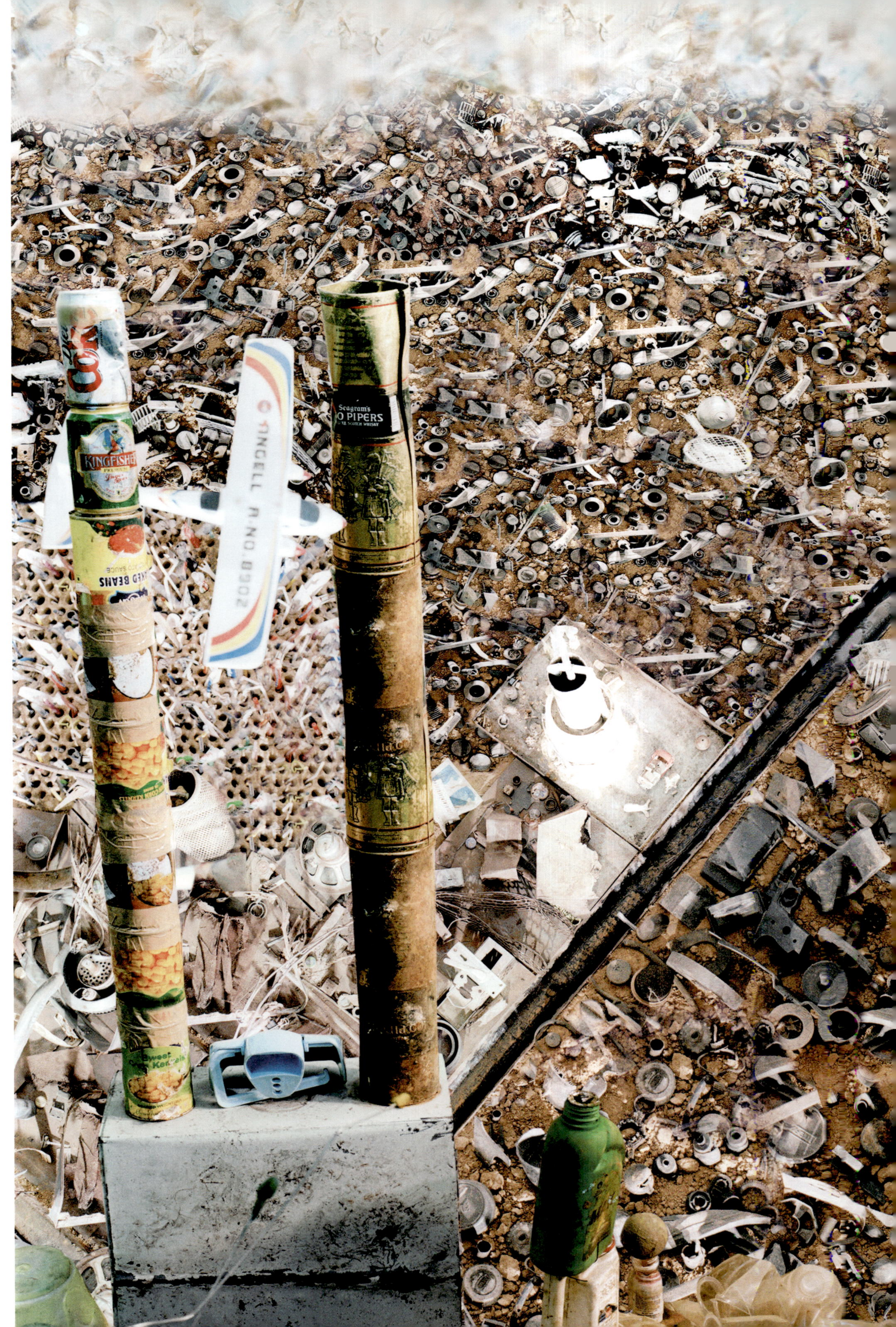

KINGFISHER
BEANS
Seagram's
O PIPERS
ANGELL R.NO.8902

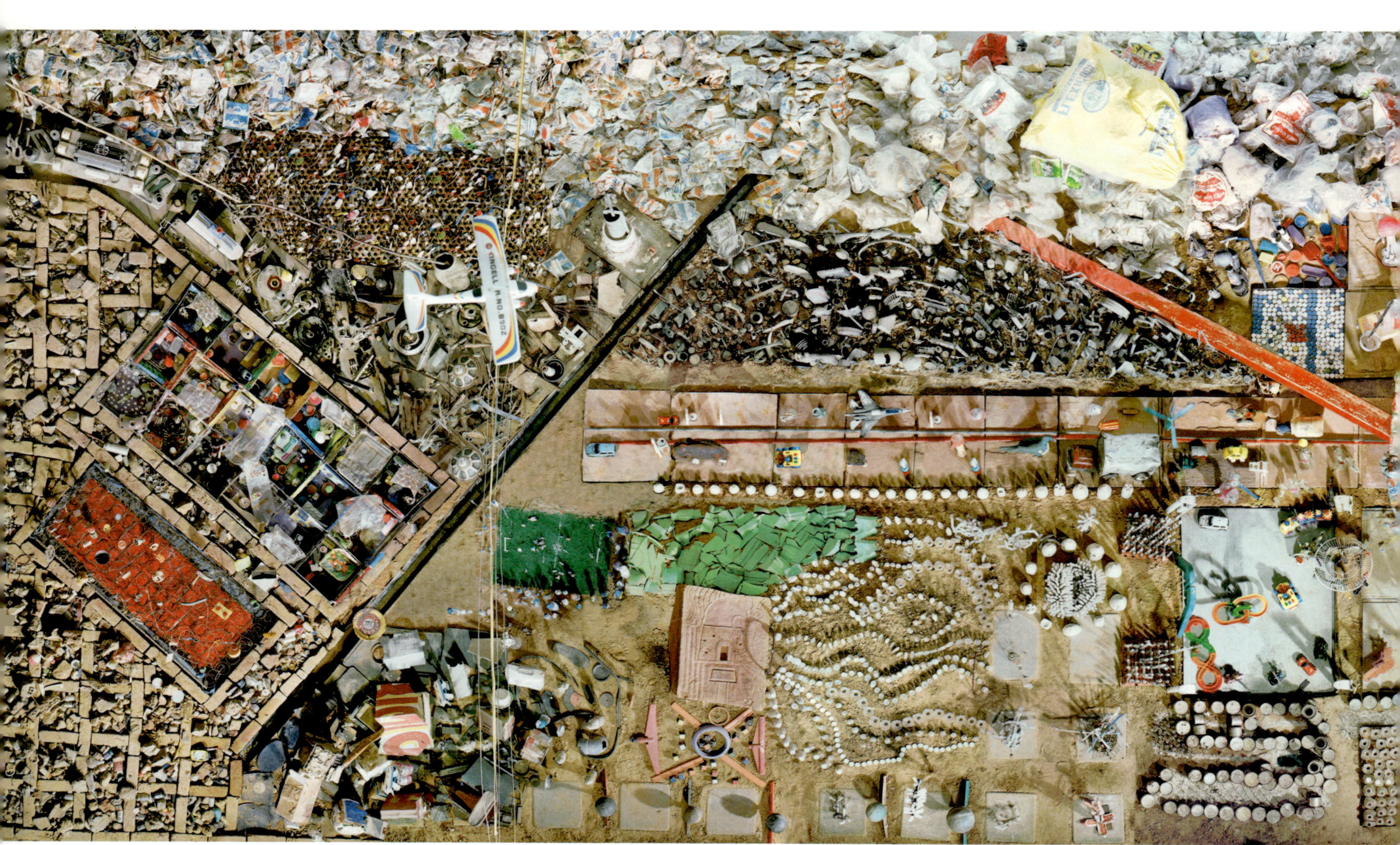

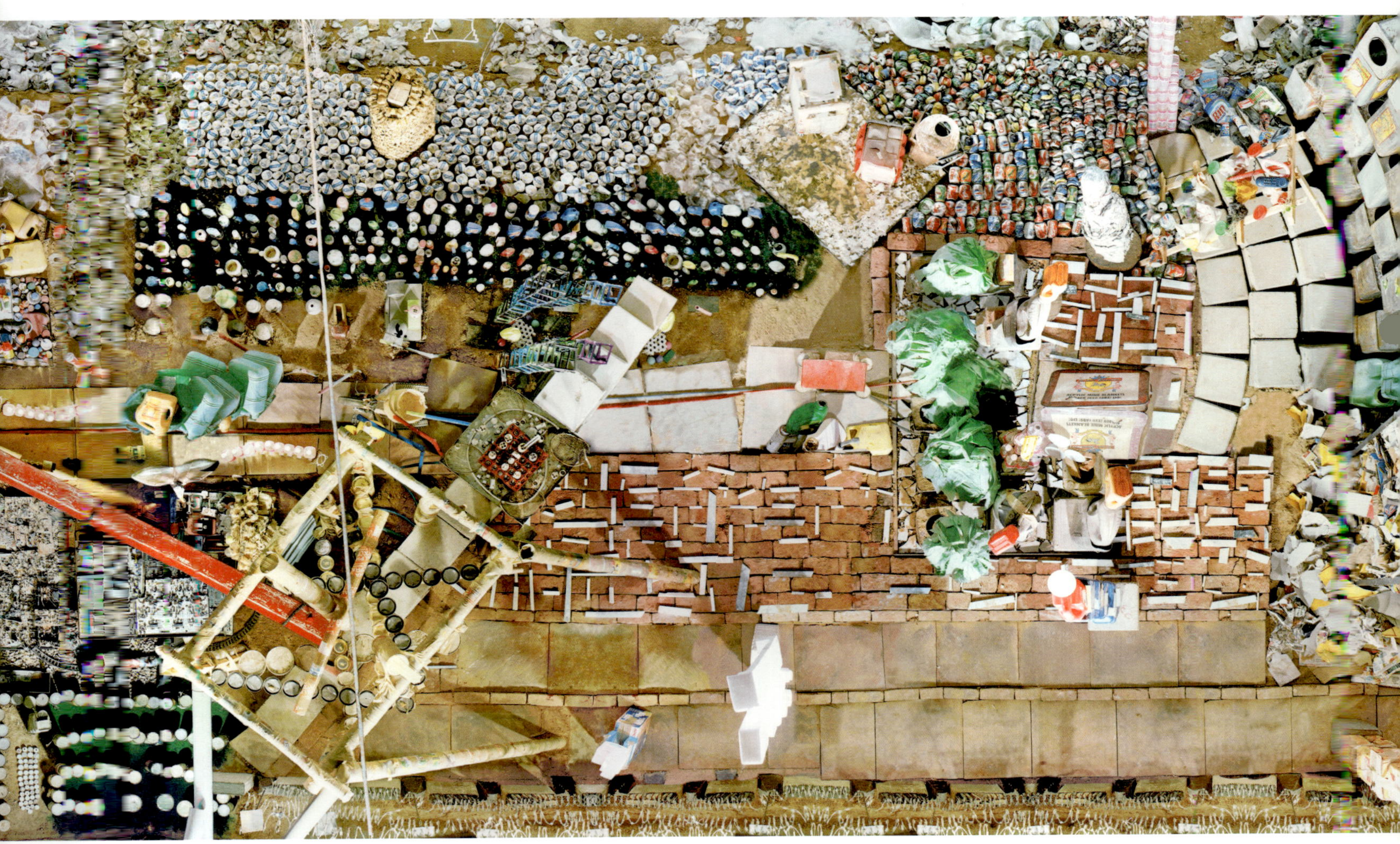

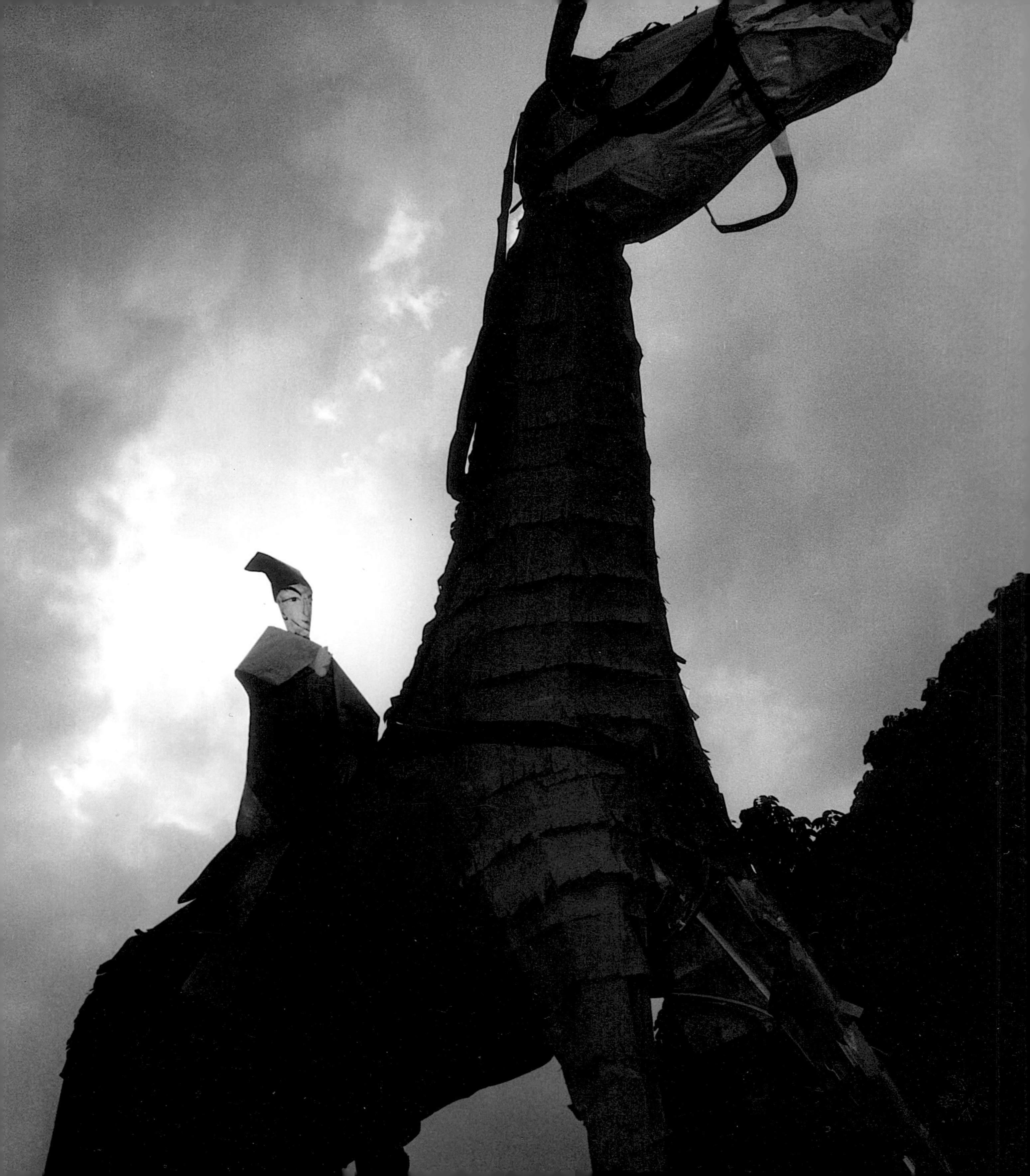

Paper Metaphors
YAN CHANGJIANG
by
Francesca Tarocco

Yan Changjiang's diverse yet coherent body of work brings to mind Susan Sontag's thoughts on the photographic enterprise and Surrealism. Sontag alludes to "the creation of a duplicate world, of a reality in the second degree, narrower but more dramatic than that perceived by natural vision" (Susan Sontag, 'Melancholy Objects', *On Photography*, 1972). In the project, *Paper Men* (1997-2007), composed of a series of photographs and a short story, Yan imbues Southern China's rural landscape, few mundane objects, and the large paper puppets traditionally burned at funerals with a powerful sense of otherness. Their previous ordinariness is transformed by the attention of the photographer.

Yan's creative dialogue with China's past was initially prompted by a chance encounter with a declining ritual tradition. His Paper Men play out a subtly humorous, melancholic, and ultimately tragic tale, echoed in the captions to each photographic tableau. At the beginning of the short story One Fine Day: The Paper Men, the narrator enters a beautiful utopian world magically concealed behind wisteria leaves in the woods of the Dragon Snake Mountain. Here peacefully live the paper people, whose skin and clothes are made of paper and whose words "sound like literature." Eventually, human beings set out to massacre them, unwilling to face a shaming comparison with the nobility of behavior and innocence of the paper people. Only a few of them survive the bloodshed, and are reduced to leading a fugitive life, away from the world of flesh men.

The paper people's encounter with the photographer/

narrator and the verbal and visual dialogues they entertain can be read as extended metaphorical musings not only on the fragility of humankind and the progressive erasure of China's traditions, but also on the decline in importance of paper and of photography itself, engulfed as they are in the unforgiving monotony and seeming inexorableness of globalization and of the digital age. Yan's images evoke China's intimate relationship with paper and bring to mind paper's intimate relationship with China's dead. The demise of such meaningful relationships is painfully foreseen. Will photography survive the death of paper? Will China survive its own amnesia?

In China, paper of a quality good enough to write on was being produced as early as the second century CE and gradually came into general use during the third and fourth century replacing bamboo wooden tablets and silk as it did so. Thanks to the technologies of paper ink and brush, Chinese manuscript culture was highly efficient. In the seventh century, China's only female emperor, the remarkable Wu Zetian, gave ulterior impulse to the widespread use of paper with the discovery of woodblock printing. Since then, printed written texts and images found a place in the daily life of China's literate elites as well as that of the illiterate or semi-literate majority. Paper 'spirit money' and objects such as those appearing in Yan's photographs have for centuries been used in funerals and death-related ceremonies and in the worship of ancestors. Such practices rest on the belief that the spirits of the dead continue to dwell in the natural world and have the power to influence the fortune and fate of the living. The goal of ancestor worship is thus to ensure the continued well-being and positive disposition of the departed towards the living. Rituals of ancestor worship most commonly consist of offerings to the deceased to provide for their welfare in the

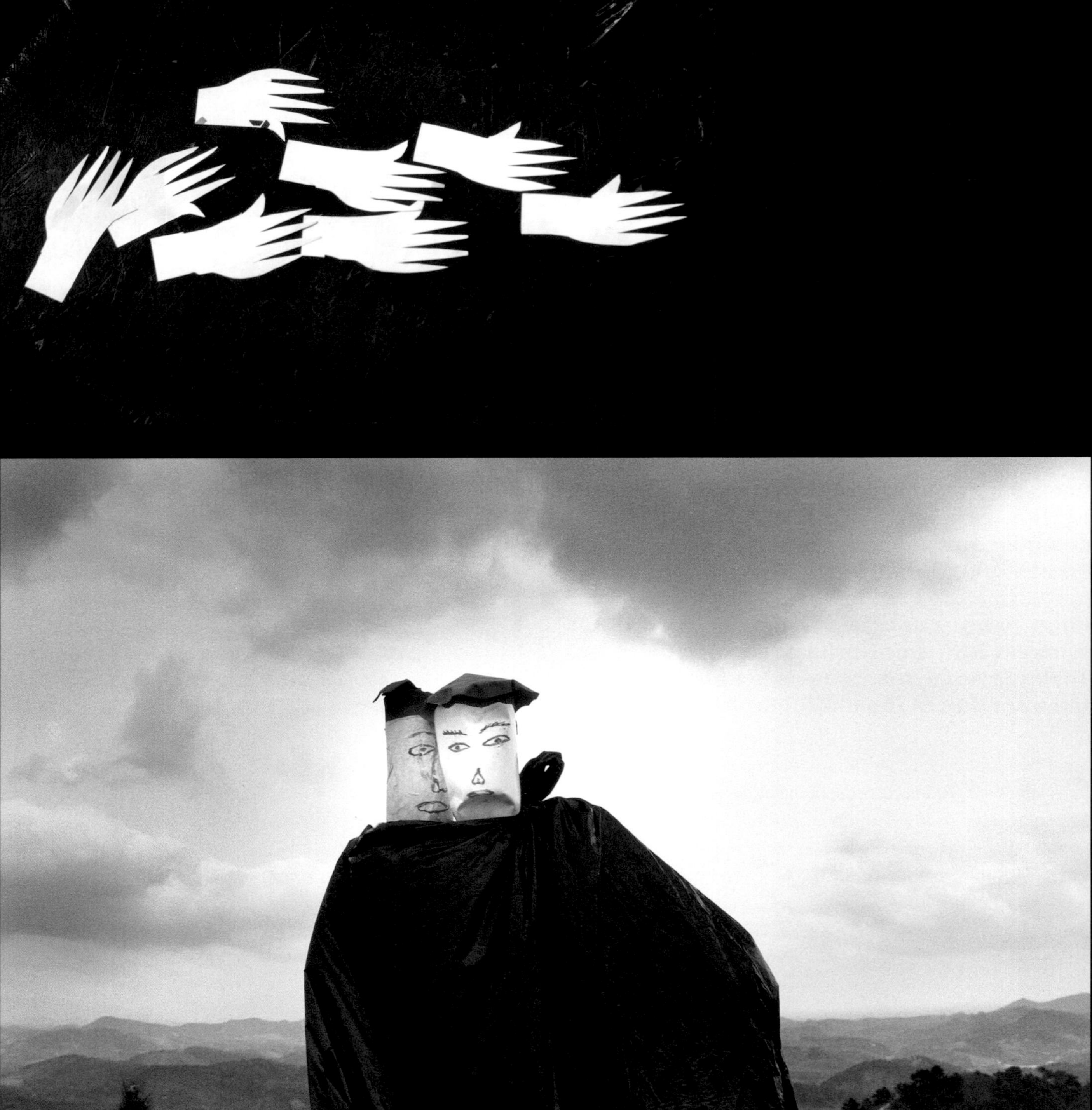

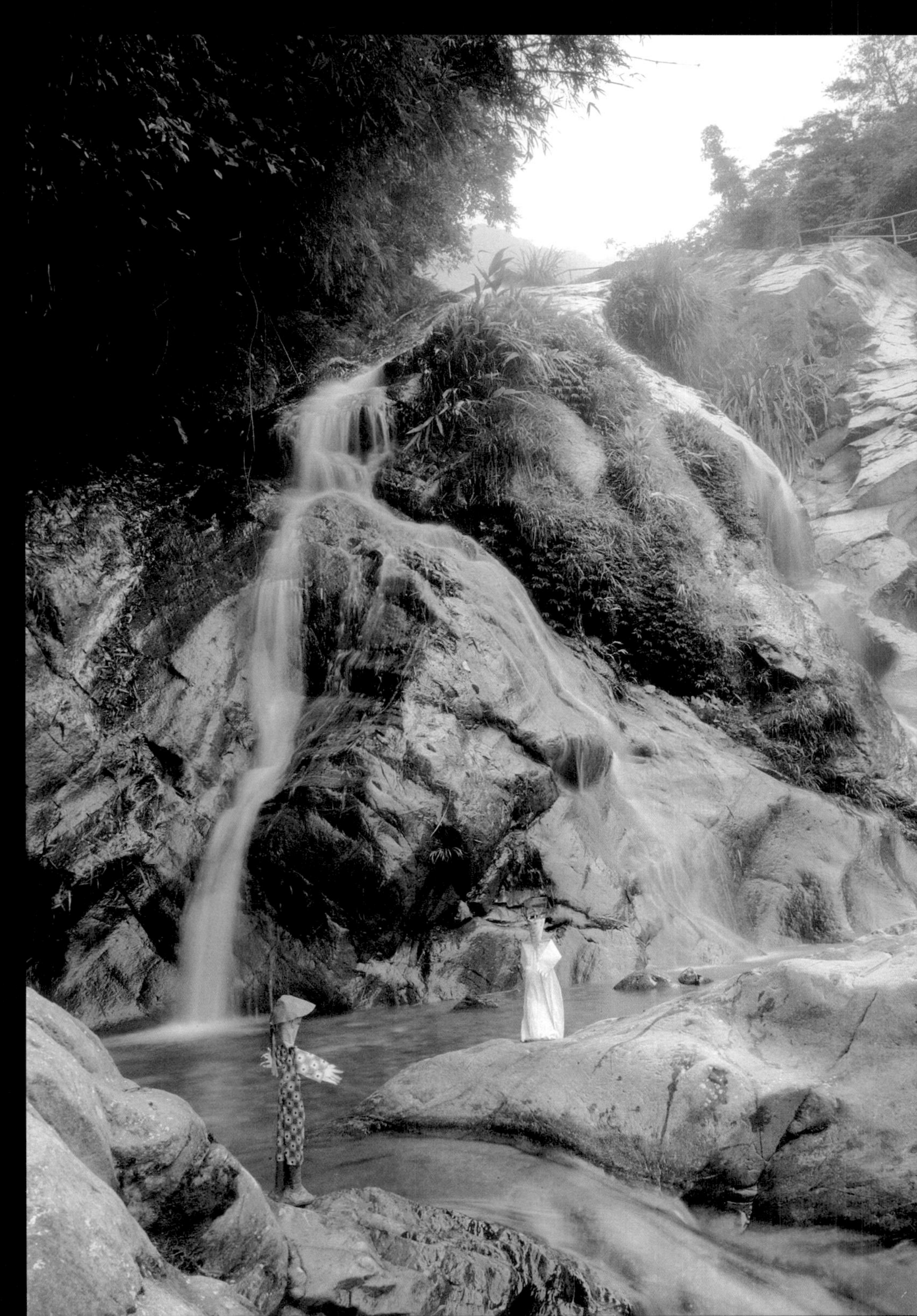

Page 18 That's how they first appeared to me out of paradise's opening. *Left above* These hands seem like indicating a direction. *Left below* Now you understand the meaning of friendship. *Below* Listening to the waterfall. *Page 22* Rolling on the river. *Page 23* Love is - like the umbrella, hanging in the air forever. *Page 25* The last picture I took of him.

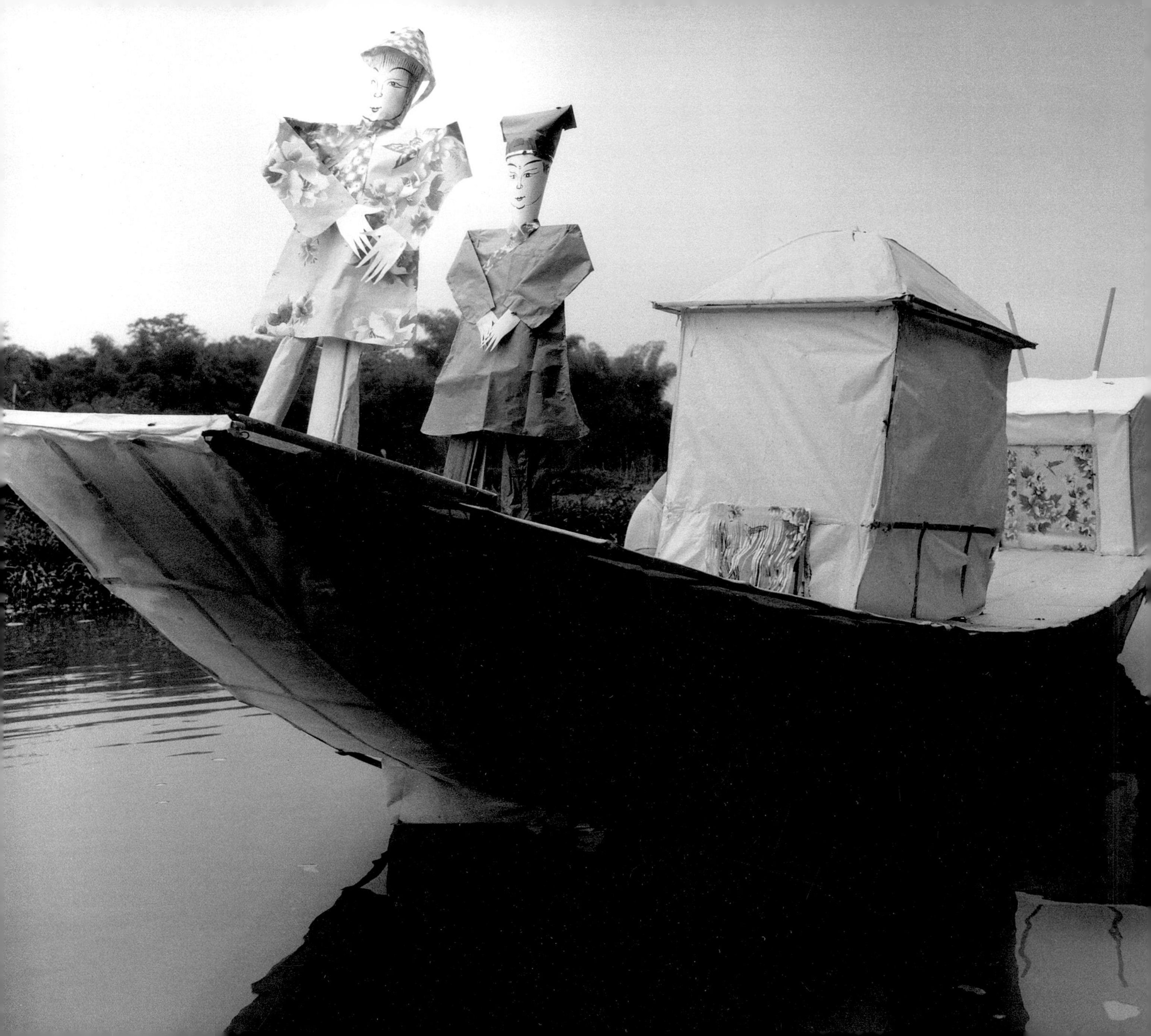

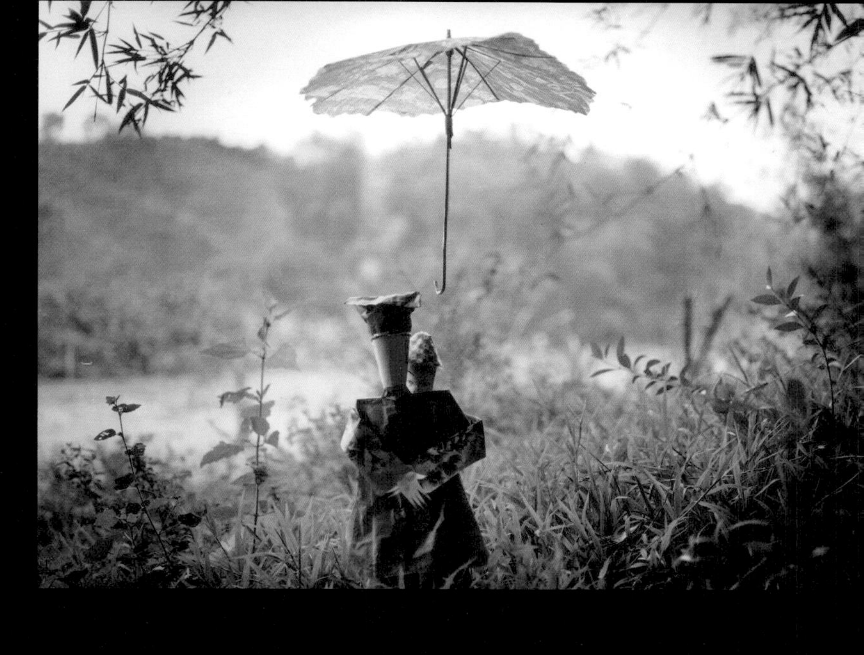

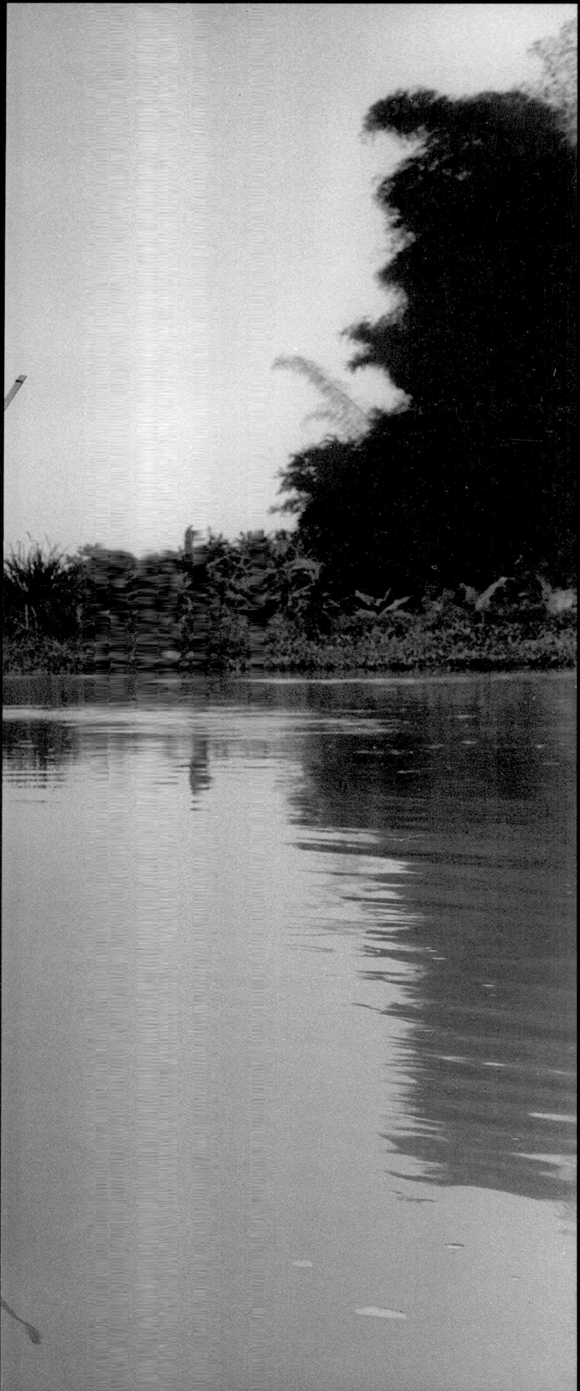

hereafter, which is envisioned to be very similar to the earthly life. The burning of spirit money thus enables the ancestor to purchase luxuries and necessities needed for a comfortable afterlife. The paper figures, burned during the funerary rites together with paper money, are destined to be the servants of the dead in the afterworld.

As if the intrinsic analogical power of light, silver and paper could confer more depth to his representation of life and the afterlife, Yan Changjiang prefers black and white to color photography. His work is concerned with photography's relationship with reality, what Barthes calls "the thing has been there", and representation. He writes, "Photography, with its capacity to 'ascertain', becomes a very powerful mode of exploration. It has a physical and material reality that one cannot find in painting or other traditional modes. When I am facing reality and depicting it with a camera, I feel fully assured and confident, and capable of convincing other people. I think even in fictional or staged photography, the essence of its appeal lies in its physical reality."[1]

In the short story, One Fine Day, the paper people claim to be 'alive'. Like all images, the artist seems to suggest that they have a life of their own. Intriguingly, recent works on icons in the fields of art history and the anthropology of art have attempted to consider the agency and power of artificial persona created by representation. An argument can certainly be made for a fundamental sense of all images having life. David Freedberg suggests for instance that by our very recognition that an image is of someone, our cognitive processes necessarily bring images to life.

"Almost every image provides its beholders with clues to the organic presences registered upon it… The smallest number of clues suffices to precipitate the search for more. Response to all images, and not only ones perceived as being more or less realistic, is predicated on the progressive reconstruction of material objects as living." Hence, he asserts, "the time has come to acknowledge the possibility that our responses to images may be of the same order as our responses to reality."[2]

Throughout Buddhist Asia, the sense that a bi or tridimensional Buddha image is a living Buddha is reinforced by the practice of consecration rituals. And nowhere is the animation of icons clearer than in the 'eye-opening' ceremony (*kaiyan*) through which ritual actions confer life to the image. Similarly, in the southern Chinese village that Yan returned to for many years to stage his photographic tableaux populated by paper people, local artists were still able to draw beautiful faces and eyebrows, to create facial expression, to give life by ink and brush.

The attention of the photographer to the thoughtful lives of the paper people, as in *Sometimes they have an argument* or *Some are hiding inside the banana grove*, remind us, to paraphrase Roland Barthes, that photography is only truly subversive when it is pensive, when it thinks about itself and the metaphors it lives by.

1. *Photography Now: China, Japan, Korea*, SFMOMA, 2009.
2. David Freedberg, *The Power of Images: Studies in the History and Theory of Response*, 1989.

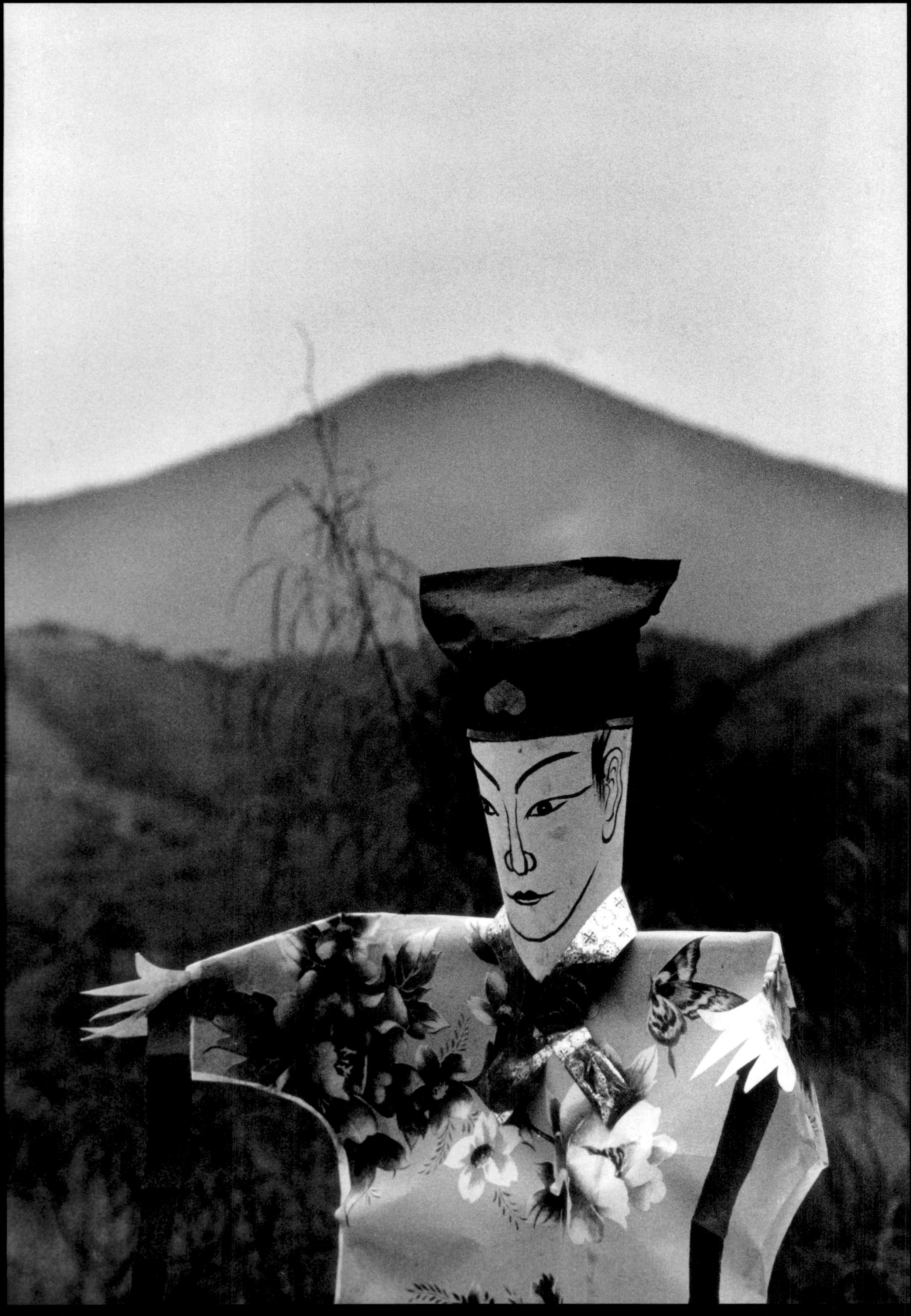

Below There is nothing to say after you die, you just return your body to nature. Right Ambush. Page 28 Happy ever after. Page 29 above This god belongs to them only; below Sometimes you can see them playing in the mist. All images cm 50 x 60 © the artist, courtesy Beaugeste Gallery, Shanghai

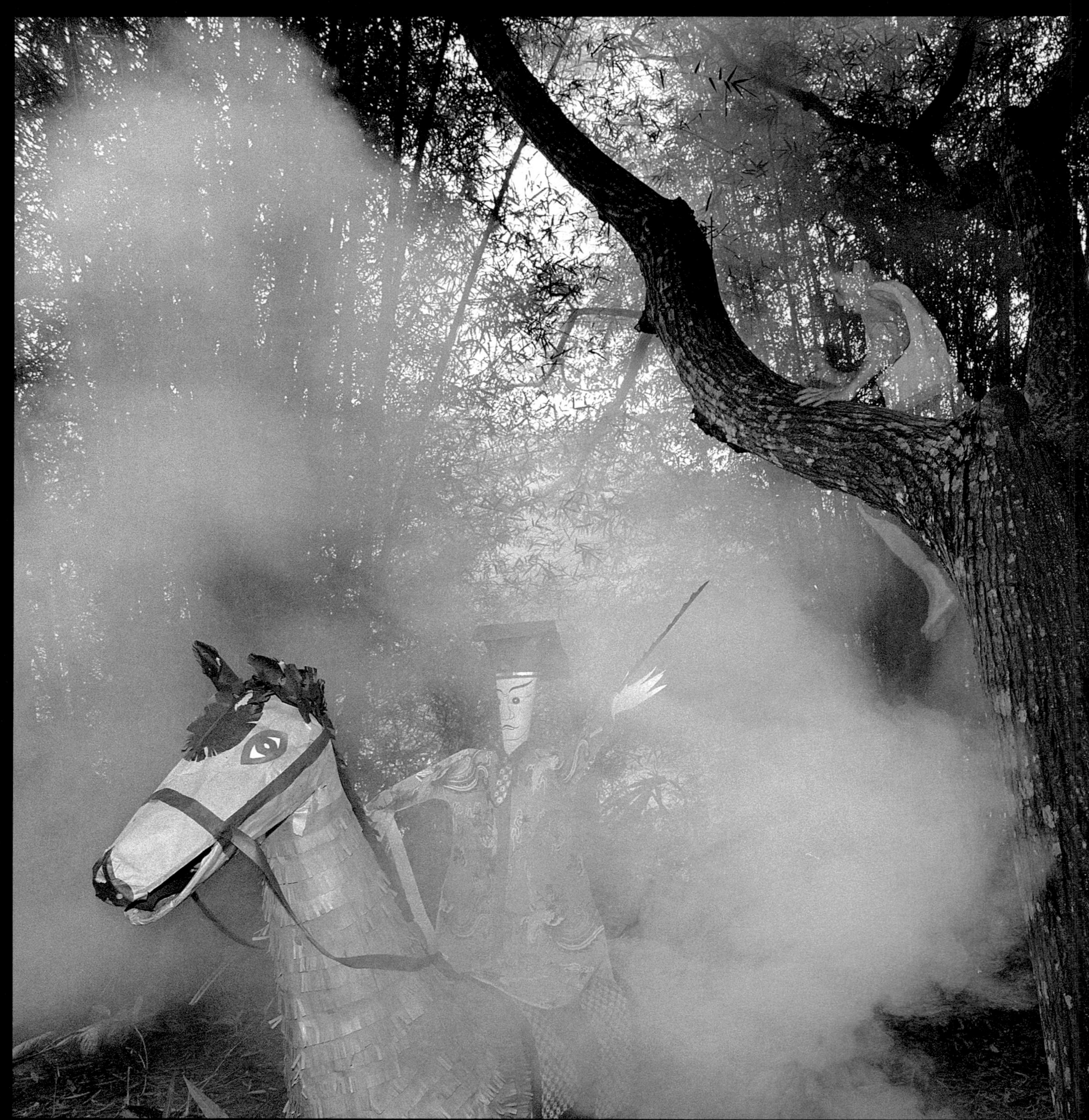

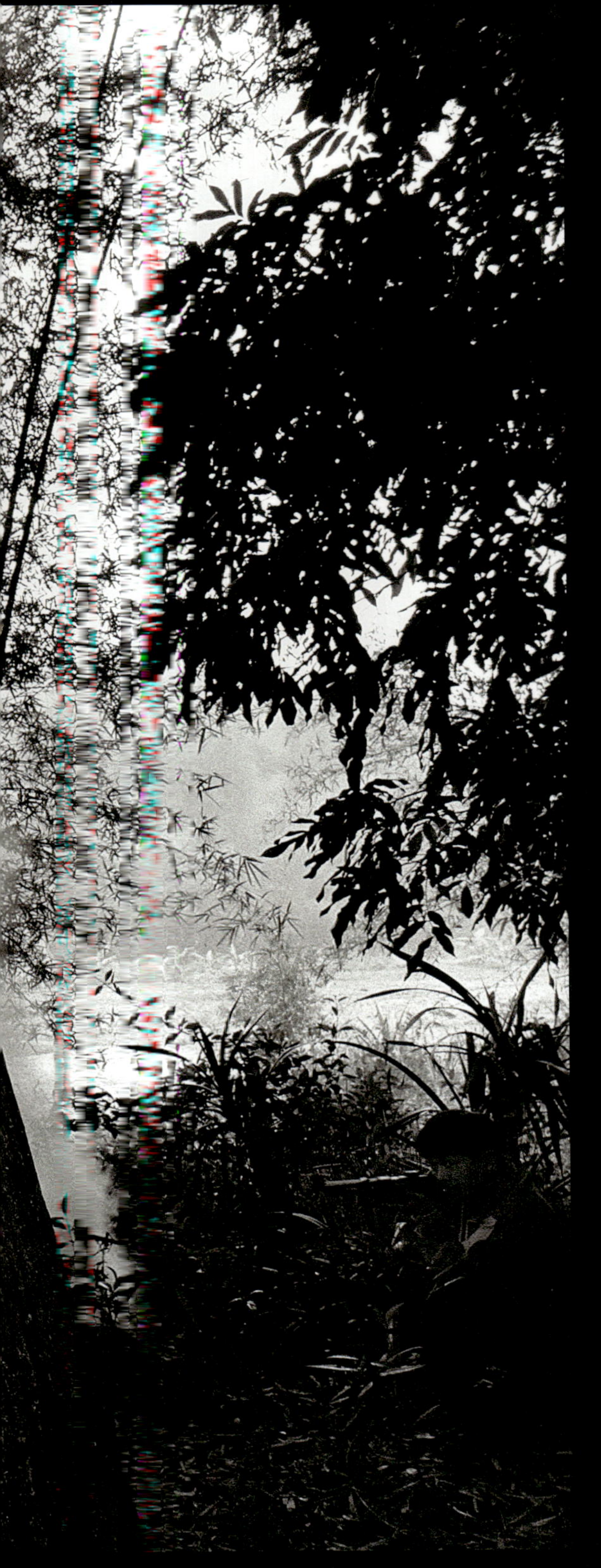
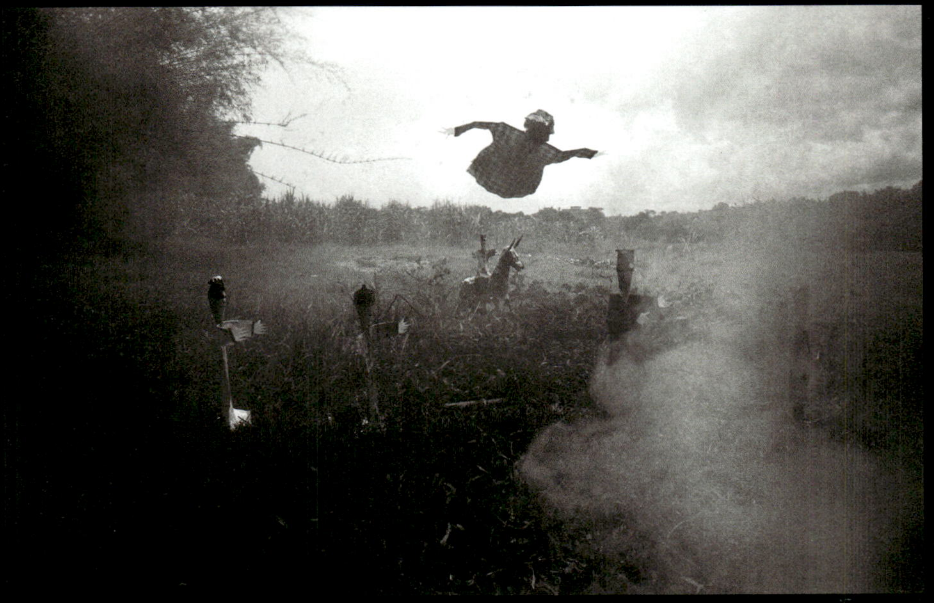

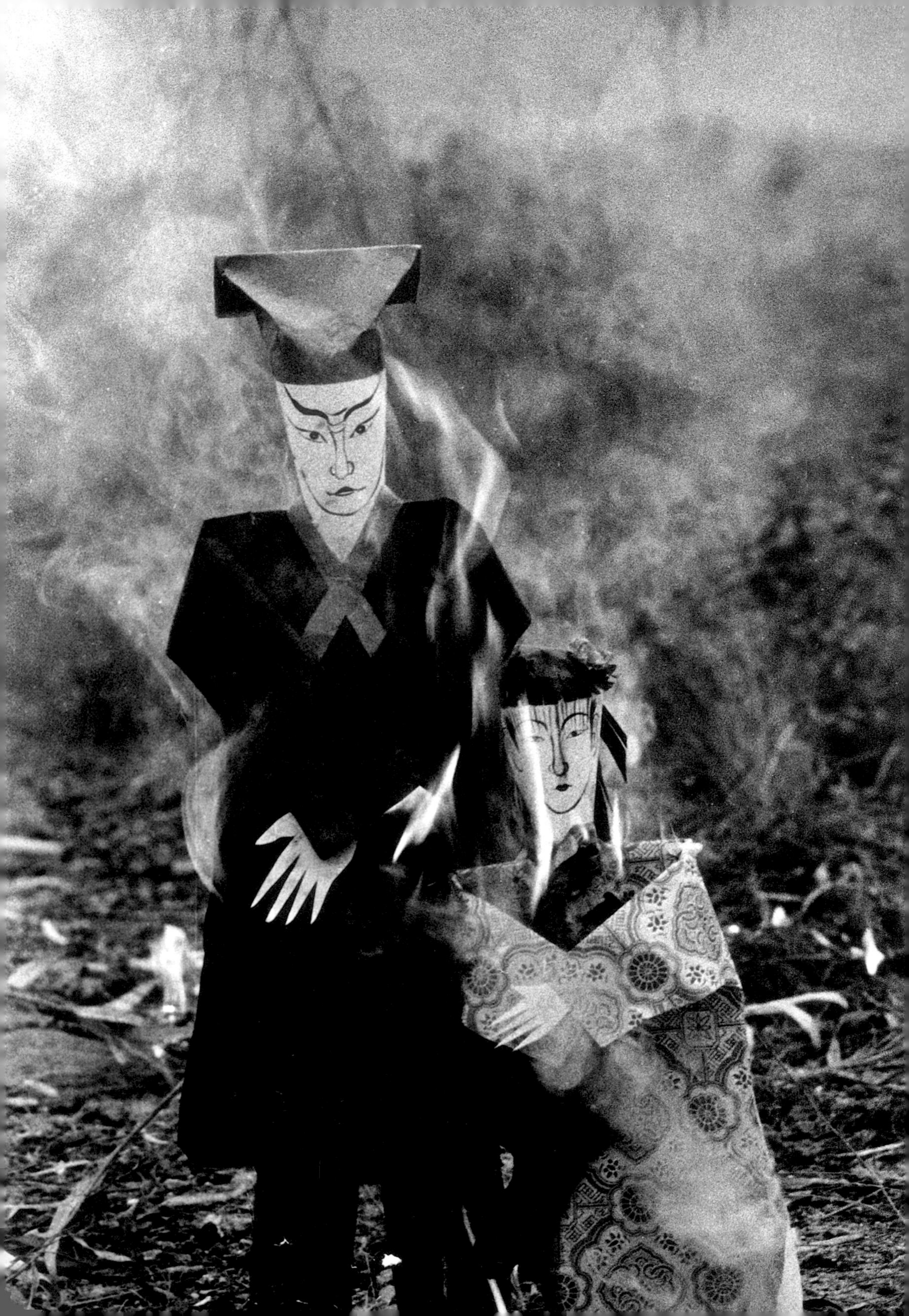

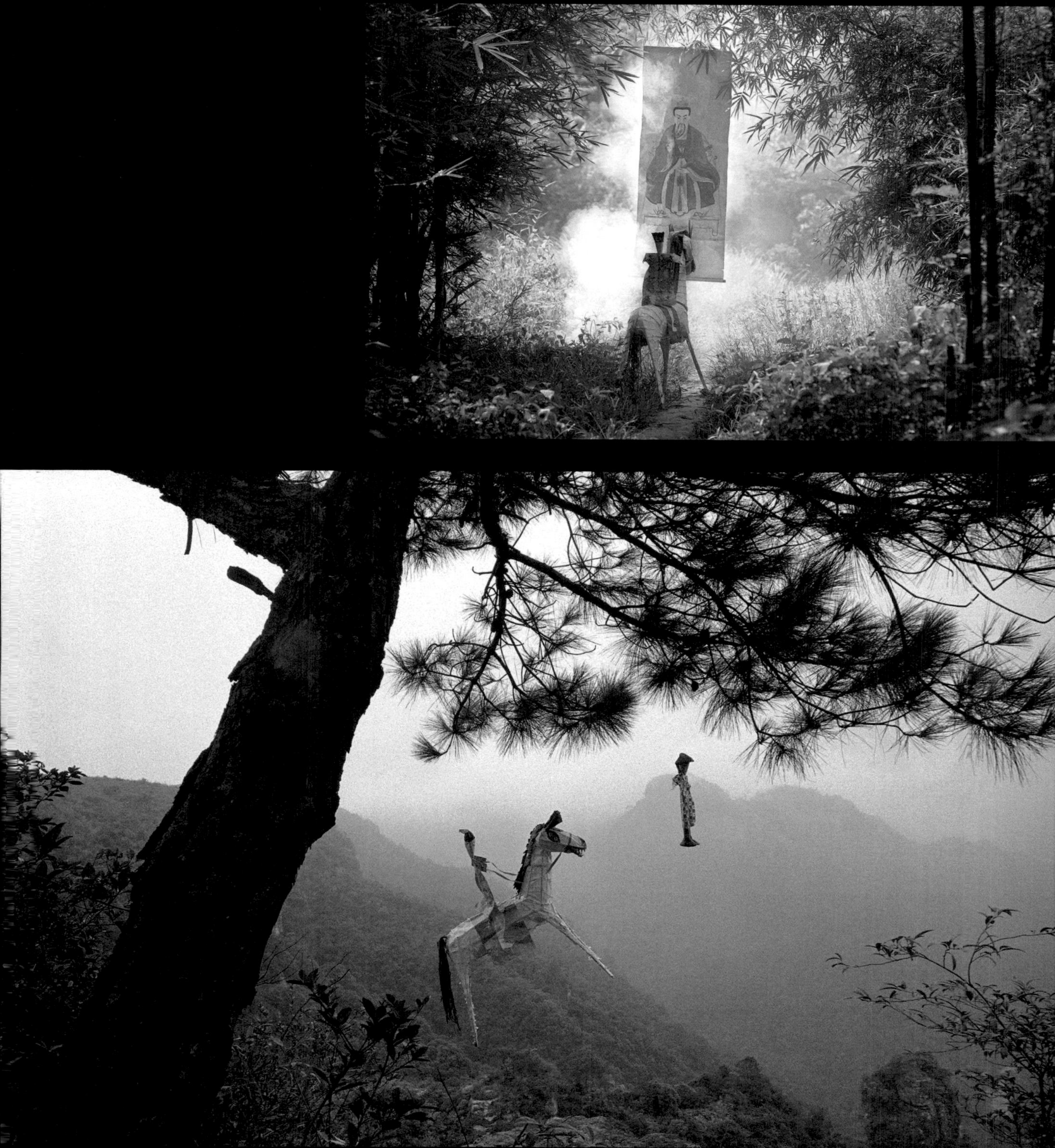

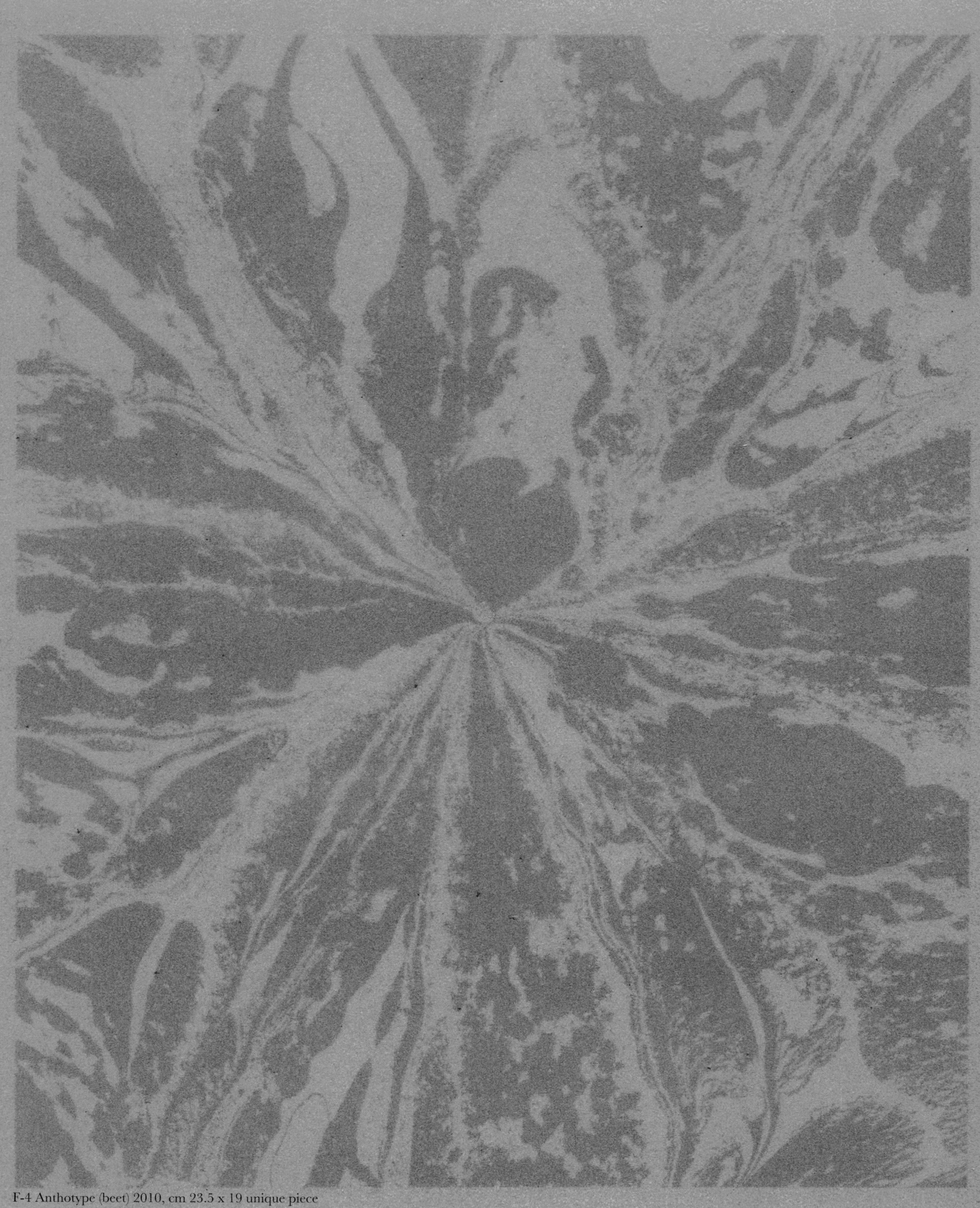

F-4 Anthotype (beet) 2010, cm 23.5 x 19 unique piece

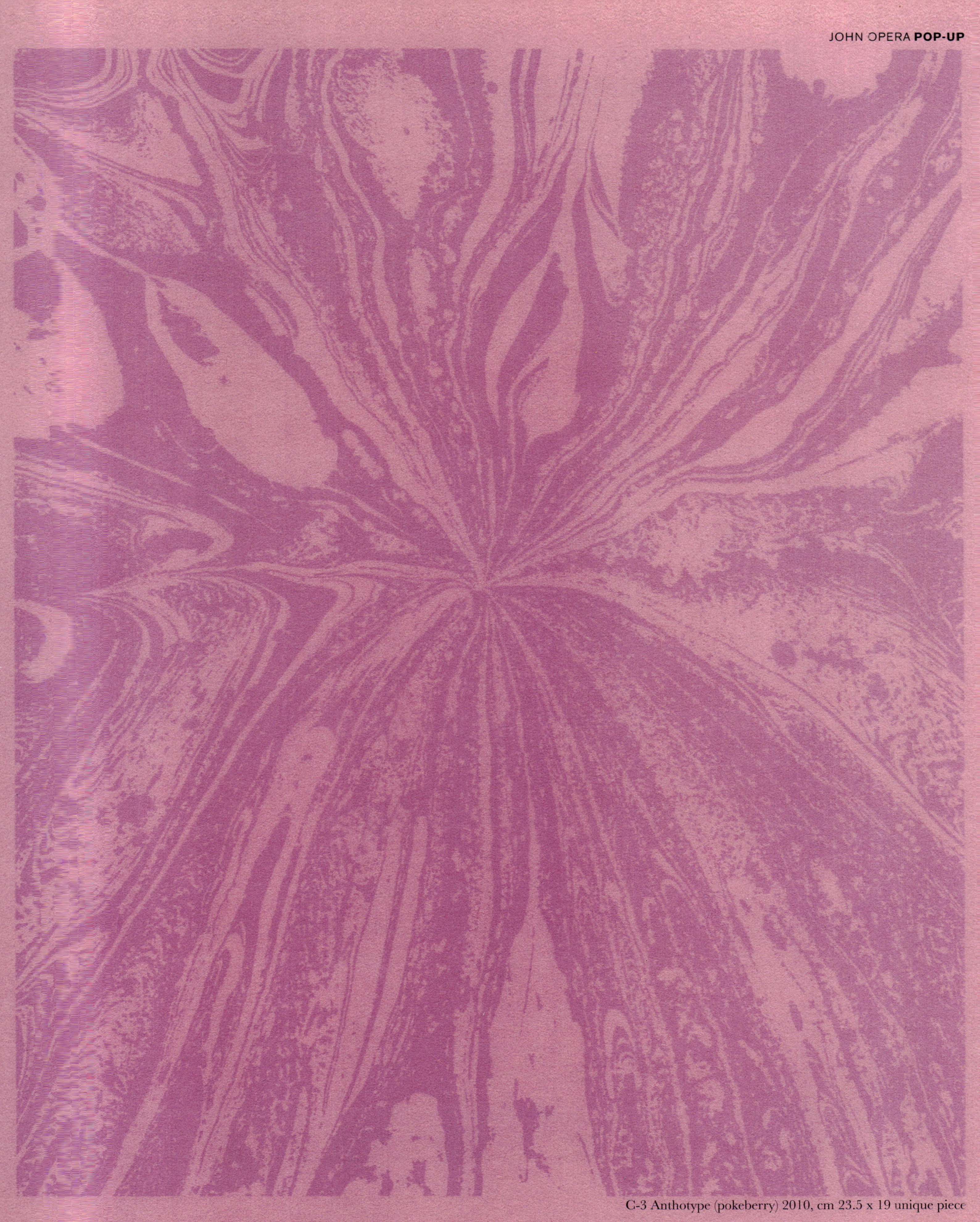

C-3 Anthotype (pokeberry) 2010, cm 23.5 x 19 unique piece

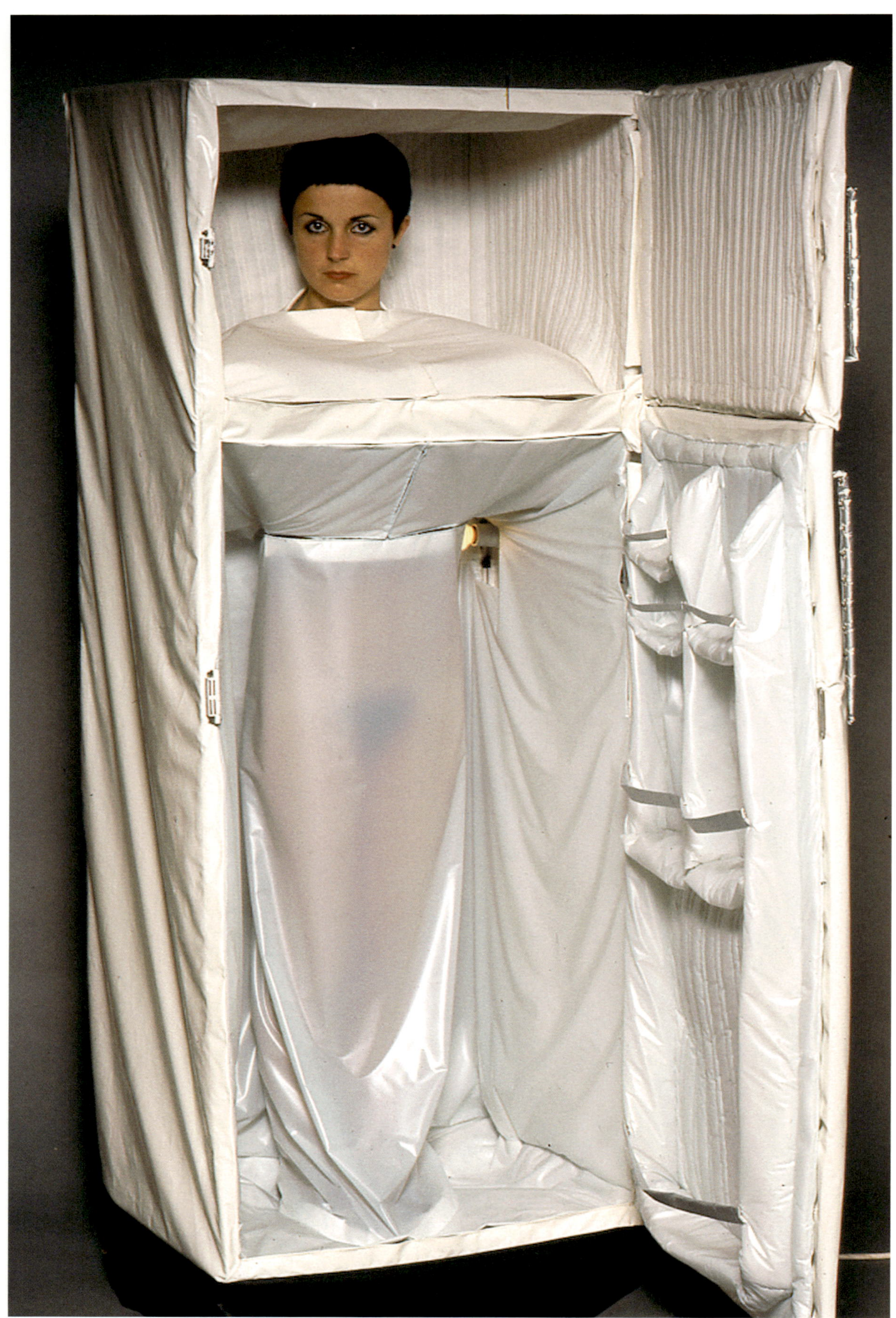

Above and right from In the Kitchen, 1977 pigment print

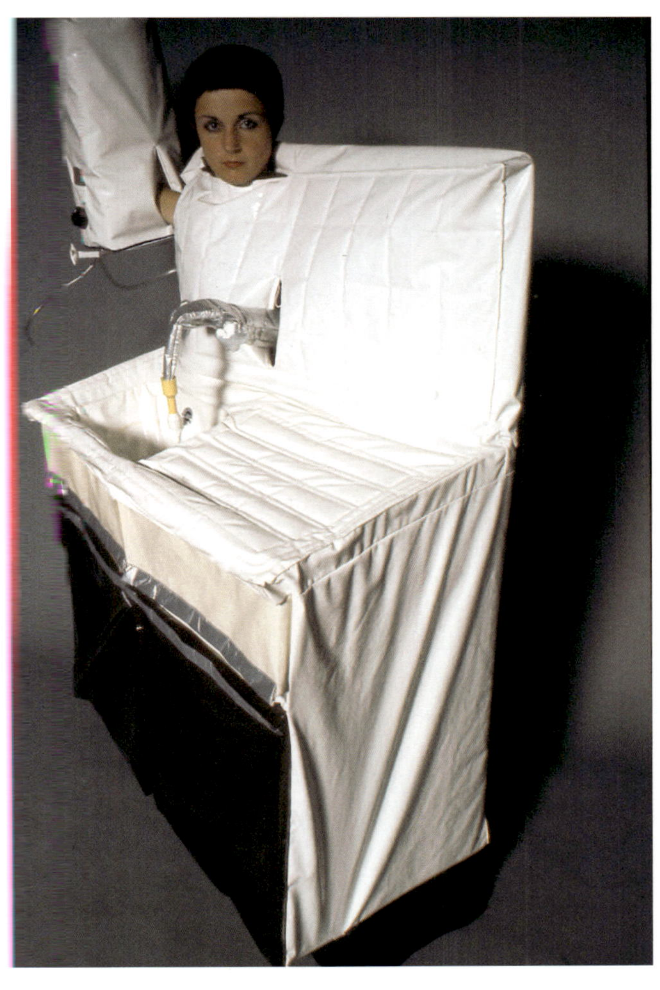

The World She Made
HELEN CHADWICK
by Amy Mackie

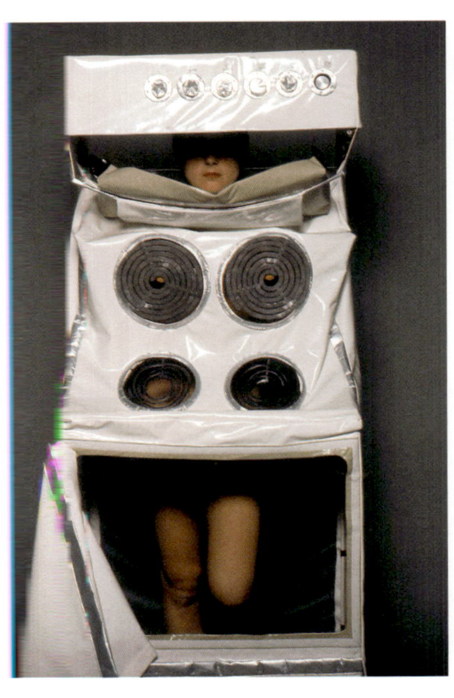

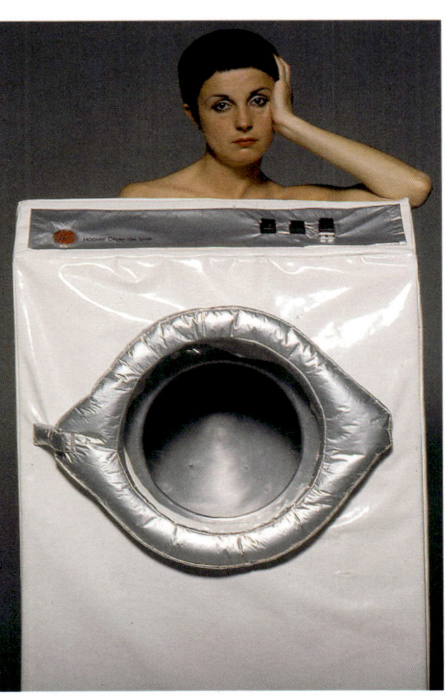

In one of her many journals from the early 1980s, Helen Chadwick writes about an "attempt to overcome alienation with [the] world around oneself."[1] She explains that as an artist, one must "leave part of yourself behind, caught within the place, a haunting."[2] Though Chadwick left many pieces of herself in this world - namely through likenesses and portraits captured on camera - she remains somewhat obscured from the annals of art history. The Barbican Art Gallery in London mounted a major traveling retrospective of her work in 2004 that regrettably did not travel anywhere else. Her last solo exhibition during her lifetime, *Bad Blooms*, 1995, an installation of her photographic series *Wreaths to Pleasure*, 1992-93, was presented at The Museum of Modern Art in New York.

Initially considered a photographer (a medium that was an integral component of her work), she was included in a number of exhibitions along such artists as Janine Antoni, Hans Bellmer, E.J. Bellocq, Nan Goldin, Roberta Graham, Mona Hatoum, Robert Mapplethorpe, and John Stezaker, though she was more recognized as a sculptor toward the end of her life. It is somewhat difficult to categorize Chadwick's multi-disciplinary practice - encompassing drawing, sculpture, performance, fashion, architecture, video, installation, sound, and photography - and this, as well as her untimely death at the age of forty-two, is perhaps in part, why she has not become canonized along with other artists of her generation.[3]

The work of Austrian artist Birgit Jürgenssen (born in 1949, just four years prior to Chadwick) has also been under-recognized, although the monographic *Birgit Jürgenssen*, 2010, by Abigail Solomon-Godeau, proves to alter this. Solomon-Godeau's essay for *Role Play: Feminist Art Revisited 1960-1980*, a small exhibition organized by Galerie Lelong in New York in 2007, brought together not only Chadwick and Jürgenssen, but also included Marina Abramovic, Lynda Benglis, Valie Export, Ana Mendieta, Yoko Ono, Adrian Piper, Martha Rosler, Carolee Schneemann, Hannah Wilke, and others. The exhibition acknowledged the challenges - especially in the 1960s, 70s, and 80s - that geography imposed on women artists. Of the many relatively unknown artists included in *Role Play*, Solomon-Godeau states, "Coming upon these works now is something of a surprise, not merely because of their unfamiliarity, but equally for their quality. Suffused as so much of it is with intelligence, wit, inventiveness and a sharp critical edge."[4] This exhibition was refreshing, primarily because it paired a group of more recognized feminist artists with lesser-known artists like Chadwick and Jürgenssen, as well as Helena Almeida, Anna Bella Geiger, and Anna Maria Maiolino in an effort to write a more inclusive history of women artists working across the globe from the 1960s through the 1980s. A series of black and white photographs from Chadwick's *In the Kitchen*, 1977, were included in the exhibition at Galerie Lelong. The work was originally conceived as a performance for Chadwick's degree show at the Chelsea School of Art and involves four women wearing Oldenberg-esque soft sculptures of household appliances (a stove, a refrigerator, a sink, and a dryer) on 'display' in a storefront. Chadwick played the role of the salesperson announcing that this was a way for a woman to "do time in her kitchen and actually enjoy herself."[5] The performance was accompanied by an audio component that consisted of a compilation of radio programs from the UK that catered to housewives, such as *Woman's Hour*, and *You and Yours*. In a letter to the editor of a Tokyo-based magazine, Chadwick wrote: "I use performance together with sculpture, photography, and sound to express the conflicts that are generated by the facets of contemporary urban life… *In the Kitchen* explores the position of women in consumer society and the dilemmas that are raised in the struggle to resolve identity and individuality."[6] Though the costumes/sculptures no longer exist, the photographs and documentation of this work, as Solomon-Godeau points out, belong with similar works that confront the politics of the kitchen: the stove of Birgit Jürgenssen, 1975; the stove "monuments" of Rosemarie Trockel, 1992, *In the Kitchen* by Chadwick (included in *Role Play*), 1977, Mierle Laderman Ukeles' maintenance works, from 1969, and Martha Rosler's tape Semiotics of the Kitchen (included in *Role Play*), 1975, are all testimonial to the ways by which women artists (who may have been entirely unaware of one another's work) were mobilized by their recognition of what Betty Friedan called "the problem with no name."[7]

There is clearly a direct link between Chadwick and other women artists working during the 1970s, though few curators have positioned her practice historically. Her relationship to feminism was perhaps more tenuous than some of her contemporaries and though she was in a peripheral position geographically, she was undoubtedly engaged in the discourse.[8] Chadwick's work surfaced recently in a very different context in the exhibition *Childish Things*, 2010, at the Fruitmarket Gallery in Edinburgh. The exhibition elaborated the dialogue between the work of Louise Bourgeois and Chadwick first addressed in *Féminin-Masculin, le Sexe de l'art*, at the Centre Georges Pompidou, Paris, in 1995.

In the catalog for Chadwick's 2004 retrospective, Marina Warner points out that Bourgeois' work, which belatedly gained widespread attention, shares many commonalities with that of Chadwick. The exhibition in Edinburgh, though chiefly a conversation about objects that recall the anxieties of childhood, positions their practices within the larger conversation concerning psychoanalysis, which dominated theoretical discussions in the 1980s. The curator, David Hopkins, focuses his attention on Chadwick's *Ego Geometria Sum*, 1983, and *The Juggler's Table*, 1984, as works that elaborate a "return to origins" and which serve as a means of capturing the spirit of her youth.

Ego Geometria Sum, which has received substantial attention over the years, is often thought of as the bridge between Chadwick's more performative work from the late 1970s and her amalgamations of sculpture and photography produced in the latter part of her career. The installation consists of ten plywood geometrical shapes that refer to milestones in childhood development. Each object (including an incubator, a bed, a piano, etc.) relates to the size of Chadwick's growing body and is covered with photographs that reference her geographical locale and experiences from each particular moment. Using an emulsion process called 'Silver Magic', that was relatively new at the time, Chadwick super-imposed multiple images on each object as a way to layer both memories and meaning. As Hopkins writes in his essay for *Childish Things*, "She seems to have understood the printed facets of the objects as slices cut through time, by means of which she was able to re-inhabit the past, and there is a weird sense in which the adult images of Chadwick imprinted onto the objects revisit (or haunt) the sites of her younger self's activities."[9]

The Juggler's Table, a miniaturized version of *Ego Geometria Sum*, contains not only machetes of the larger sculptures, but includes the original source photographs of the sites and objects that inspired Chadwick's process. *Ego Geometria Sum: The Labours*, 1984, as series of photographs Chadwick produced in collaboration with Mark Pilkington as part of her installation at the *Aperto* exhibition at the Venice Biennale in 1984, adds yet another plane of meaning to this work. In the photographs, Chadwick's naked body wrangles with each of the ten sculptural objects. Her face is obscured, her gaze removed, leaving only the haunting presence of her figure embracing the likeness of herself captured in each object. It is as though she is parting ways with each memory, each experience frozen in time. It seems impossible not to think about the Latin phrase 'memento mori', as Chadwick has so successfully captured the instant where life and death merge and where the self dissolves into the void.

The Oval Court, 1984-86, part of Chadwick's exhibition *Of Mutability*, 1986, at the Institute of Contemporary Art in London, led to her nomination for the Turner Prize in 1987.[10] Marina Warner, who championed Chadwick's work from the beginning, gives due attention to both *Ego Geometria Sum* and *The Oval Court* in her essay for the exhibition's catalog. Interestingly, both Warner and Richard Cork, who also wrote for the catalog, focus on alienation and mortality as dominate themes in Chadwick's work. As Cork writes, "Even though all Chadwick's work could be described as a form of struggle against alienation, she has never been willing to suggest that a victory is inevitable."[11] Resulting in a spectacular bacchanalia-like still life installation, *The Oval Court* was created by means of an average business photocopy machine (which had become easily accessible in the early 1980s). Using blue photographic paper, Chadwick made numerous copies of her body, dead animals, and a variety of organic materials, which were arranged on a large platform along with five gold spheres. Like *Ego Geometria Sum*, the arrangement of the images appears at first to be random, but Chadwick's extensive writing about both works indicate that this could not be further from the truth. Chadwick purposely laid out each installation according to mathematical calculations, historical precedents, and in relation to her own body. Chadwick endured harsh, though misdirected criticism following her Turner Prize nomination for the use of her naked body in the work. Thus, it is interesting to note that she was included in an exhibition entitled *New Perspectives on the Nude* in 1983 (along with Roberta Graham, Robert Mapplethorpe, and others), which addressed a subject that Chadwick was greatly concerned with throughout her career: the naked body vs. the nude body. Susan Butler's essay for the exhibition elaborates: "In linking body imagery to objects representing stages of growth, Chadwick effectively removes the nude image from the realms of easy symbolism, abstraction and self-indulgent fantasies on the part of the spectator. The nude image resists being reduced to a field of projection because it both undergoes and asserts the specific nature of its own experience."[12]

Chadwick's archive contains numerous accordion books of photographs from the late 1970s and early 1980s that recall the unabashed, vibrant sexuality of Mapplethorpe's oeuvre. *Ego Geometria Sum*, however, is reminiscent of the early 19th century self-portraits of Eadweard Muybridge where his (mostly) nude frame imparts a melancholic reflection on mortality. It would be a challenge to claim Muybridge's body as 'naked' in his photographs, and yet Mapplethorpe's subjects were clearly much more than simply nude. Somehow Chadwick found a way to explore both understandings of the human form by calling into question the way we perceive ourselves.

In the early 1990s, Chadwick began to pursue other means of representing the self. This was a major turning point in her career and explains the break between her early work that relied on traditional photographic methods and her later work, in which she utilized light boxes and chromogenic prints. In many ways, it seems that Chadwick was simultaneously working in the past and the present, looking both backwards and forward in terms of photographic processes, art historical precedence, and narrative. From the obsessive documentation of her soft sculptures, costumes, and performances produced as part of her degree shows at Brighton Polytechnic and the Chelsea College of Art & Design to her embrace of both lo-tech and well as emerging photographic methods, it is evident that photography, the ability to seize an experience indefinitely, was always the guiding force of her work. It appears that Chadwick has something in common with Davos Hanich, the main character from the non-linear cinematic masterpiece *La Jetée* (Chris Marker, 1962), whose obsessive childhood memories foretell his own death. The film, which is constructed of thousands of still photographs, is a poignant reflection on the boundaries between the human spirit and the expansive landscape of the mind. Whether framed by feminism, the history of photography, or the politics of the body, Chadwick's insight and innovation during the few short years of her artistic output remains an enduring presence - even if only captured eternally in a world of her own.

1. Helen Chadwick's extensive archive has been maintained at the Henry Moore Institute, Leeds, UK since 2004. The quotes from this particular journal have been digitized and can be perused on the HMI's website.
2. Ibid.
3 Born in Croydon, England in 1953, Chadwick died unexpectedly in London in 1996 at the age of forty-two.
4. Abigail Solomon-Godeau, *Role Play: Feminist Art Revisited 1960-1980*. Exhibition brochure. (New York: Galerie Lelong), March 15 – April 28, 2007.
5. Helen Chadwick as quoted by Niclas Östlind. *Helen Chadwick* (Stockholm: Liljevalchs konsthall, 2005), 17.
6. Helen Chadwick in a letter to Hideo Kaido, Chief Editor of *Sogetsu Shuppan Magazine*, Tokyo, August 30, 1979 (in the HMI archive).
7. Abigail Solomon-Godeau, *Role Play: Feminist Art Revisited 1960-1980*. Exhibition brochure. (New York: Galerie Lelong), March 15 – April 28, 2007.
8. Chadwick's omission from many (if not most) conversations about art informed by feminism in the United States, recalls the great divide between American and British feminism that Lucy Lippard wrote about in her essay, "The Pains and Pleasures of Rebirth: European and American Women's Body Art" , originally published in *Art in America* in 1976.
9. David Hopkins, *Childish Things* (Edinburgh: The Fruitmarket Gallery, 2010), 35.
10. This was the first year that a woman was nominated for the Turner Prize. There was in fact two women nominated in 1987, the other artist was Thérèse Oulton.
11. Richard Cork. "Contesting Alienation" in *Of Mutability* (London: The Institute of Contemporary Art, 1986), 18.
12. Susan Butler, *New Perspectives on the Nude* (Cardiff, England: ffotogallery, 1983), 7.

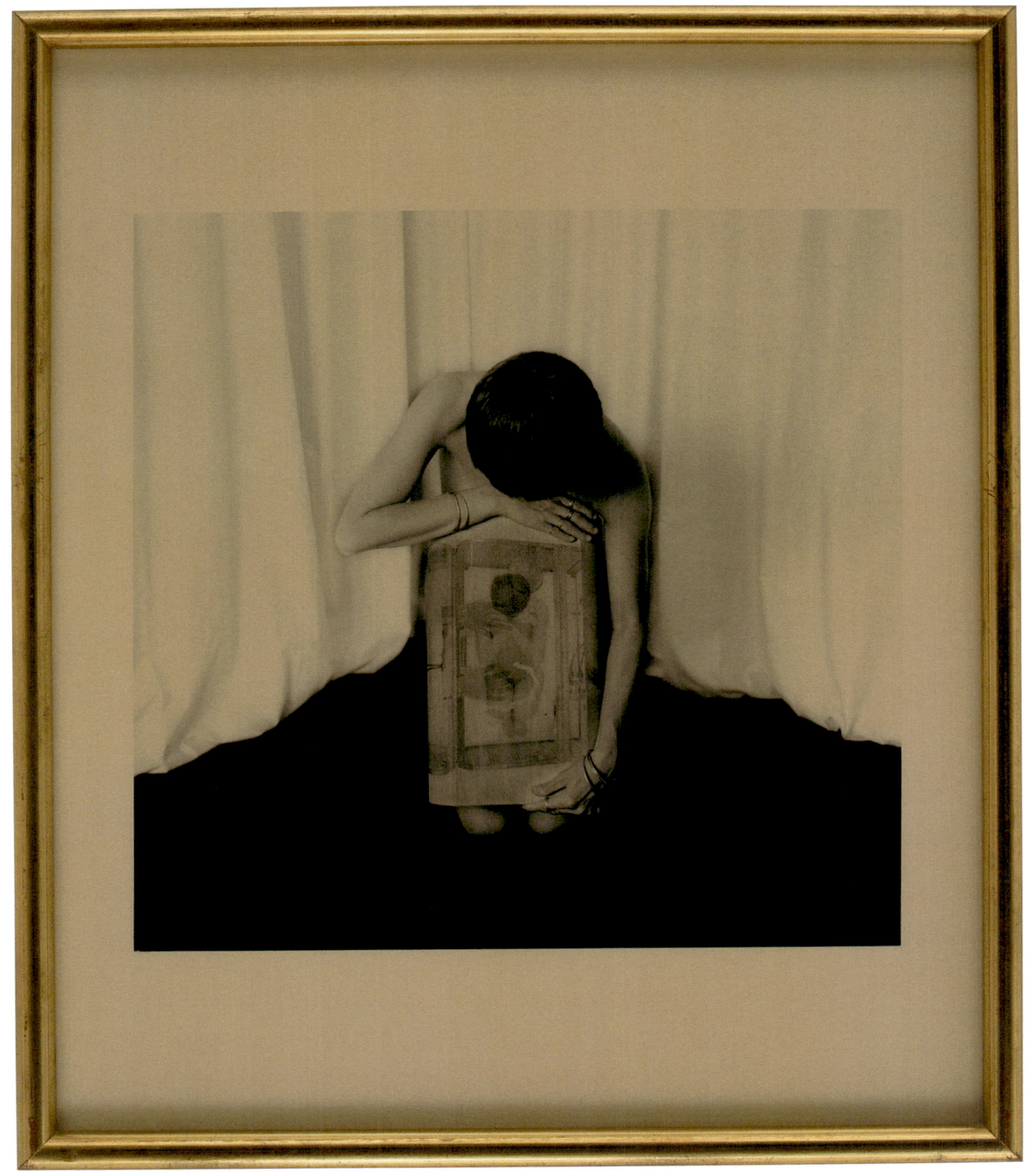

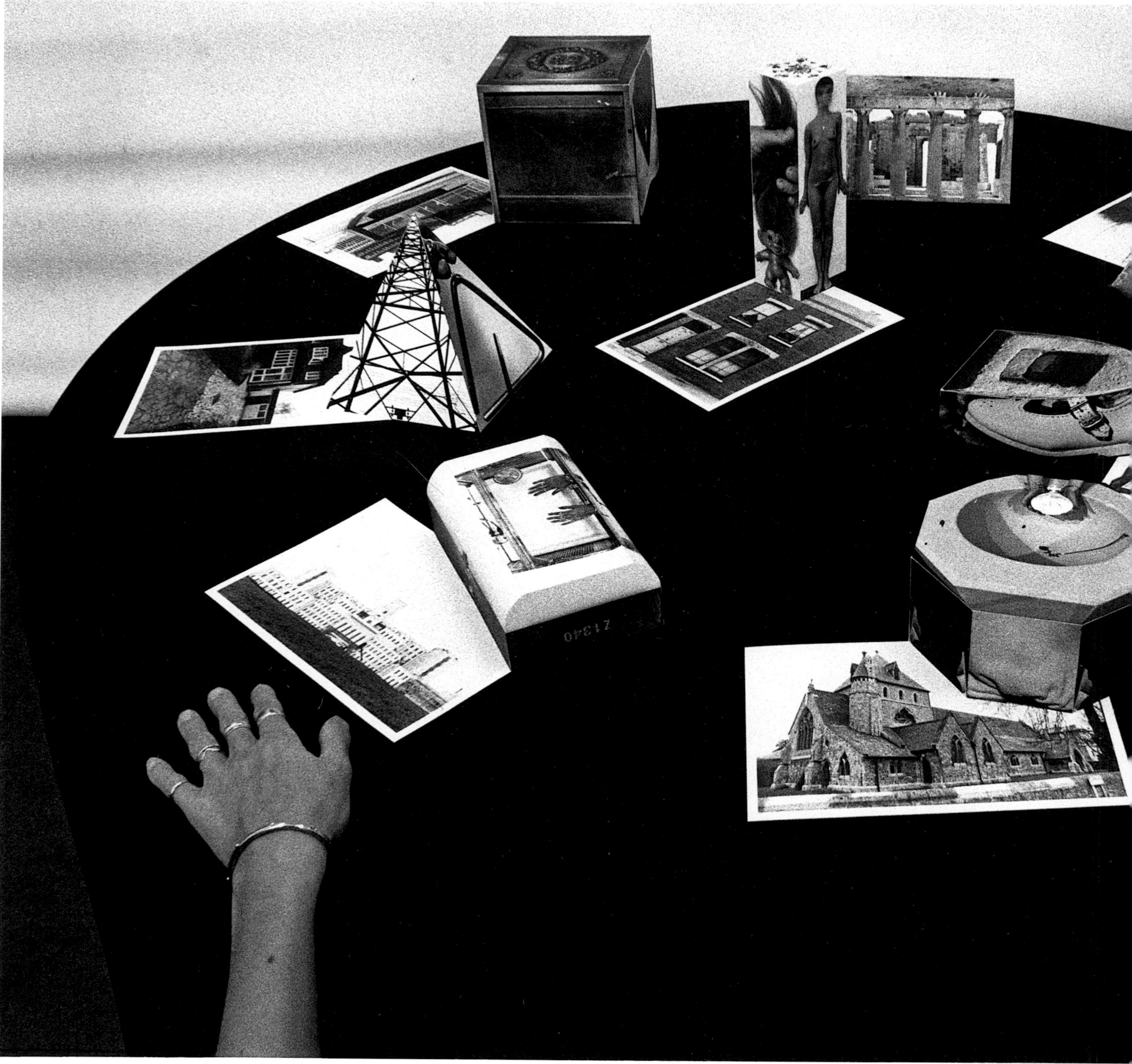

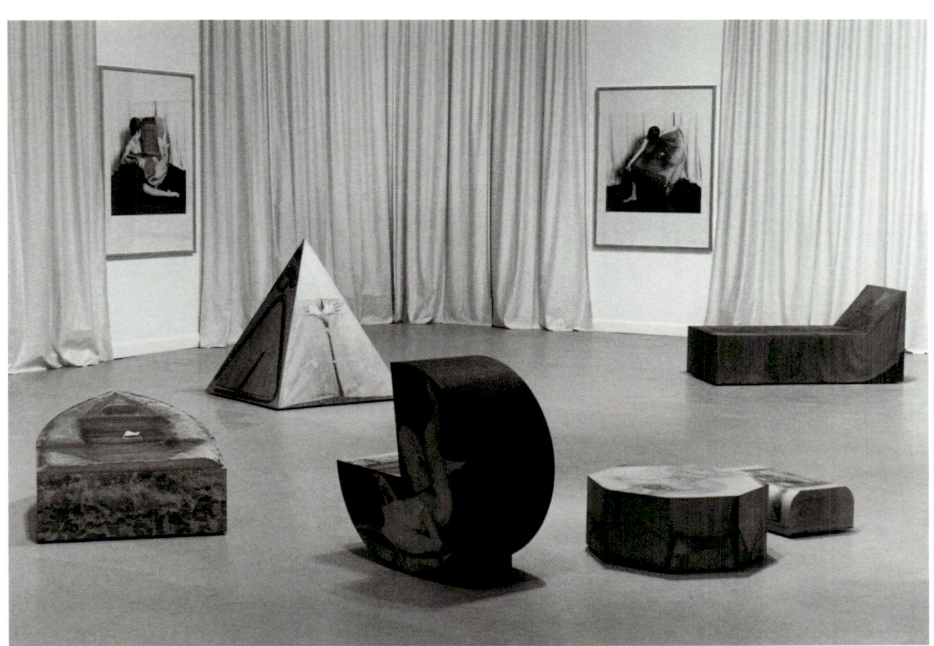

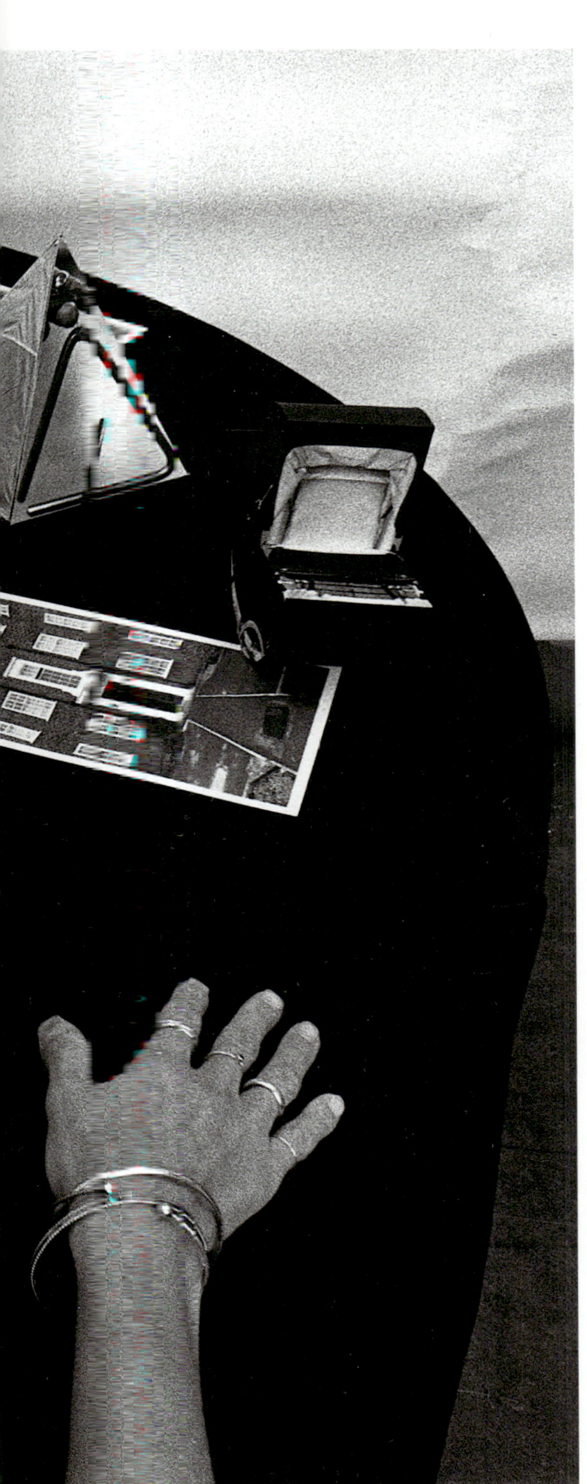

Page 37 Image from Ego Geometria Sum: The Labours I, 1984. *Previous spread left from* The Juggler's Table 1983; *right from the installation* Ego Geometria Sum, Venice Biennale 1984. *Below from* Domestic Sanitation, 1975. *All images © Estate of Helen Chadwick, courtesy of Leeds Museums & Galleries (Henry Moore Institute Archive)*

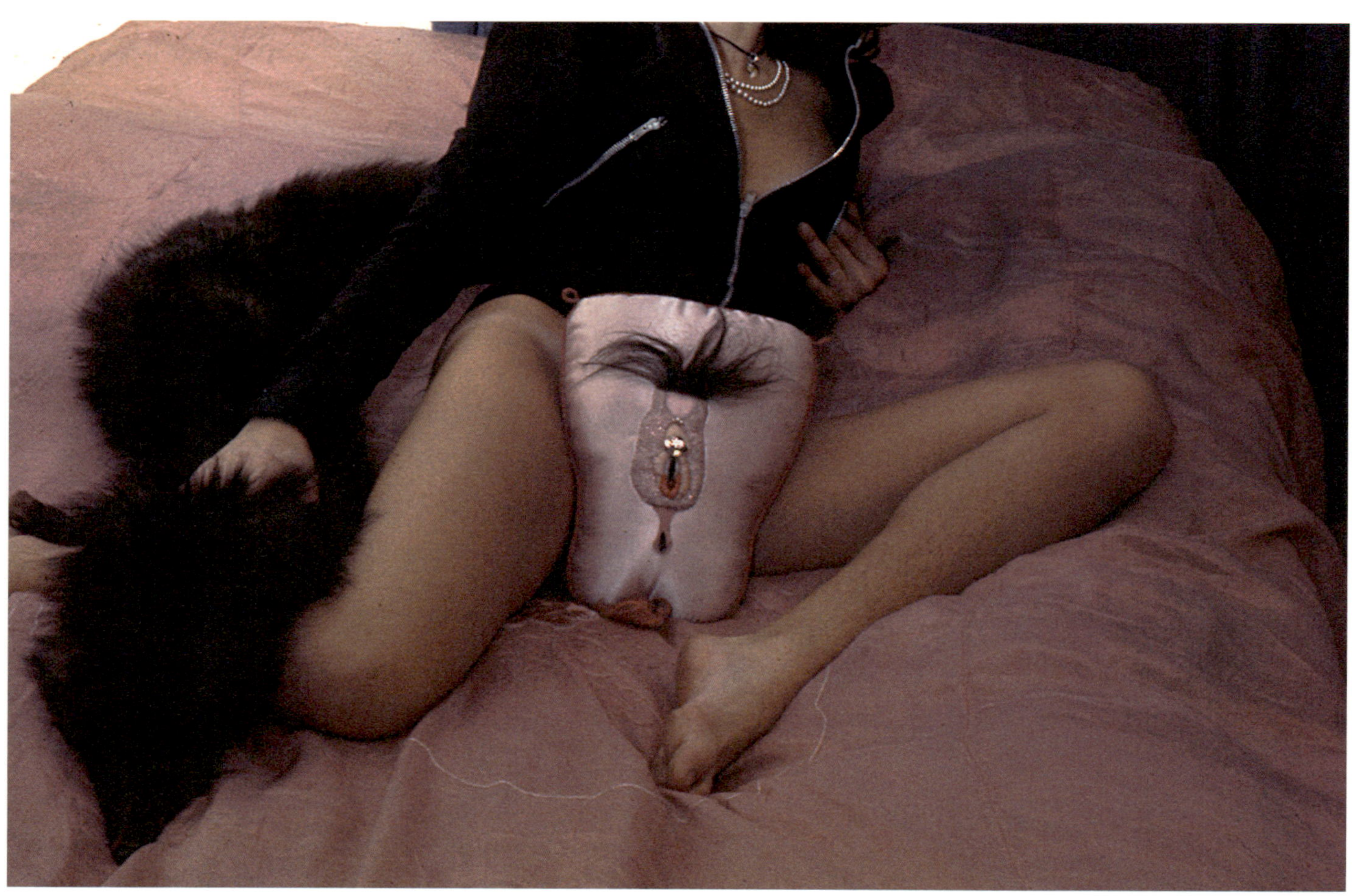

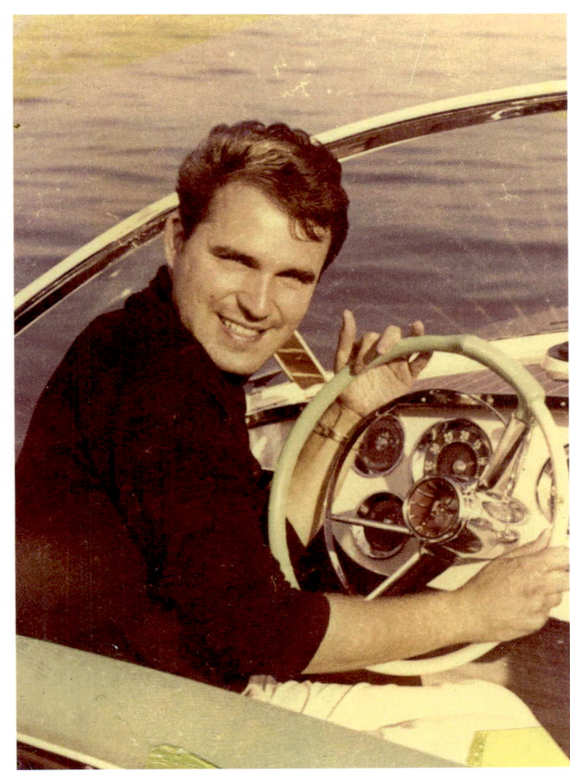

LIVIO
told by Katia Fiorentino

Suddenly in 2006 I have inherited, along with an impressive assortment of hair rolls, brushes and hair dyes, a variety of photographs signed by famous people. Livio, my mother's business partner and the official coiffeur for the Hotel Regina Isabella in Lacco Ameno, Ischia, had been collecting them during all his career. The Hotel Regina Isabella is a five star luxury hotel founded by Angelo Rizzoli in 1956. Lacco Ameno, until then a tiny village of fishermen and farmers, suddenly became a V.I.P. tourist destination.

My long-term friend Camillo remembers Livio's gentle manners, which developed as a result of being an only child with no family. In fact, Livio soon became the adoptive child of the entire island community.

I went back to my native Ischia to meet Rosalia Taliercio and Salvatore Monti, respectively the first receptionist and massage therapist of the prestigious hotel since its opening in 1956. Through their tales and memories, I had the opportunity to get a first hand portrait of those years that they describe as "the golden age" of Ischia, precisely the years between 1956 and 1980. They remember how their village became an exclusive tourist destination. It happened so quickly that many professional figures had to be 'imported' to work at this hotel, as the local population still lacked specific skills.

Rosalia and Salvatore describe Livio's Salon as the real 'stage', where prestigious guests went not only for hair and beauty, but also for informal meetings. Anna Magnani, Monica Vitti, Alberto Sordi, Delia Scala, Mina, Gina Lollobrigida, Liz Taylor, John Wayne, Gabriella Ferri, Luchino Visconti and many others were able to access the Salon directly from the beach, more often than not in a very casual and relaxed fashion.

Livio and my mother Dora were the perfect hosts. She joined him at the Salon as the first beauty therapist in 1963. In addition to the business, they shared a passion for music, dancing and being beautiful: she was soberly elegant, ironic but discrete, while he was flamboyantly colorful, sophisticated and a true aficionado of jewels.

Celebrities from the world of cinema and stage, esteemed aristocrats and industrials, along with local brides were all welcome in the Salon, all treated with equal humanity and privacy, but moreover, all with respect.

In those years it would have been extremely easy for them to leave the island for a more lucrative and prestigious career, but they are remembered for kindly turning down many once-in-a-lifetime offers. They remained faithful to that little world where everything they needed was included, especially the sense of family and belonging.

Through these photographs, and the memories of Camillo, Rosalia and Salvatore, I was allowed a vision of Ischia as a special and precious place, one that adds to my personal memory of my mother and of Livio.

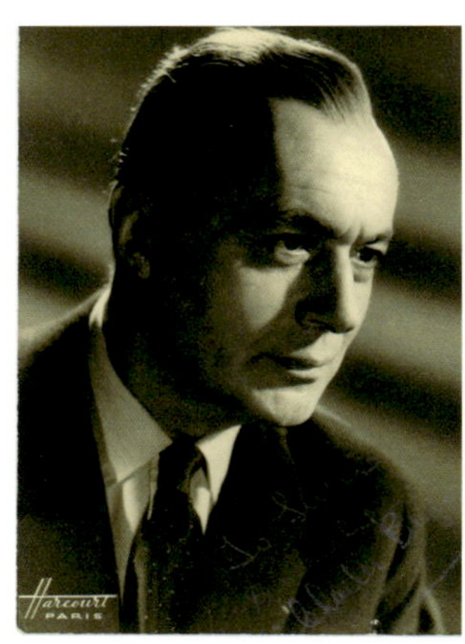

Harcourt
PARIS

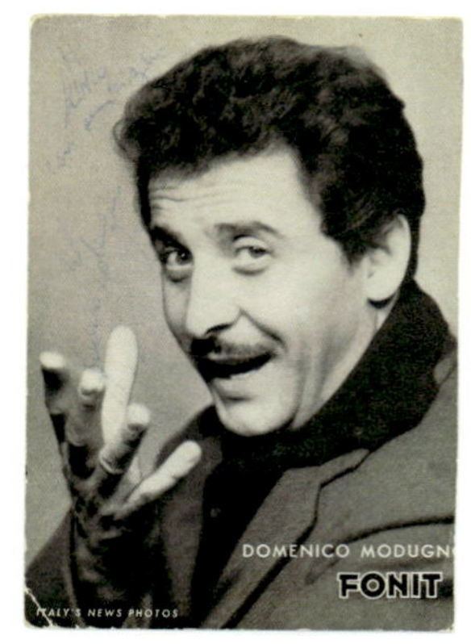

DOMENICO MODUGNO
FONIT
ITALY'S NEWS PHOTOS

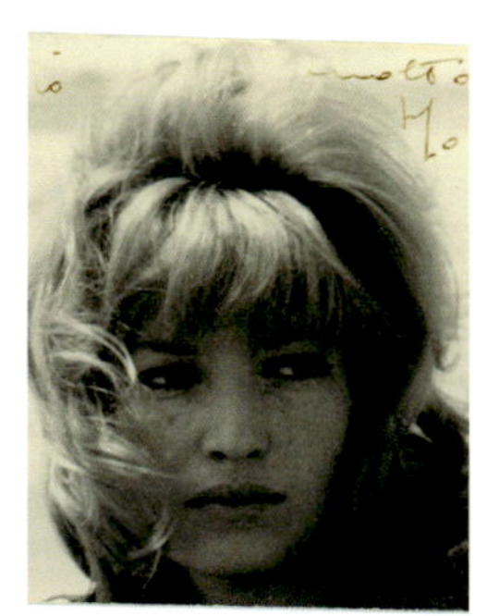

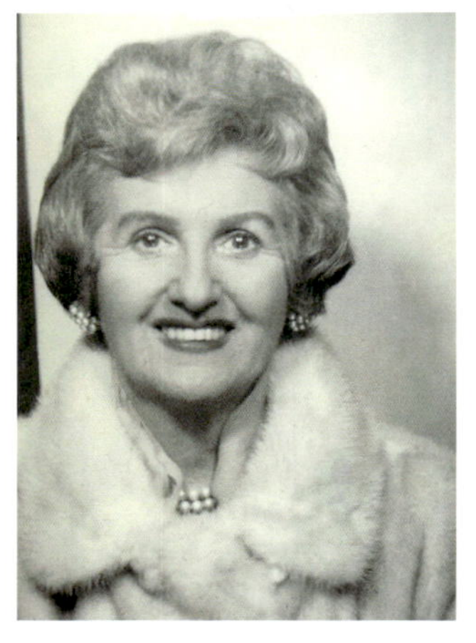

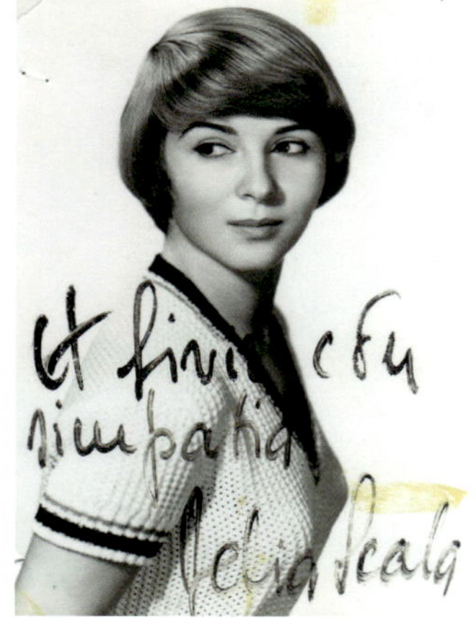

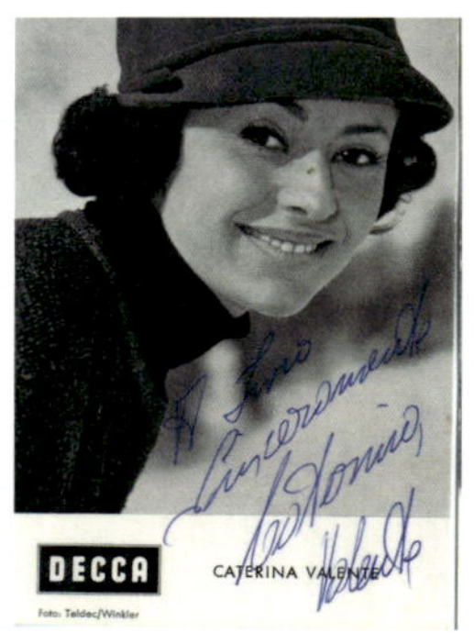

DECCA
CATERINA VALENTE
Foto: Teldec/Winkler

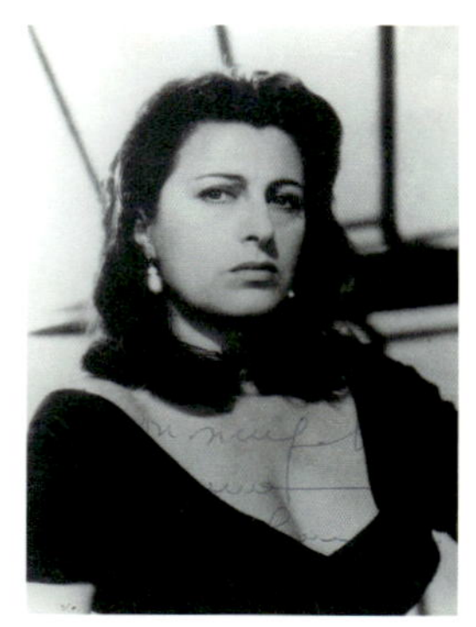

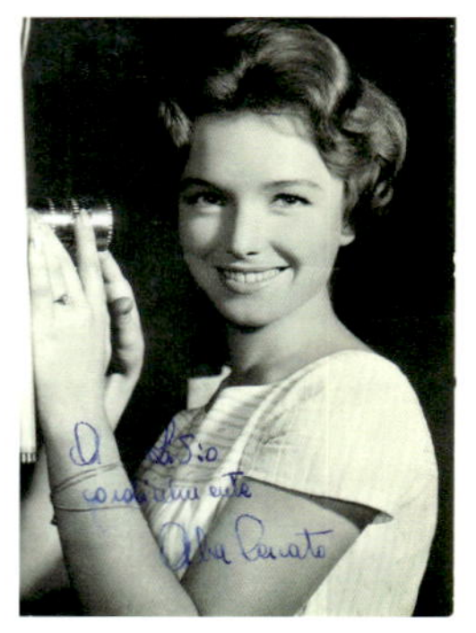

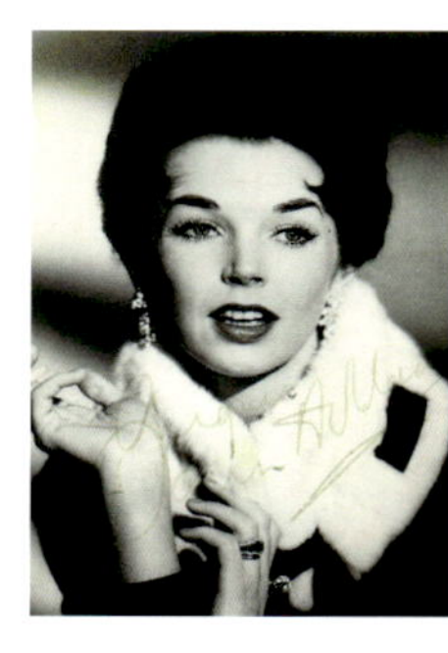

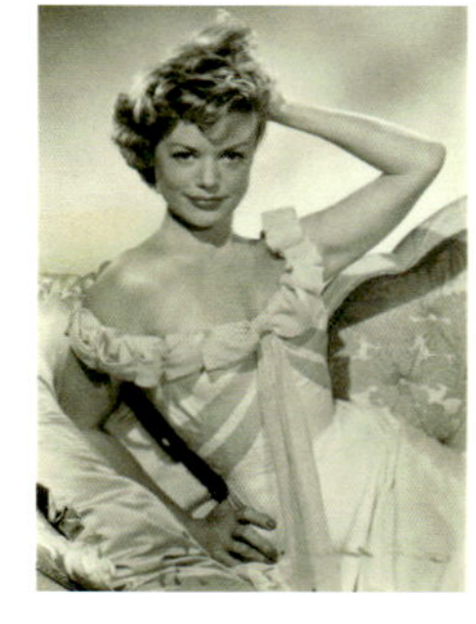

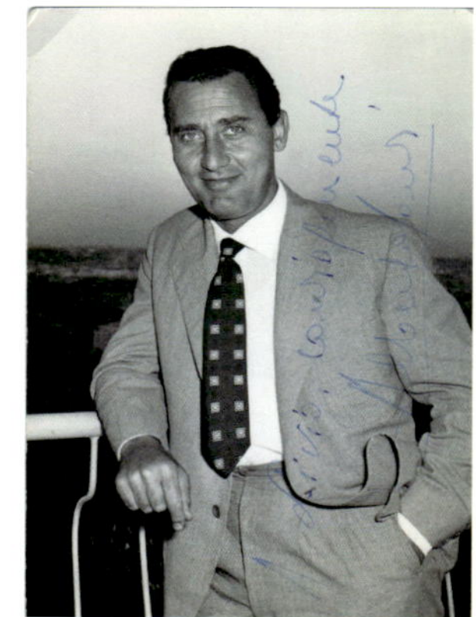

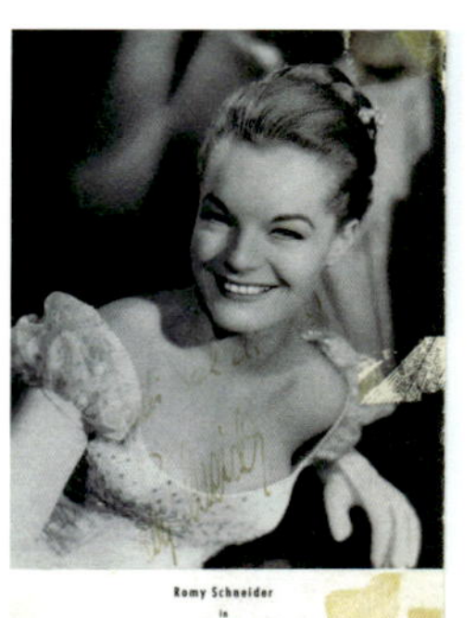

Romy Schneider
in
»DIE SCHÖNE LÜGNERIN«

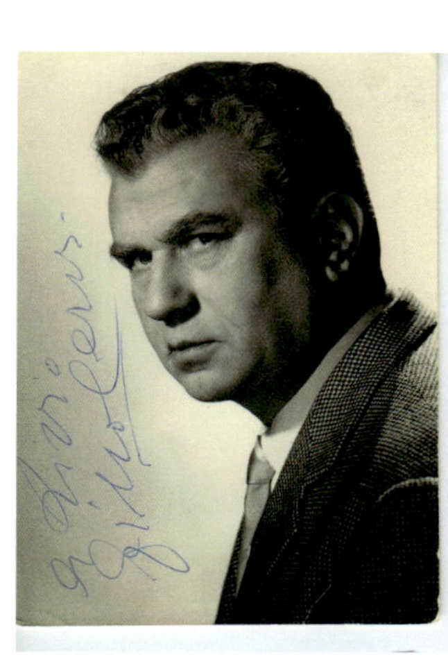

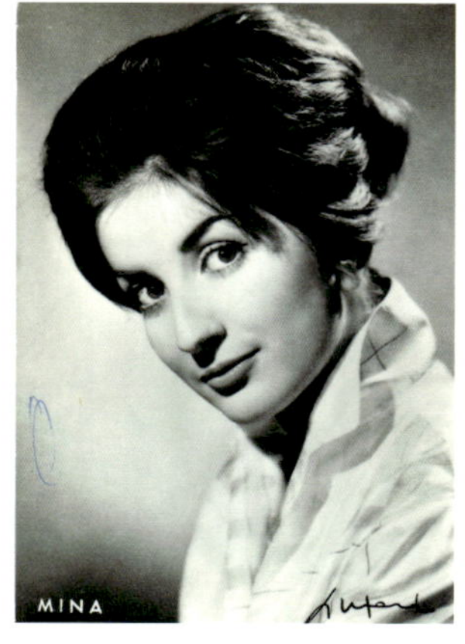

MINA

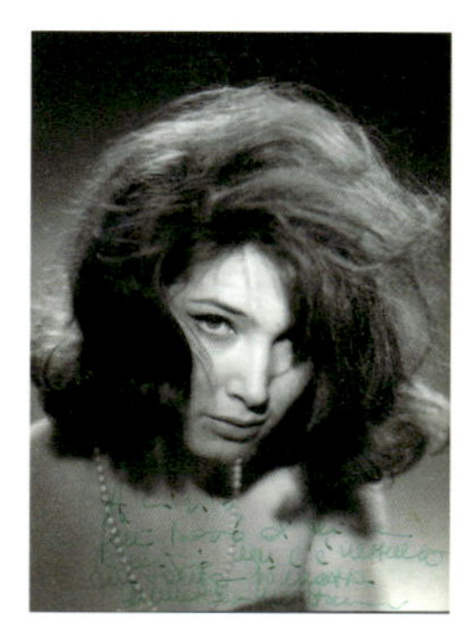

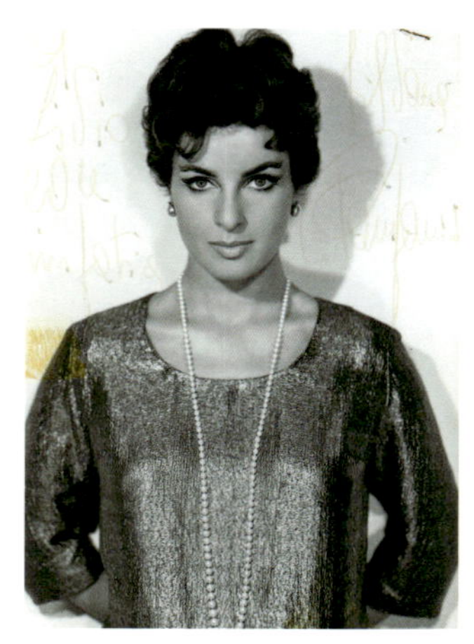

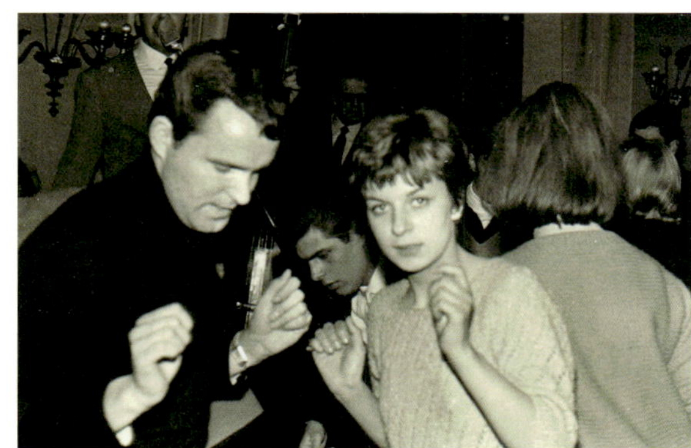

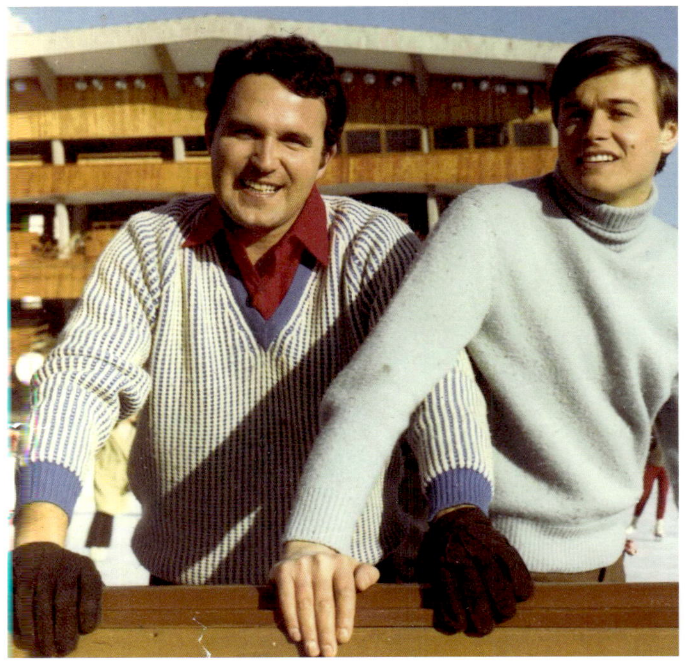

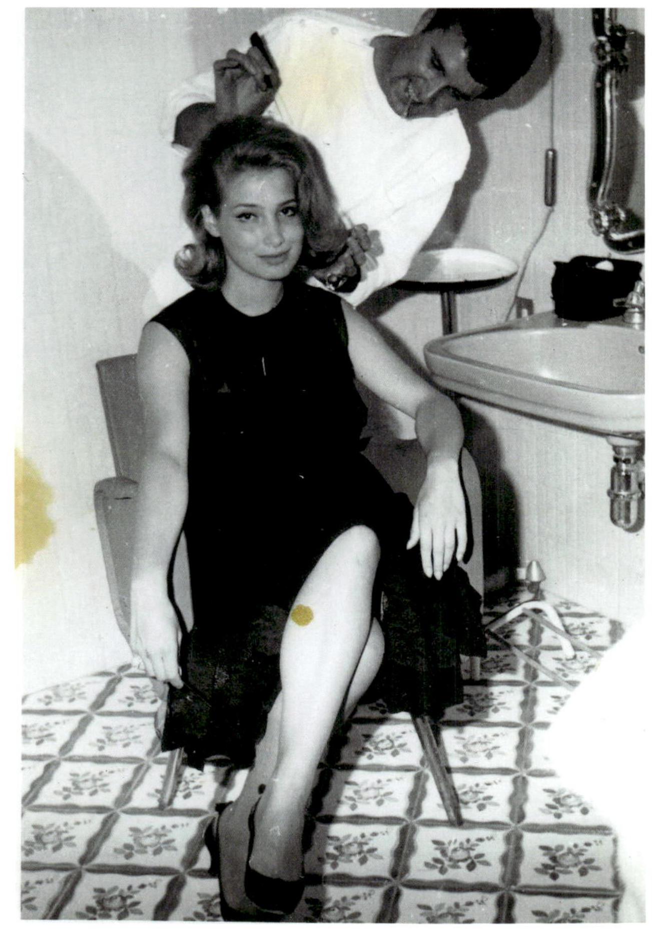

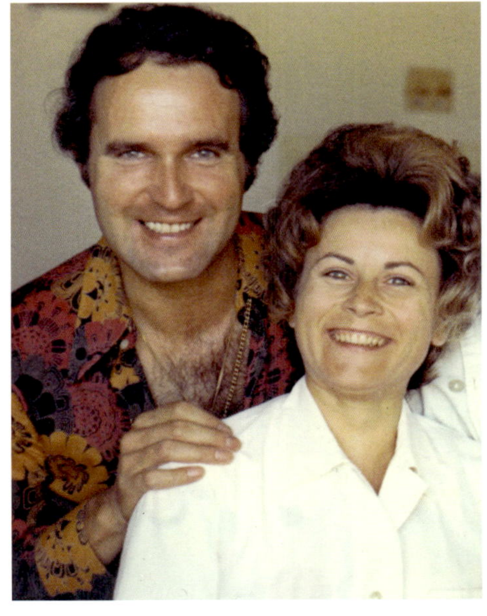

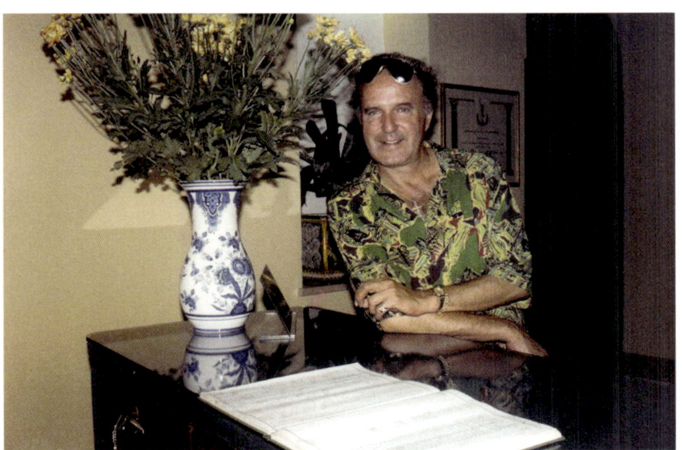

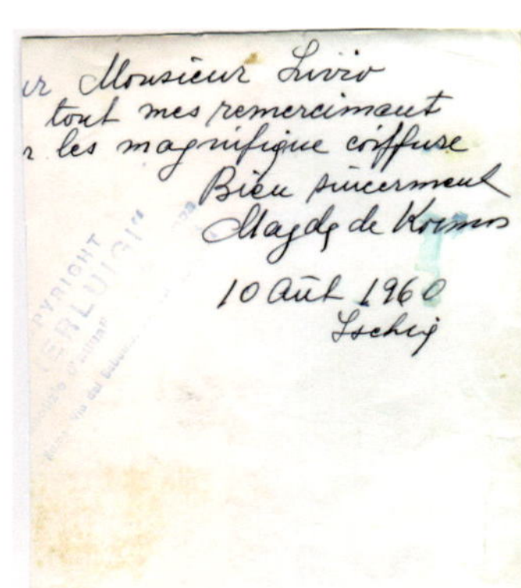

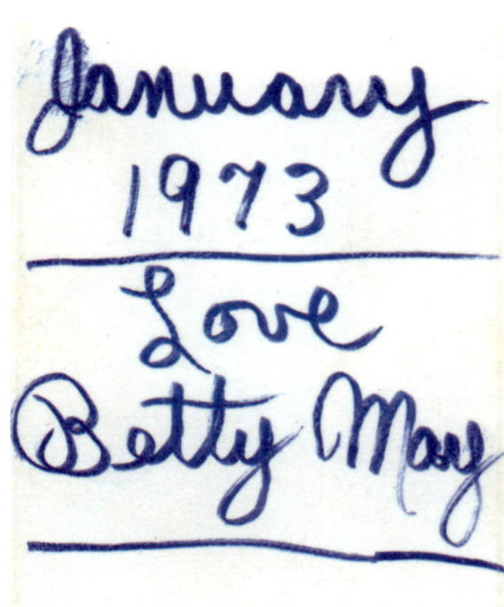

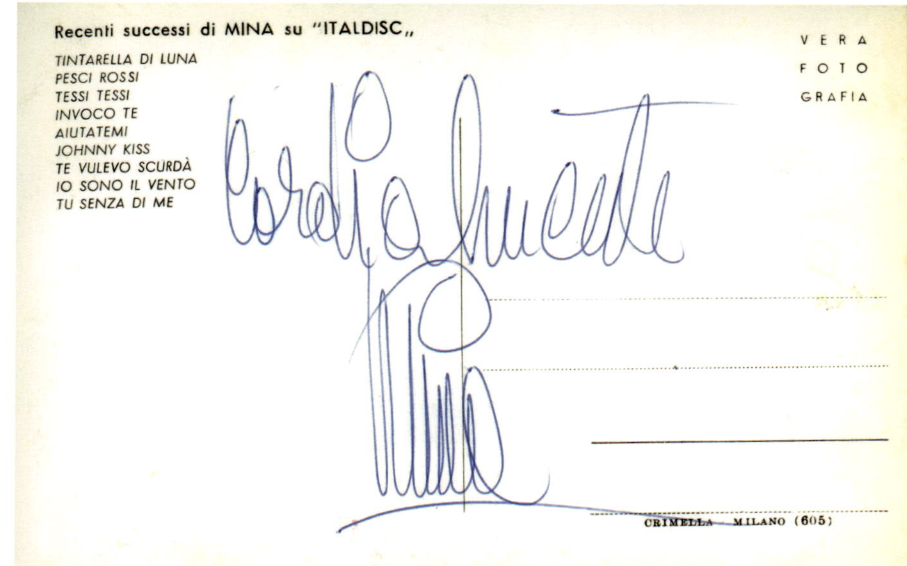
Recenti successi di MINA su "ITALDISC„
TINTARELLA DI LUNA
PESCI ROSSI
TESSI TESSI
INVOCO TE
AIUTATEMI
JOHNNY KISS
TE VULEVO SCURDÀ
IO SONO IL VENTO
TU SENZA DI ME
VERA
FOTO
GRAFIA
CRIMELLA - MILANO (605)

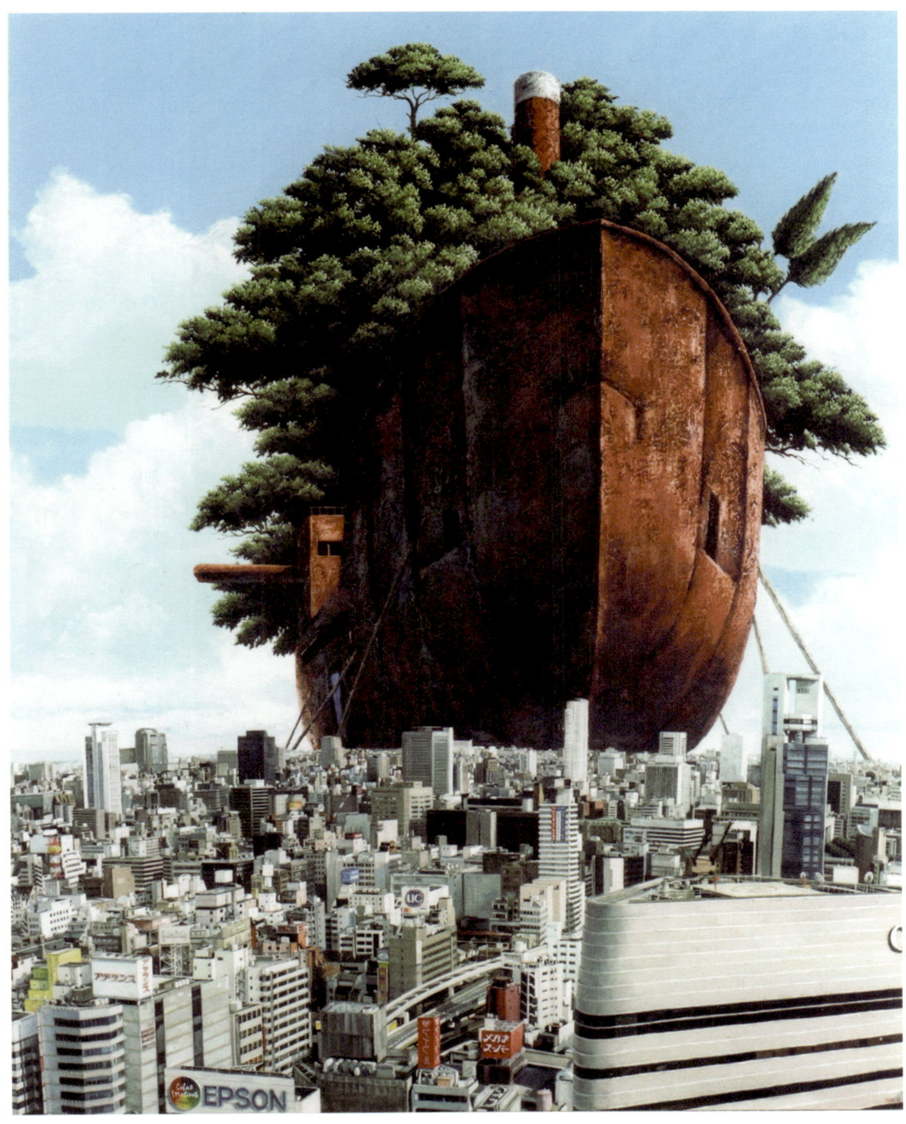

SHUICHI NAKANO

In his latest series, *Searching for Paradise*, Nakano paints surrealistic scenes of wildlife as they eclipse various Japanese cityscapes. These are not frightening scenes, ominous perhaps, but in some sense, tranquil, inquisitive, with a detailed technique that playfully draws attention to imbalances in proportion and scale. Are the animals too big or is the city too small? What relationship do these creatures have with their urban landscapes, as if embarking on a reverse Safari? The man-made world is dwarfed by the species that humans have long attempted to dominate, and Nakano's large scale images depict and empower an environment where wildlife can recapture its domain. Nakano was born in 1966 in Hokkaido, Japan. He studied at the Hirosaki University and the Aichi University of Education, where he completed his M.A. He currently lives in Yuzawa-shi, Akita.

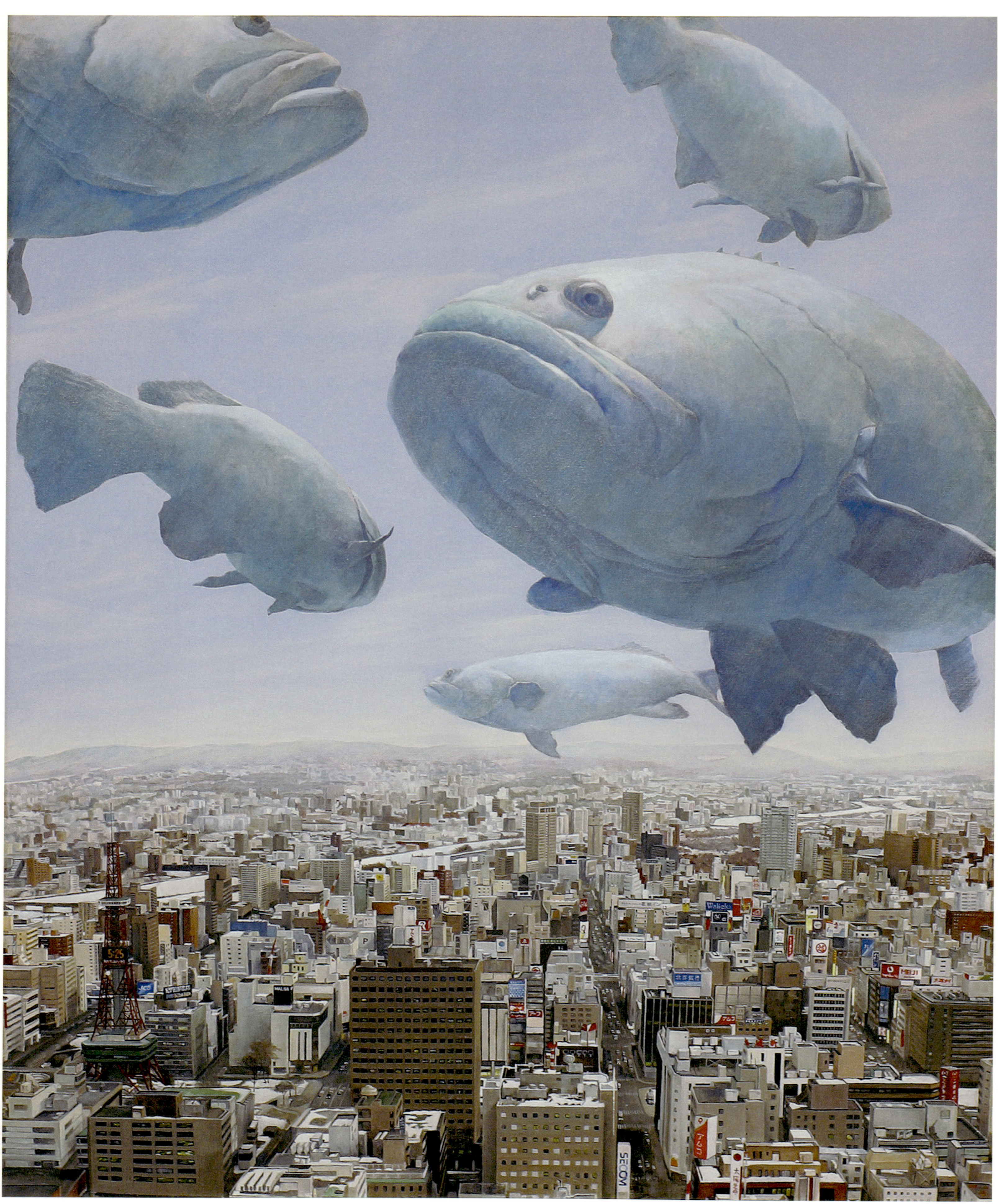

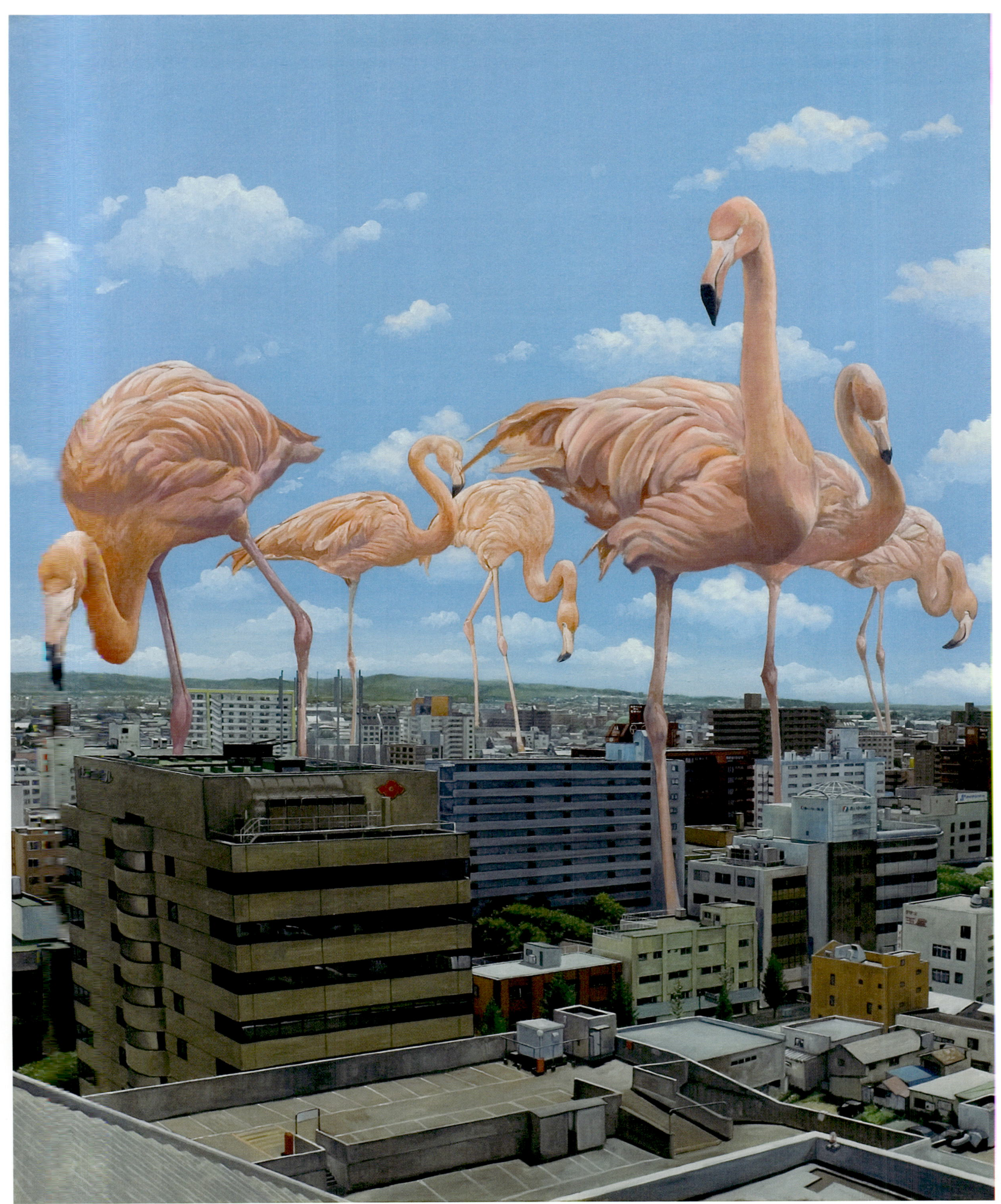

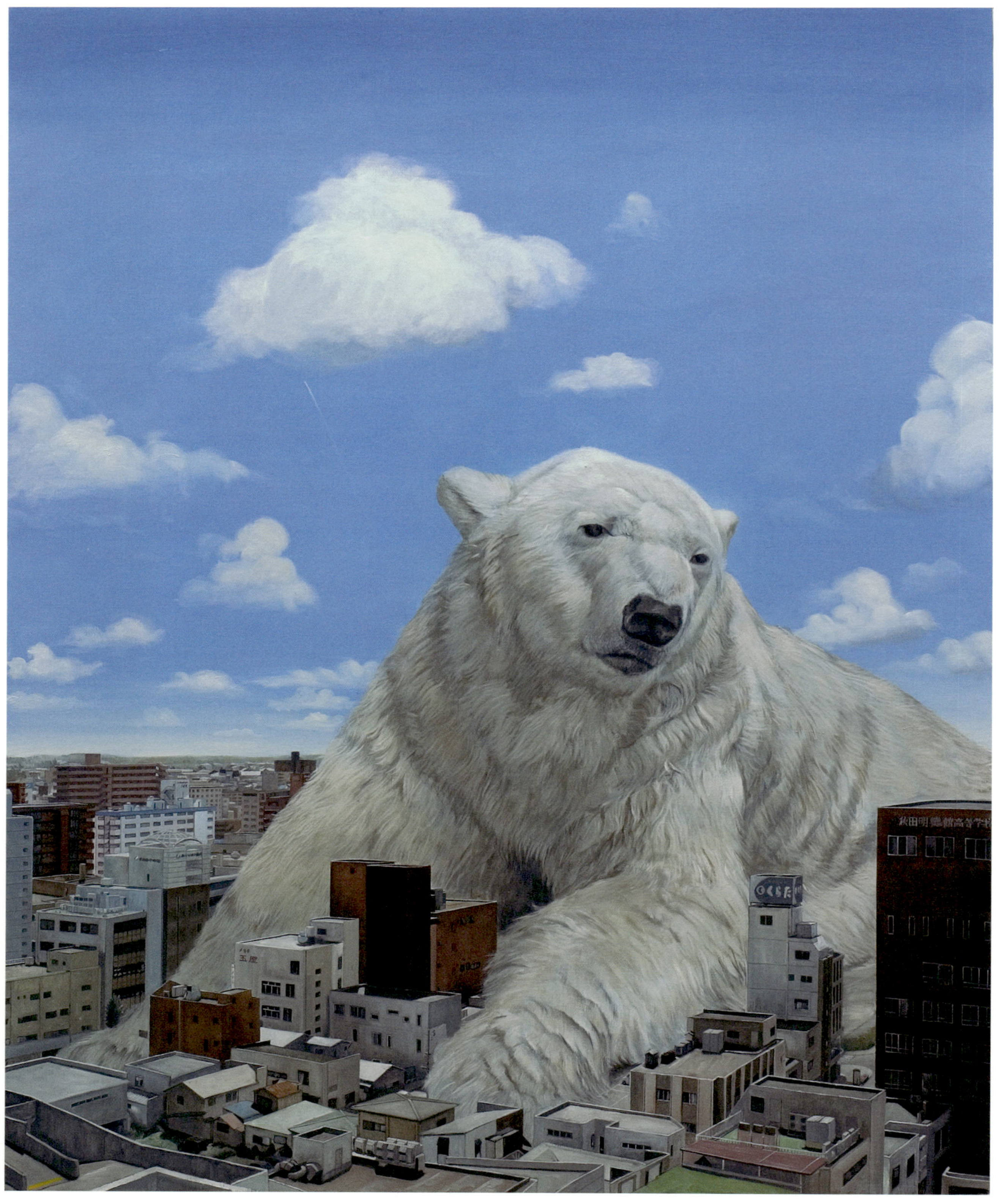

Page 45 Silence, 2004, cm 162 x 130.3, *from the series* Searching for the lost story. *Page 46* Chill at 5:25, 2008, cm 162 x 130.3, *from the series* Searching for Paradise vol.1. *Page 47* In the place where sea breeze blows, 2010, cm 162 x 130.3, *from the series* Searching for Paradise vol.2. *Above* By sleepiness, 2010, cm 162 x 130.3, *from the series* Searching for Paradise vol.2. *Rigth above* Till find the forest, 2010, cm 91 x 116.7, *from the series* Searching for Paradise vol.2; *below* At the end of spring, 2010, cm 130.3 x 162, *from the series* Searching for Paradise vol.2. *All images oil on canvas and panel © and courtesy the artist*

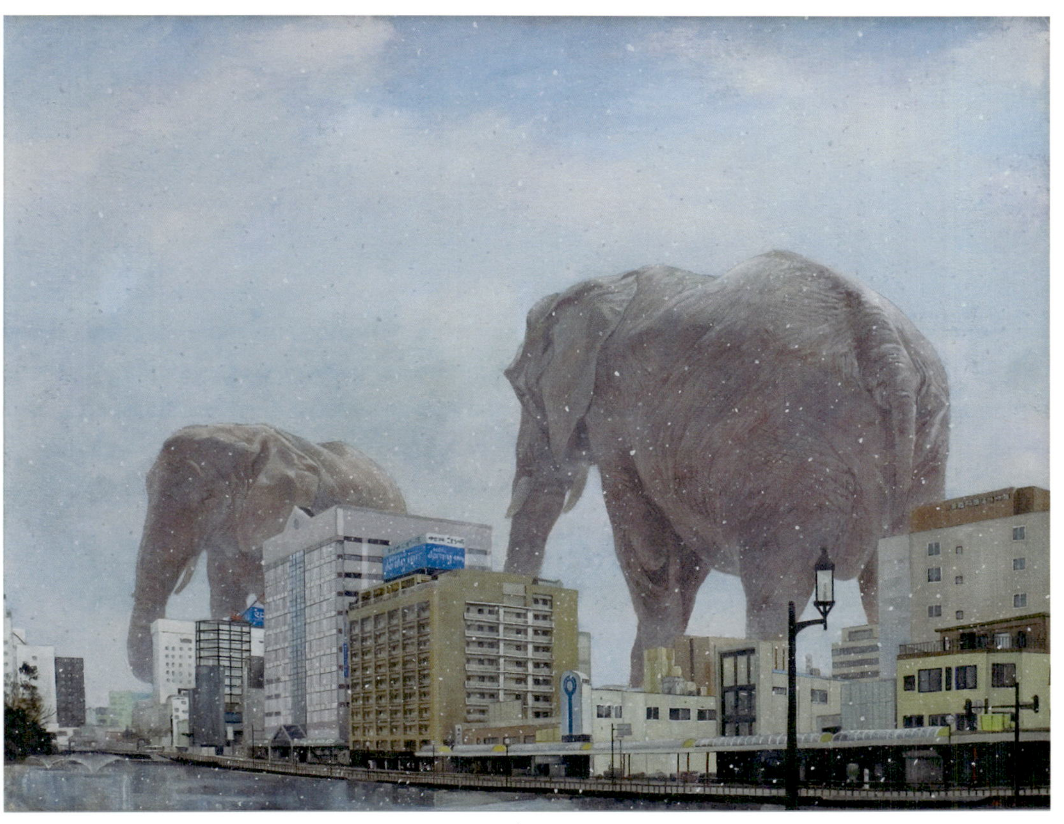

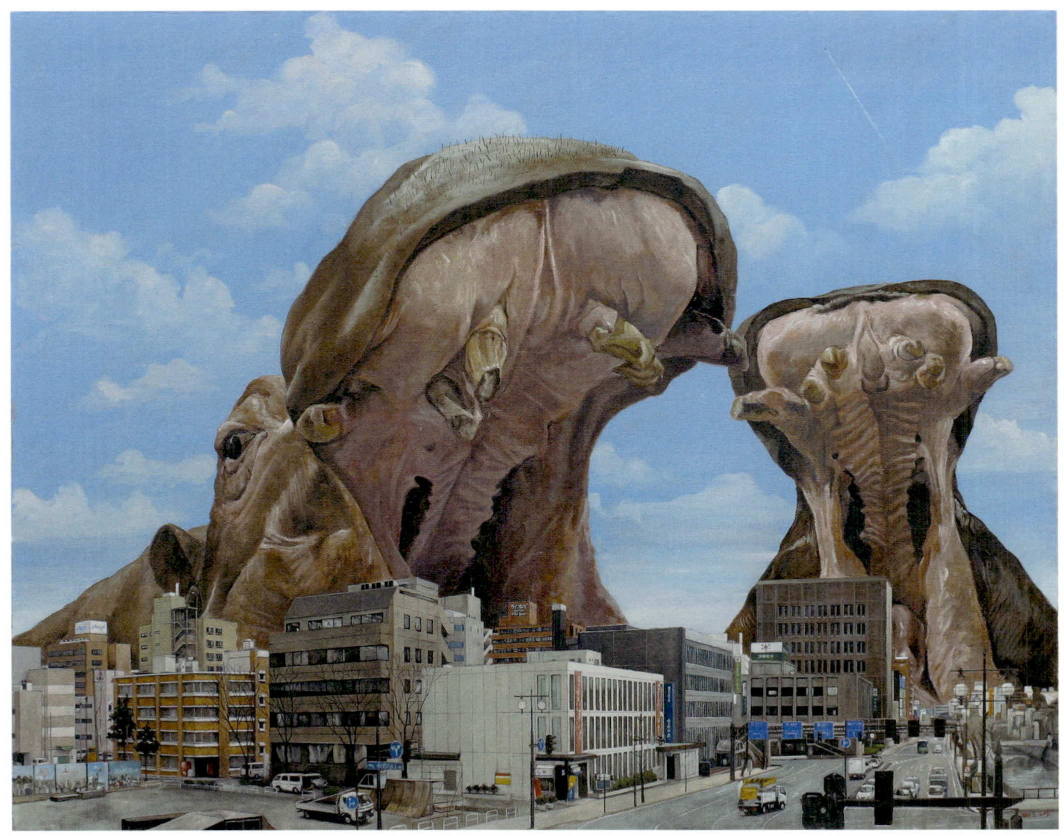

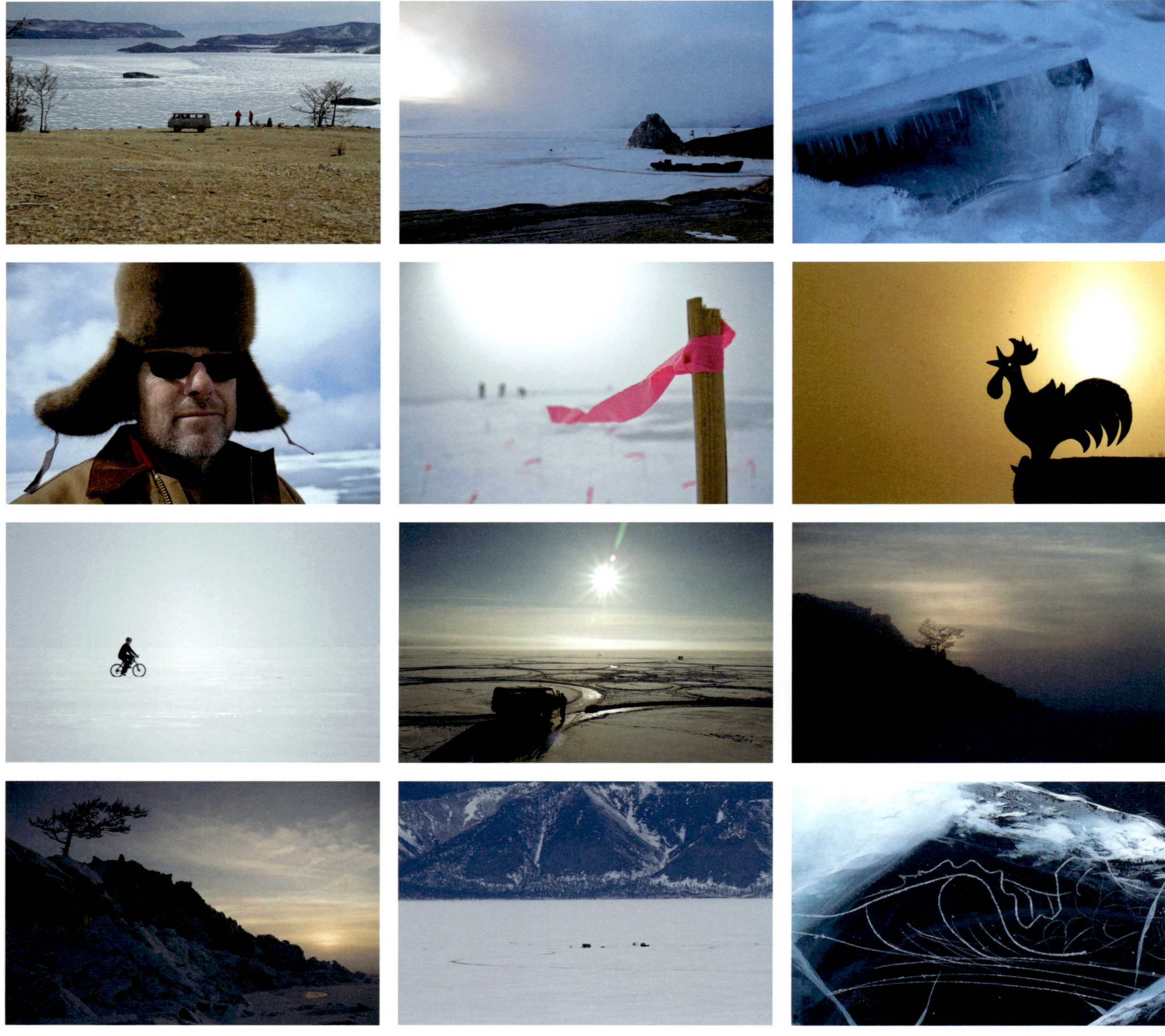

ART DOCUMENTING ART
Emma Reeves on
MEREDITH DANLUCK

On the 31st March 2010 Jim Denevan, an American artist, and his team of four collaborators broke the record for the largest artwork in the world. It took the form of concentric circles perfectly mapped out over a distance of 9 square miles. The feat took place on the frozen surface of Lake Baikal, in extreme Siberian weather conditions, to the bemusement of the one hundred or so local villagers on the island of Olkhon where the team were based for the duration of the project.

Art Hard, a film created by Meredith Danluck brings the project to a wider audience. A video artist in her own right Danluck does all she can to defy specific classification in art world terms. She admits, "at some point I just decided that I wanted to have a really interesting life and that I couldn't necessarily control the parameters of that life." Faced with the task of documenting an artist she had never met in a place she had never visited, she decided that the film would be more of a meditation on creativity. "This, to me was this perfect opportunity to strip it down to this very basic question as to why people really do anything." An early encounter with one of the local villagers sets up the underlying premise of the film in the most eloquent and philosophical way; when asked what her definition of art is, Nina Kursheva, an elegant woman in her 60's, unhesitatingly opines, "Art is a conversation with man's soul, with the thin substance of man. A monologue, a dialogue in different ways. Man consists not only of flesh, but also of something else and this something else seeks expression."

A conventional approach to creating a film about the making of an artwork would dictate that Denevan become the central character. In Danluck's film she purposefully avoided interviewing him until very late in the process, choosing to focus her attentions on the team working with him to create the artwork. "It is not a celebration of him. It is the idea of art in his context. It is portraiture. I think that that kind of documentary is more informative on an emotional level than a traditional kind of biopic. You understand more what a relationship with that person would be like." Her film is also just as much about the physical surroundings, the context in which the artwork is made. Lake Baikal becomes an extraordinary brooding presence, an immense body of thick audible ice. The weather rages around them all, often threatening to sabotage the project entirely overnight. Local people are enlisted to help and Danluck has no hesitation in including their often negative and humorous responses to the task at hand. Humor is important to Danluck. "The absurd in the situation is just there. Everyone always wants to be more serious, work with conflict, but if you balance it out with humor it is more dynamic."

Ultimately, Danluck gradually allows an intimate and moving portrait of Denevan to evolve. The personal reasons for his compulsive need to create are gradually revealed. "I think maybe to draw on a very large surface is a distillation of human experience. To make a mark on the ground, it's something that everyone does when they go from birth to death, or from home to the 7/11."

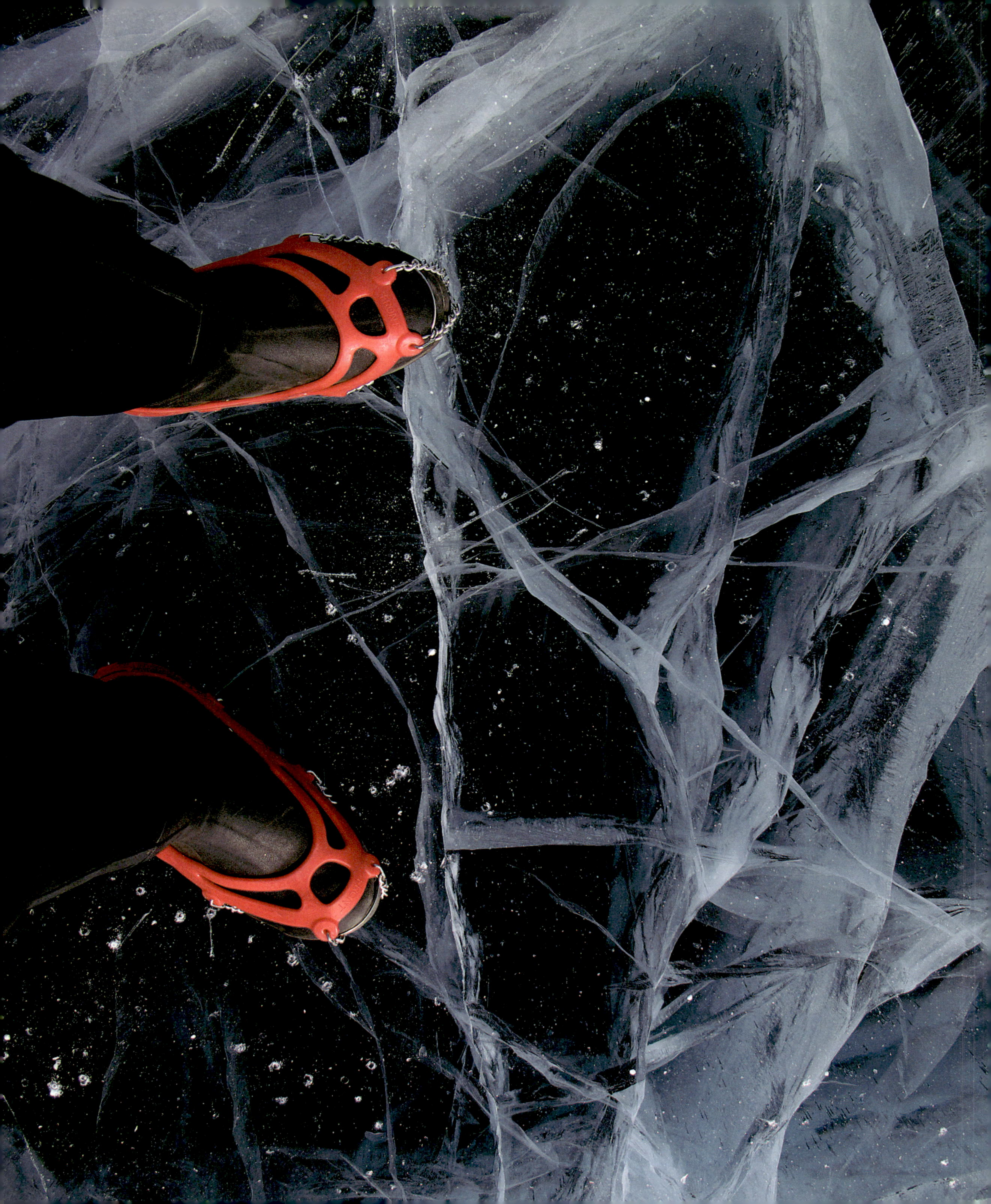

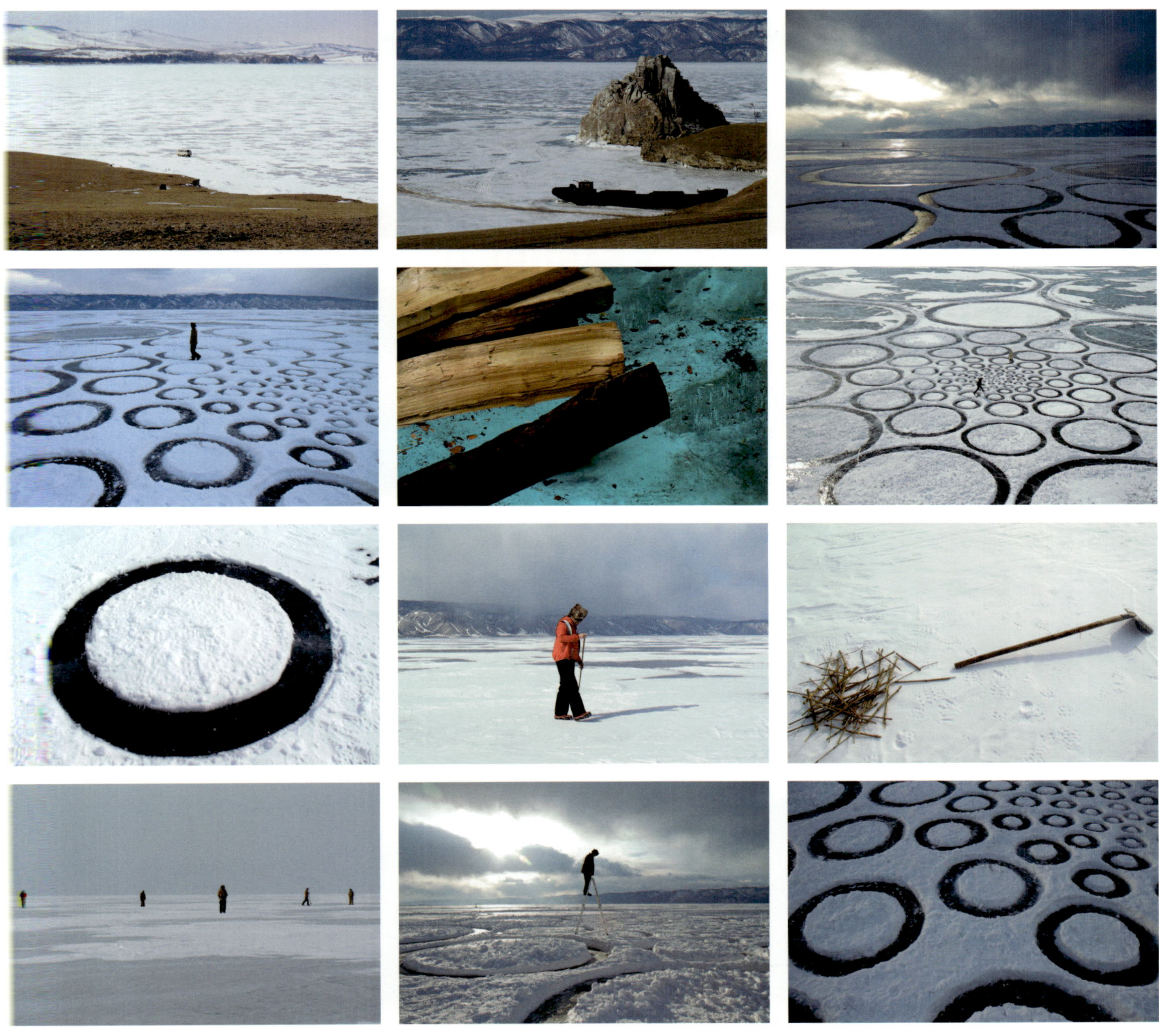

All images © the artist and Jake Burghart, courtesy Renwick Gallery, New York and theanthropologist.net

M. E. BRUGSCH: THE TREASURE OF DEIR-EL-BAHARI
by Gerry Badger

This article, in the September 1970 issue of *Creative Camera*, was said to have greatly inspired Richard Avedon. I do not know how true this is, but if we look at some of Avedon's later portraits, especially those of his father, one can perhaps detect the reason for such an assertion.

The photographs in the article were taken by Émile Brugsch, an archaeologist at Cairo's Bulak Museum (now the Egyptian Museum), following the discovery of the Deir el-Bahari cache in 1881. On the West Bank of the Nile near Luxor, near the temple of Hatshepsut, the mummies of forty pharaohs, queens, princes and princesses of ancient Egypt, including some of her greatest rulers, were discovered down a rough shaft by two inhabitants of the nearby village of Gourna, an event that inspired one of Egypt's finest art films, Shadi Abdel Salam's *The Night of Counting the Years (1969)*.

I have always been intrigued by this discovery, the political machinations surrounding it, and by Brugsch's straightforward, but startling photographs. The caption to the article states that these photographs came from an album in Auckland, New Zealand, where Brugsch is named M. E., and not Émile Brugsch. Many years after the *Creative Camera* piece, I was very pleased to acquire a print of one of the greatest ancient rulers, Sethi I, at a photo-fair for next to nothing, and enclose it as a supplement to the scan.

Recently, it was reported that during Egypt's impressive people's revolution, the Cairo Egyptian Museum was broken into, and the heads torn off two mummies. Perhaps the violators had not heard of the 'curse of the pharaohs', and are now suffering for this act of wanton vandalism. Sloppy journalism had described Hosni Mubarak as a latter-day 'pharaoh', but all the archaeological evidence points to the fact that, while not exactly presiding over democracies, the rulers of Kemet (as Egypt was known), cared rather more for their subjects than the late, and unlamented dictator.

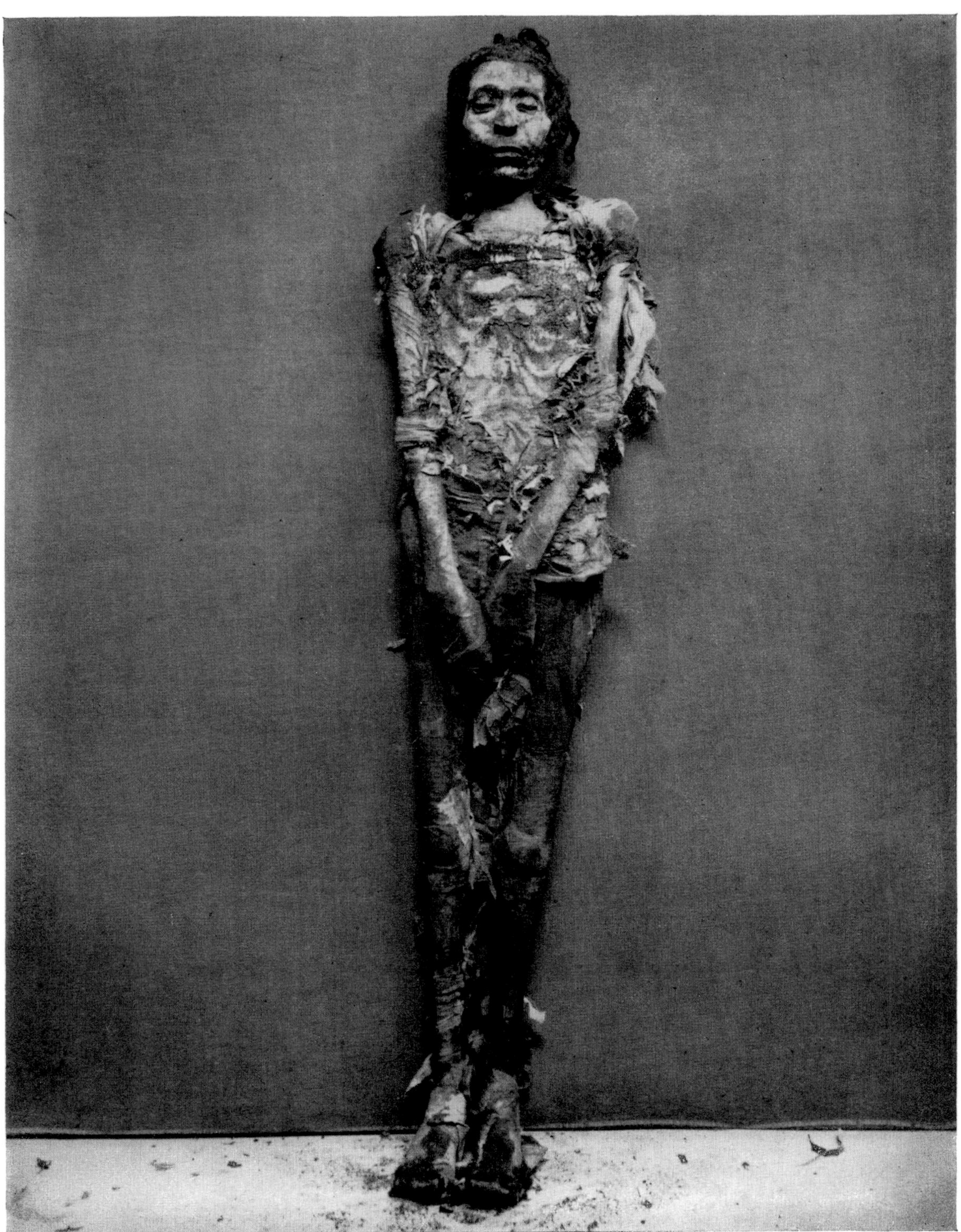

Egyptian Prince Djet-ptah-any-ankh, twenty-first dynasty (1000-900 B.C.).

285

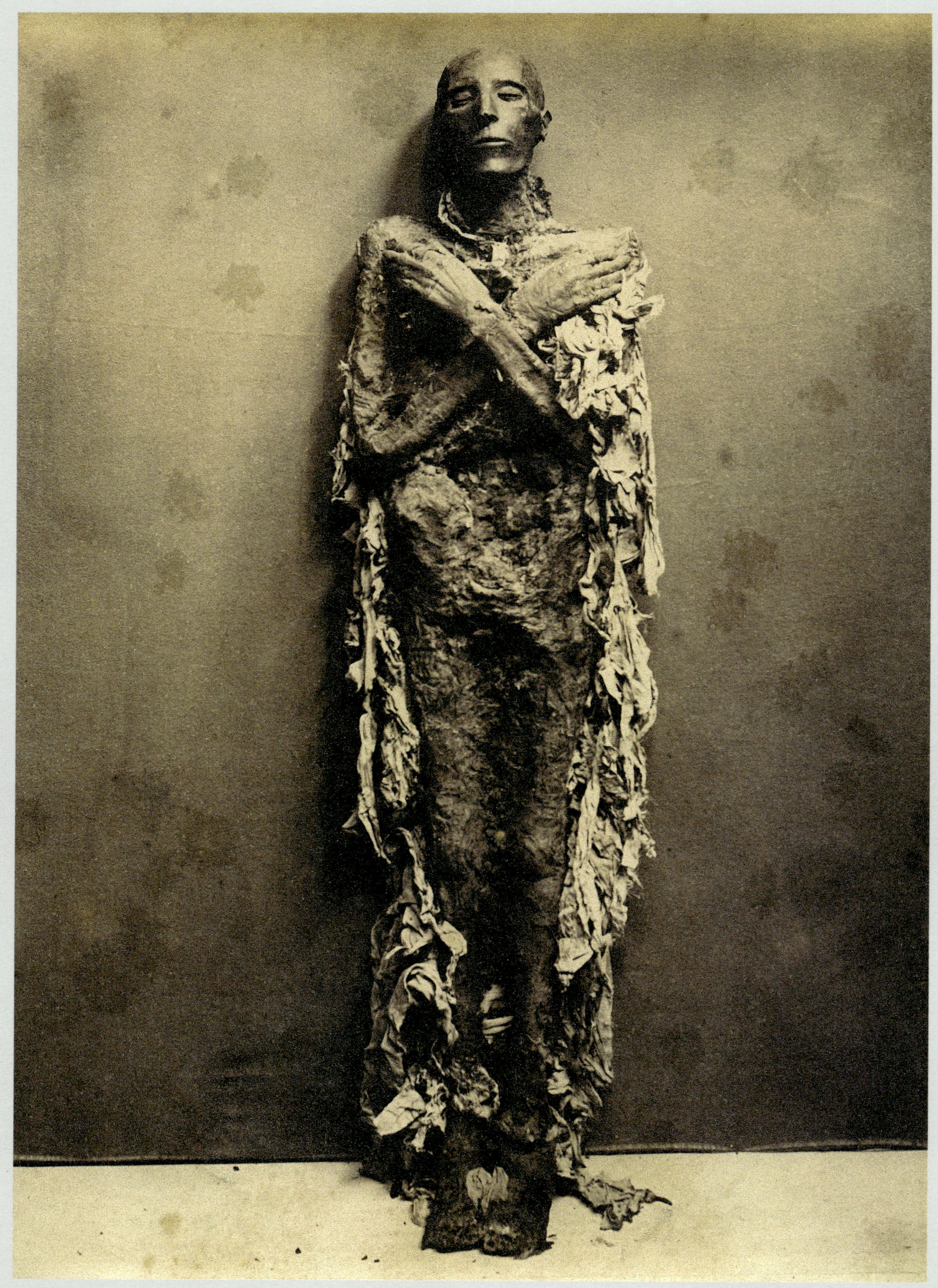

photographs by **M. E. Brugsch**

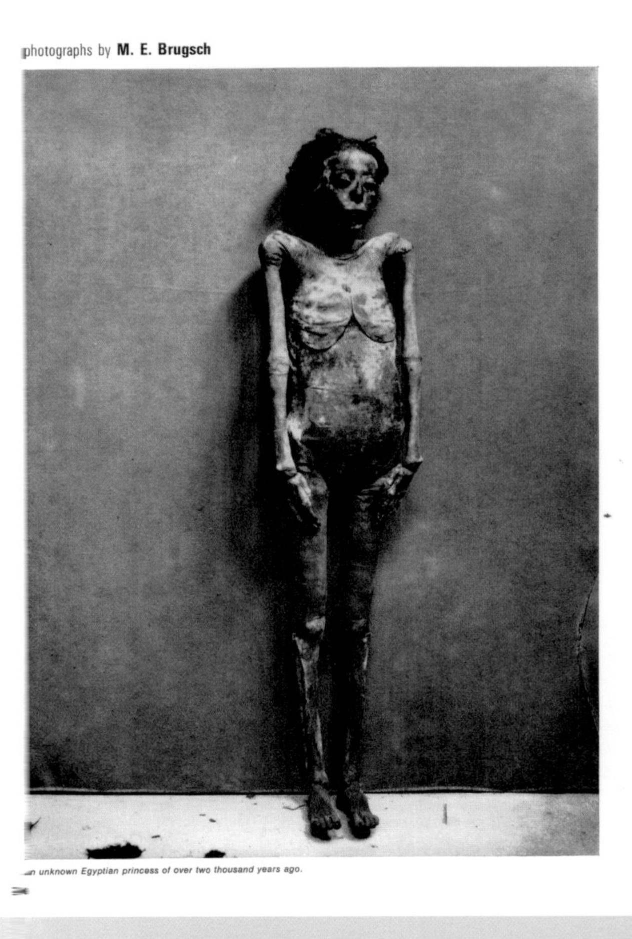

an unknown Egyptian princess of over two thousand years ago.

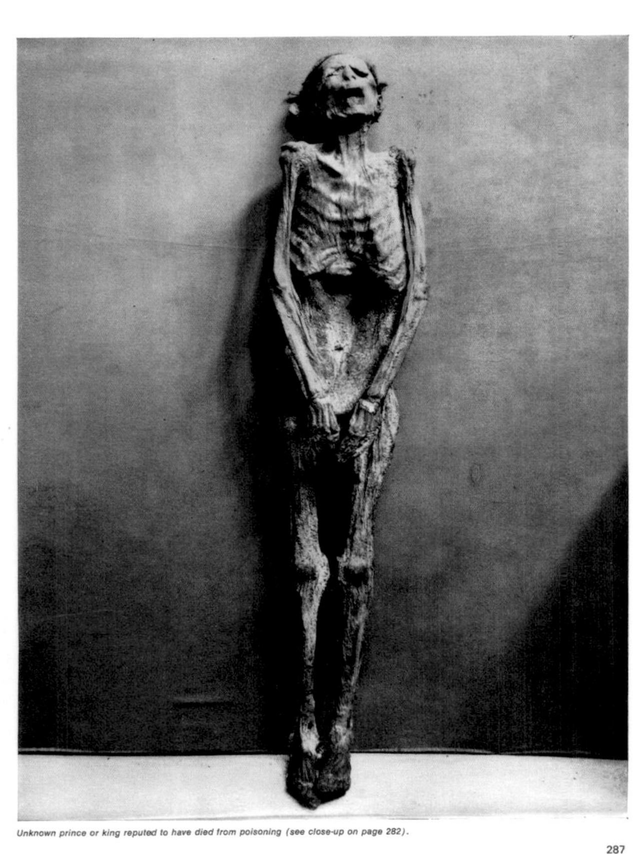

Unknown prince or king reputed to have died from poisoning (see close-up on page 282).

287

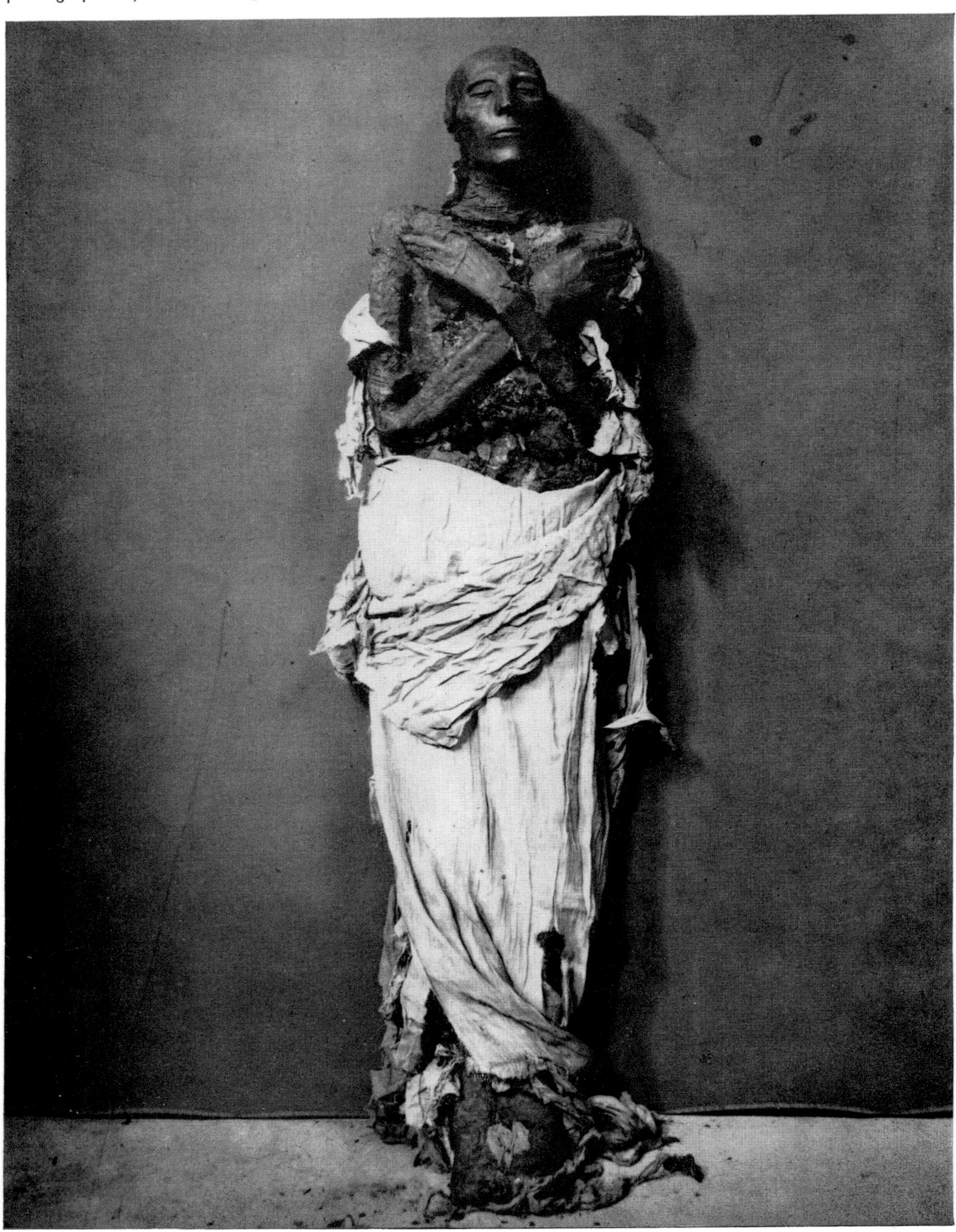

Egyptian King Seti I, nineteenth dynasty (1378-1304 B.C.)·

284

M. E. Brugsch the treasure of Deir-El-Bahari

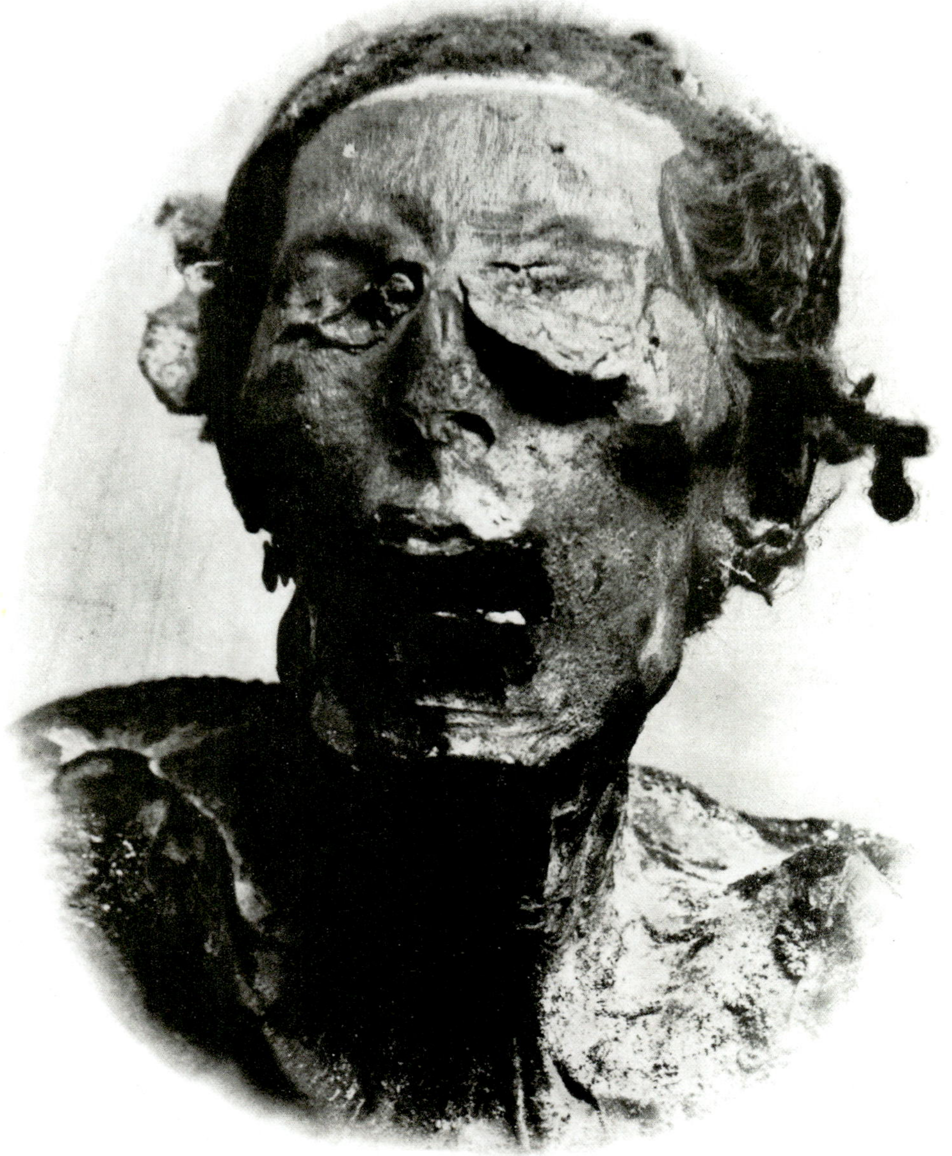

Close-up of mummified unknown prince or king reputed to have died from poisoning.

**These photographs are from 'The Treasure of Deir-El-Bahari', by the famous Egyptologist G. Maspero.
The account, with original photographs by M. E. Brugsch for illustrations, was published in France in 1881. The
original photographs and text are in the collection of the Dominion Museum, Wellington, New Zealand, and
were sent to us by John B. Turner.**

282

ry poe try poe try poe try poe try poe try poe try poe
ry poe try poe try poe try poe try poe try poe try poe
ry poe try poe try poe try poe try poe try poe try poe
y poe try poe try poe try poe try poe try poe try poe t
ry poe try poe try poe try poe try poe try poe try poe
ry po trey poe try poe try poe try poe try poe try poe
ry poe try poe try poe try poe try poe try poe try po
oe try poe try poe try poe try poe try poe try poe try
oe try poe try poe try poe try poe try poe try poe try
ry poe try poe try poe try poe try poe try poe try poe
ry poe try poe try poe try poe try poe try poe try poe
ry poe try poe try poe try poe try poe try poe try poe
ry poe try poe try poe try poe try poe try poe try poe
ry poe try poe try poe try poe try poe try poe try poe
poe try poe try poe try poe try poe try poe try poe tr
try poe try poe try poe try poe try poe try poe try po
y poe try poe try poe try poe try poe try poe try poe t
e try poe try poe try poe try poe try poe try poe try p
ry poe try poe try poe try poe try poe try poe try poe
ry poe try poe try poe try poe try poe try poe try poe
poe try poe try poe try poe try poe try poe try poe
ry poe try poe try poe try poe try poe try poe try
ry poe try poe try poe try poe try poe try poe try
oe try poe try poe try poe try poe try poe try poe
y poe try poe try poe try poe try poe try po try poe try p
ry poe try poe try poe try poe try poe try poe try
ry poe try poe try poe try poe try poe try poe
y poe try poe try poe try poe try poe try poe tr
y poe try poe try poe try poe try poe try poe
ry poe try poe try poe try poe try poe try
ry poe try poe try poe try poe try poe try
ry poe try poe try poe try poe try poe

What do you mean overexposing to become a wiser person?

André Príncipe in conversation with

JH ENGSTRÖM

JH Engström is an errant figure. He was born in Karlstad, Sweden, in 1969, spent most of his adolescence in Paris, moved to New York at 29, traveled around Europe, and then moved back to his native Värmland more recently. During his life he developed an equally multifaceted and unique photography style made from the combination of a number of different codes: from documentary photography to fashion, from reportage to family pictures. He made it into a paradigm through the publication of numerous books starting with *Shelter* (Bokförlaget DN, 1997) and continuing with *Trying to Dance* (Journal, 2004 - short-listed for the Deutsche Borse Photography Prize), *Haunts* (Steidl, 2006), *La Residence* (Journal, 2009) and many others.

The conversation between Engström and André Príncipe took place in Paris on November 17th, 2010. They met just after discovering that they were both staying on Rue du Faubourg Saint Martin, a few steps from each other. In the following minutes they also found out, among many other things, that they share the ritual of always drinking red wine when flying, play the same soccer positions (wide midfielders or left wing) and love Albert Camus' *L'Etranger*. The conversation took place over lunch. Even though they were not really flying, they shared a bottle of red wine.

ANDRÉ PRÍNCIPE *When editing your books, do you leave a lot to chance, or do you plan everything very carefully?*

JH ENGSTRÖM The most difficult thing is to be totally in control and at the same time totally intuitive. That's the most challenging and the most interesting part, to be in different levels. Photographing comes naturally, it's like breathing. It's not an effort, comes out of necessity, just comes. So, that is not really the work, maybe the work is the editing, and there also, like in everything, like in writing or making films, you have to have a method.

I think photography is writing. That's what photography means, writing with light. Do you see yourself as an image maker or a storyteller? Does this question make sense to you?
To be honest, I'm always quite curious with words and all, but I don't really care if I'm this or that. I'm more interested in… I'm very keen in expressing myself. I don't really care if I'm a storyteller or an image maker.

Would you do it with music?
It's less complicated when I do photography because I've been doing it for a while, so I know that language better than music, which I don't know at all. We only have one life, I'm quite sure about that, so how do you use that? For me it became photography, it was through photography that I expressed myself.

And it's going to be like that.
Yeah, you know and accept that. But that's a classical one. How many photographers, like you, and me too, envy people that make films? You know I envy them, I'm like, Wow! Or writers, I have so much respect for words. People that say, "I'm going to write a novel." That's impressive for me. How to get that together? Musicians, writers, filmmakers, they impress me, because I don't know how they do it. To make a photography book is quite complicated, both me and you, now, we know how it goes, it's a big thing, it's a long project

before you have the photos and then you have to work with the editor and do the editing, but compare that to making a fiction film - it's nothing. To have the strength to carry your vision from the beginning to the end. But that's also the reason why I don't do fiction films, because I know a lot of people that do and they say it's very rare that you keep your vision to the end because there are too many interests, too much money involved.

Would you do films with actors and actresses, with scripts? Would you stage? I don't want to stage too much, I could stage a bit, but that's like a secret, you know?
It's not a secret, I always say that I do stage and for me there is no difference between staging and not staging.

Exactly, I feel the same! People don't understand this! There is something I call relationship photography and there are the ones in which I'm trying to be invisible.
So, these relationship photographs, are they, more or less important to you than the ones you do when you are a fly on the wall? Is there a difference?

No, doesn't matter.
Neither for me. Not at all. For some people it does, it's very important if it's staged or not.

I have no kind of morality.
You do! Well, not in that way. [laughs]

[Laughs] Not in that way! Morality is like underpants, I don't want to wear my underpants on top of my pants.
The book I did with Anders Petersen, *From Back Home*, it's not relationships, it's not people that I know. The relationship I

have is with the landscape or the region where I did these photographs. But the people, I don't know them. We didn't spend time together. I have a really strong relationship to that region. That makes it easy for me to do it, so it's kind of relationship photography as well, but in other ways.

These people, you know the way they talk, you know what they think, their beliefs! So, that's already relationship photography. I wanted to ask you about those books, because you have La Residence, From Back Home, *the book about the Charles de Gaulle airport. These books are organized. I mean the theme or what they announce to be, the title, etc, it has to do with a place, which is something very classical in photography.* Trying to Danc*e and* Haunts *are books which are about, I mean, they get more complex, but they announce to be about your relationship to the world and your relationship to photography.*
Well, I totally agree. I feel very clear about that. The books that are about specific geographic places, and the books where the frame is in my head. I did *Trying to dance* and then I did *Haunts*, and I'm now doing this project on Paris, which is totally… I mean, Paris, what is Paris? It's abstract, there's no way you can tell about Paris. So what is it? You have to put frames on it yourself, except that it is Paris, and for me, it becomes more and more the concrete story that I have with Paris, so it's quite far away from *Haunts*. But at the same time it's complex because, for me, *Haunts*, it's my story as well, you know?

A territory. It can be physical or it can be emotional, but you need a territory. It's actually always both. You start on one and then you make the movement to the other. You started by making books, which were an exploration of the world and photography, and then you did books organized around a specific place, more classic photo books, and I felt like you didn't need to make such a big effort anymore. You can make a

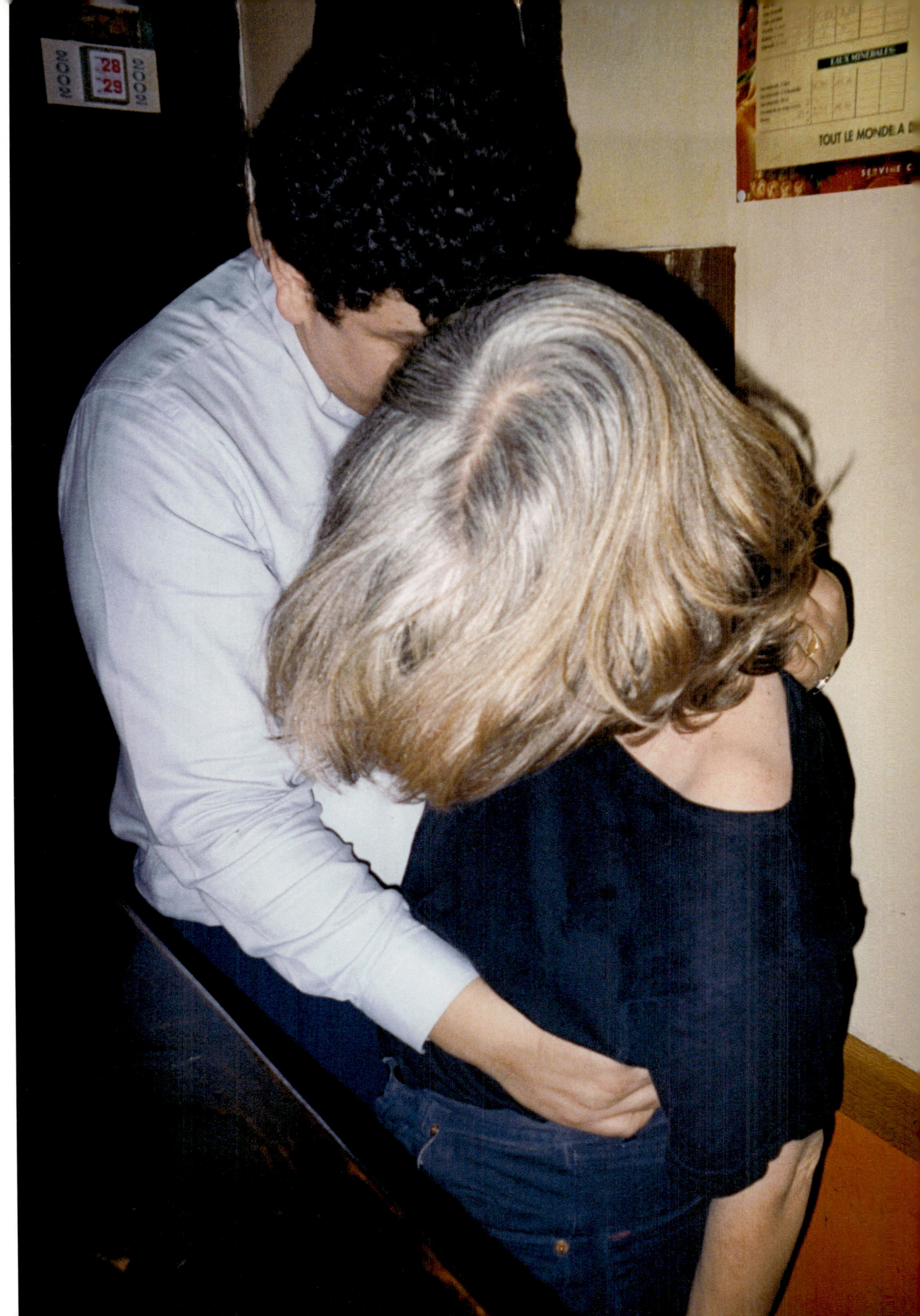

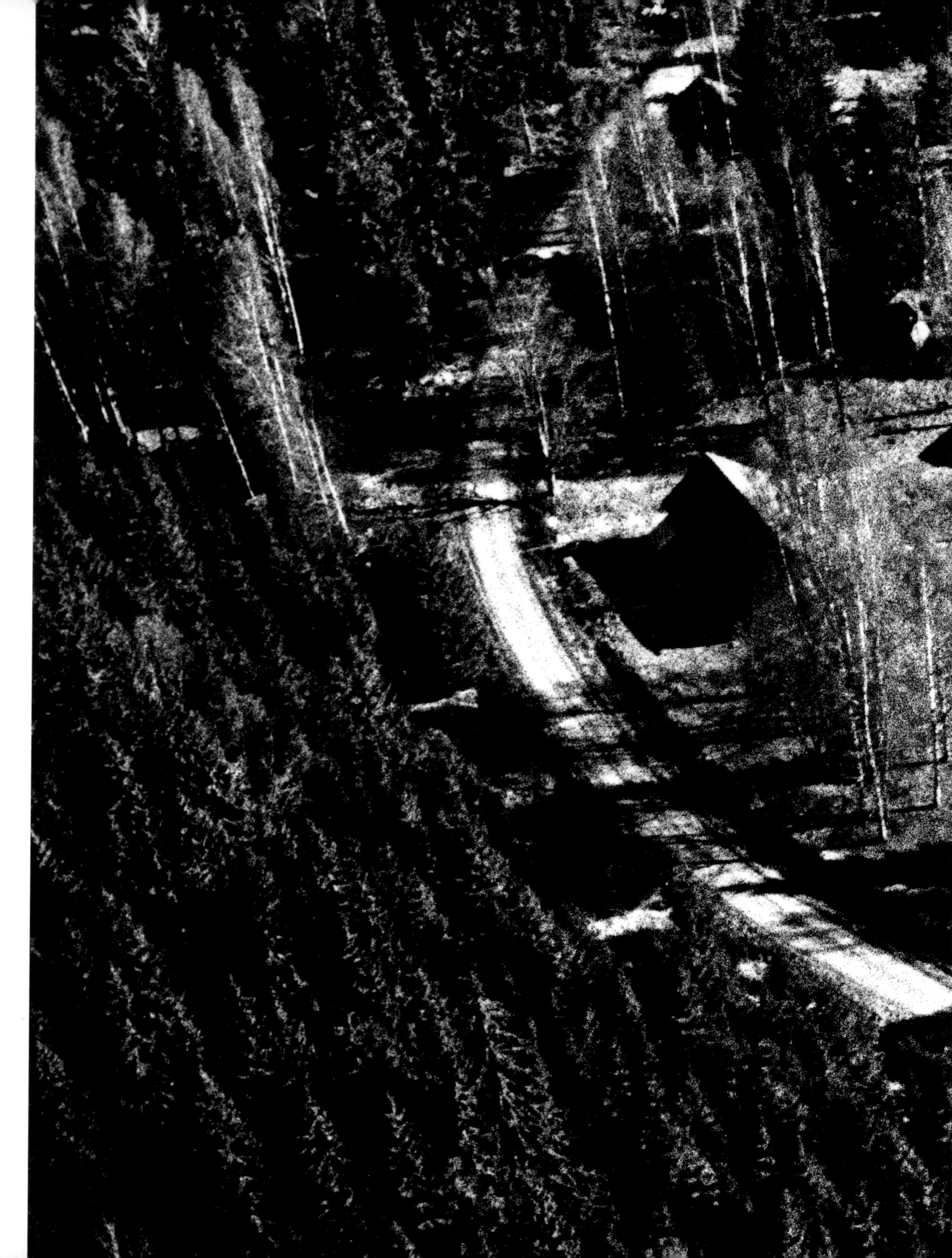

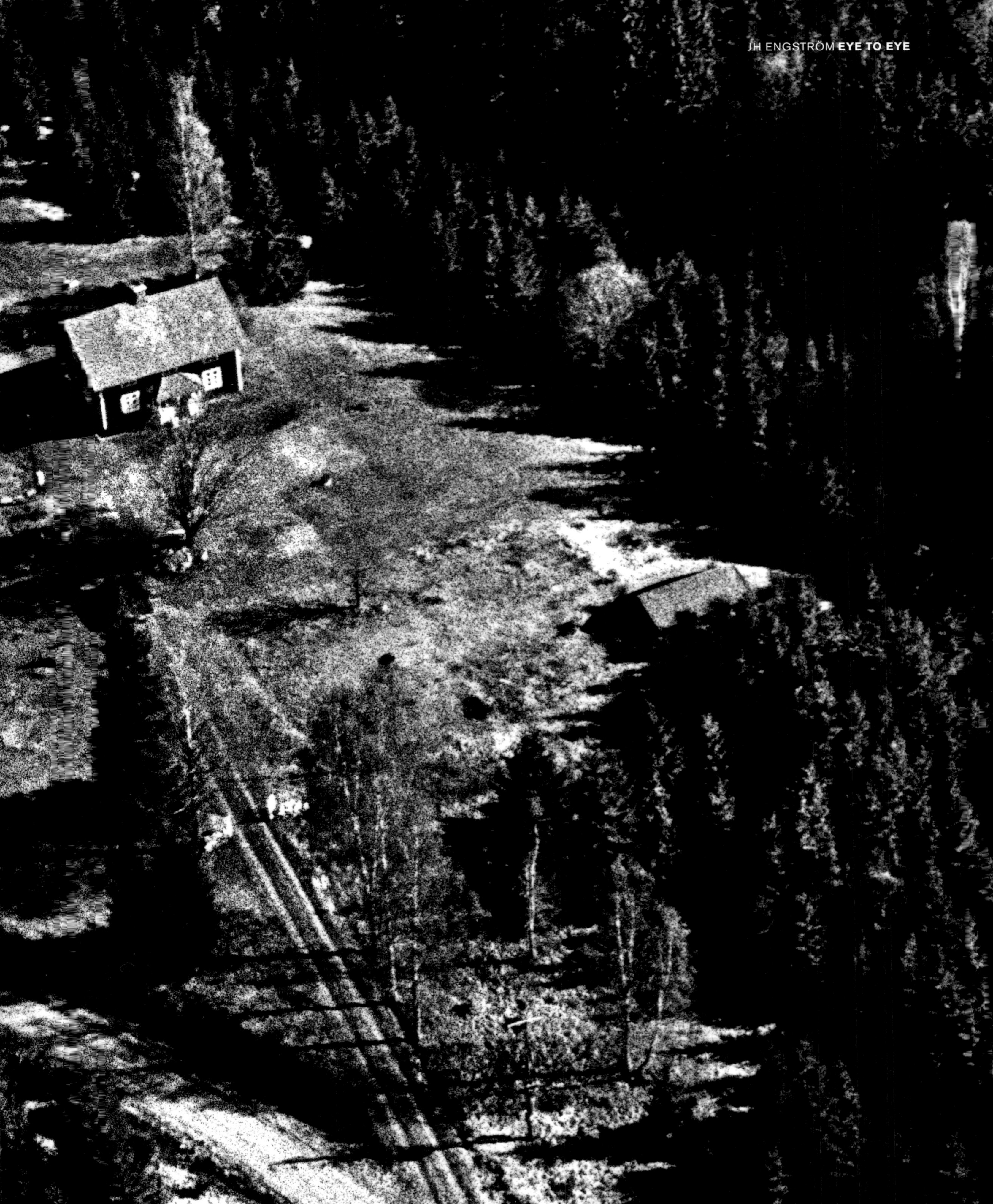
JH ENGSTRÖM EYE TO EYE

book about Shinjuku and it will also be about you, your relationship to photography and as Daido Moriyama says me in Shinjuku.
But, what interests me more, I think a lot about this too, I wrote about this yesterday. I think that what makes photography not so easily accepted in the art world is that it is always, however subjective it is, there is always the objectivity that is there and what is most interesting is it will become a document. The book that I did with Anders about Värmland… now it is very subjective, it's our view of Värmland but in 100 years they won't care about us and what they will see is how was it in that region in 2007.

That is a real document. You know, documents are done…
That's what I'm saying, that is my wish. I'm considered to be very subjective, and I am. My starting point is very subjective but at the same time I have this wish and I know that when they will look at my work in fifty years, when I'm dead and everything, forget about me, what they will see is how it was back then, they will see the people in the beginning of the 21ˢᵗ century and they will see how they dress and all that kind of stuff and how photography was, which is not the case in, for instance, painting.

Yes, and that is the generosity of making a document that you can trust. Because when people do a document they do a passport, they try to be objective. If I would find a passport from 100 years ago, that would be interesting, that would give me some information, but passports are done to gain power over something, to control. Machines do them. The kind of work you do is much more interesting as a document. I don't like that word document; I mean I like it the way we are talking about, the way you do it. I feel it is a noble word, but often misused.
All these words are misused. You know, what can you say? That's why it's so difficult to talk about it… a lot of words within photography: fiction, documentary, all that is misused. Talked

about too much, maybe.

Yeah, we should shut up. Speaking of which, I wanted to ask you about, photography as life… but you are also trying to become a better person when you are doing that, becoming wiser, knowing more about yourself and other people, about the world…
When I do photography?

By doing your work.
Oh, I have a lot of difficulties with that!

*I was seeing your books last night and this is what I thought; you overexpose… those photographs of, you know, the large format photographs of places [*Trying to Dance*]. That's overexposed?*
Yes, that is overexposed. But what does that have to do with me becoming a wiser person?

[Laughs] Yes, exactly. It doesn't.
What do you mean overexposing to become a wiser person?

[Laughs] Ok. It's not even a question. I was going to tell you what my insight was.
Ok.

And you can say no, no, you're totally wrong… In some of your photographs, I have the impression you saw something and decided to photograph it, overexposing it. To give too much light to it. And on the other photos, which are in the flow of life, many times you use flash…
And sometimes I don't.

Sure, there are no rules and no shortcuts, but maybe we can say that you tend to give things more light then they have; and this is just language, but again, I was thinking about the word enlightenment, which

...ally means giving more light and I was thinking...how to say this? Somehow you are aiming at some kind of enlightenment. I don't know if you are aware of it or if you disagree with that...
In a way, yes, it's right. But it's not like you wake up and you decide something like that. It's true that I had this sentence in my head that I wanted to... to kind of infect the negative with too much light and that's what I did with these overexposures. I don't know, it's difficult; you shouldn't really explain why you do things. But, it's true that I have this obsession, which is totally existential with the... facts, the facts of things. For example, when I lived in New York and was doing the landscapes for *Trying to Dance* and I saw something, nothing about it, it was very banal, just there, except that it is there, and that is very, very strong, that thing that is there, so I had this urge to kind of impose that very, very, very strongly in the fucking film, like 10 times more than what was supposed to be. It's also true that the use of flash is not to make things look ugly or raw, it's because of the urge to show things as they really are.

We need more light to show those things. It's our job.
We also need mystery, we also need shadows, we also need... we need everything.

Enlightenment is also inside the shadows, and it's also in accepting that you don't see or that you can't possibly see everything. And it has to do with who you are as a person, as you go along. Don't you feel that, I don't know, you're trying to understand life or yourself or the others? I feel that I'm totally obsessed by the mystery and the abstraction and now I think I reached this kind of acceptance that there is no understanding. So, I don't have this goal to become more enlightened or to know what's going on, maybe what I'm trying to do is very difficult, it's more and more to accept things.

Exactly, but that is the way to enlightenment, Socrates says, the only thing I know is that I don't know, or the Zen masters...
Yes, it's that, and as you say it's very classical so it's not... but it's that, you know? That is why I love Paris, because I have a personal relationship to it, that's a starting point, but then it's also this chaos that will never be explained. Which is about human beings being concentrated in one area and human behavior, and it's right here on the streets, in the bars, and sometimes it's really ugly and sometimes it's beautiful, but to have this side by side, this ugliness and beauty, it is beautiful... it's very raw this city, it's very fucking cruel!

All those big cities are like that.
Yes, but I think it's like that even in small cities, but I like it here, because you can see it.

Right, I agree, here it's more visible and it's faster. But, isn't it a book, and putting photos next to each other, isn't that, right there, the photo book medium, isn't it the temptation of seeing everything equal? Accepting everything in the same light? Because that's diptyches.
For you, it is. And maybe, for me as well, but I don't think that everybody thinks that way. You know, when I did *Haunts*, which was four years ago, how many books before that, maybe you can count them on one hand, how many books had you seen that had mixed...talking now about the language of photography, not the work, but how many books had you seen that mixed color, black and white, 35mm and 4x5? Only this ridiculous thing had not been made before, because we are so rigid in how we use the language of photography.

Page 60 from the series Haunts, 2006. *Page 63 from the series* Haunts, 2006. *Pages 64-65 from the series* From Back Home, with Anders Petersen, 2009. *Right from the series* Wells, 2011. *Following spread from the series* Haunts, 2006. *All images © the artist, courtesy Gallery Vu, Paris and Gun Gallery, Stockholm*

It balances between trying to tear everything down and to communicate, you know? It's a language and communication built on different agreements and arrangements, so that we understand each other.

Well, you are making a book to be completed by the viewer and you just do your part.
Yes, but these 50% that are supposed to be completed by the viewer have to be open, so it's possible for the viewer to finish it. I did a dummy, in which I worked for about two or three years that was totally, totally interior and I liked it; to me it made total sense, you know? I showed it to some people that know photography, and they said this is not communicating, you are so inside yourself, that I'm not getting anything… I know you, and I'm trying to put all my energy to read this but I can't because you are not communicating, so you just have to throw it away. But for me it was also a very good feeling, because it was two or three people that told me this and every time I thought not communicating, that's exactly how I felt!

In film, they talk about this off space, it's what you don't show in the movie, but you kind of create it by not showing it in a particular way, and what you can do with a film is to create an off space, a certain off space which is for the viewer. I feel that. I'm generally not interested in the photos I do, per se, I'm interested in organising them in a certain way that will make it about the images I haven't seen.
But, I'm the same there, as I told you before. I'm both. Not interested in the single photograph and I can be totally sentimental about a photograph.

In a personal way?
Yes, because it means something to me and that's why I put

it in. There is no other reason. So there are two levels, the editing, organizing level and then the very, very personal level. I have to feel something, you know? I cannot only organize with the distance. I have to have a connection with what I organize.

Wow! It's like a song or a song sung by someone who is feeling what they sing! So, you need to have this feeling. When I did my first book, Tunnels, *I didn't believe that you could photograph anything, anything that was outside of me, so it was always about absence… when I saw your* Trying to Dance, *it made a big impact on me. I felt, this guy he knows that it's impossible, but he is still trying, he is still making an effort.*
Yes, it was a kind of struggle there, it still is. The question about intimacy and distance. Of course I'm distant as well. But at the same time, what is distance? What is close? What is that? Who knows? I don't know. I can try to be close to someone and it will be a very distant thing. And I can be very far away from something or someone and feel very close. I try to express that in putting the images together. But photography is about that; it's about what is close or far away. All languages have to do with that. I care about the kind of discussion about what is it to be a human being, that comes from literature. That interests me. This discussion is about us as human beings and also, actually, about language which is a big part of us being humans.

Sure, language started with drawings and the drawings become more abstract, until the Chinese characters, and that's why I also think that image making and storytelling is the same thing.
Maybe that's what I mean when I say I don't care if I'm this or that.

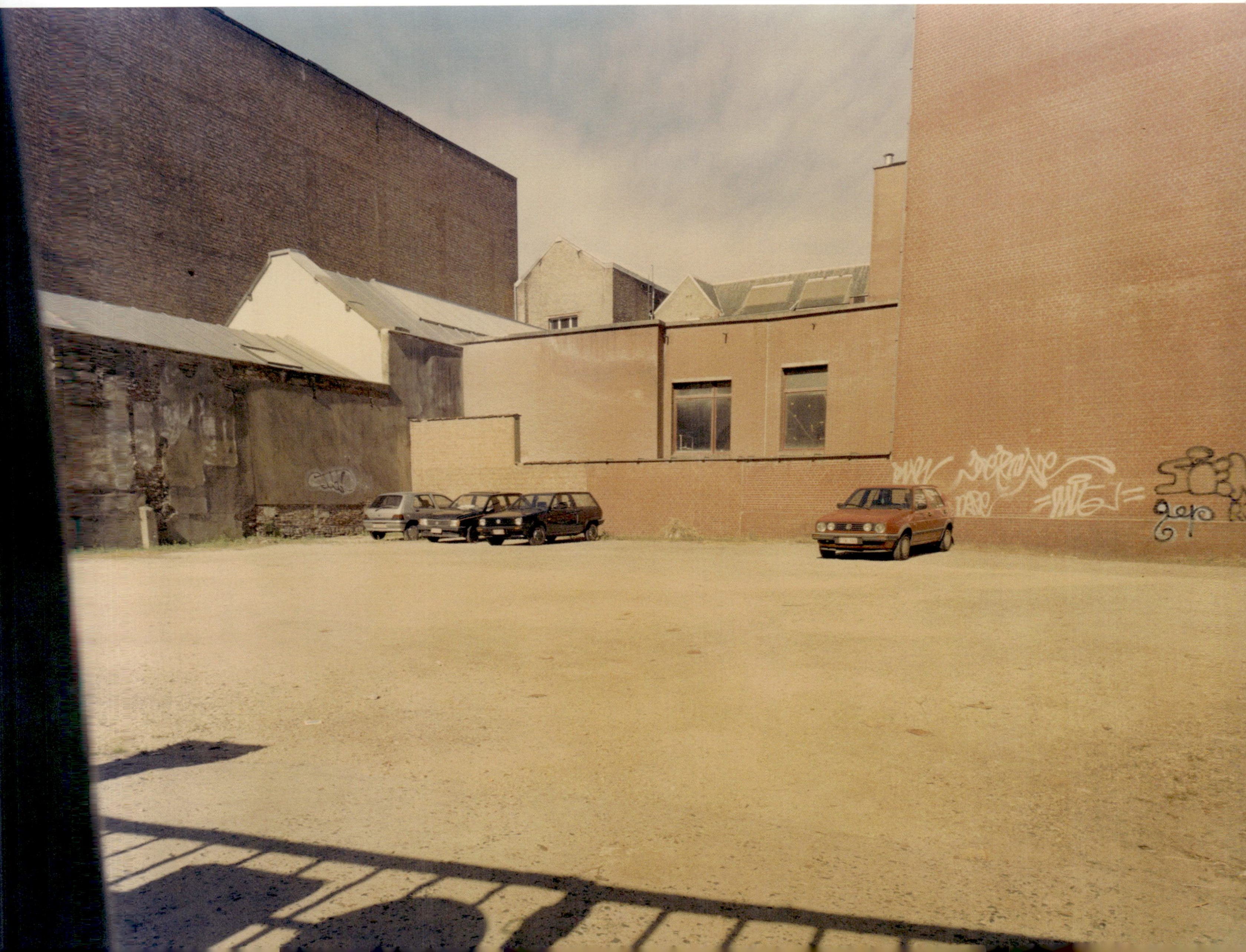

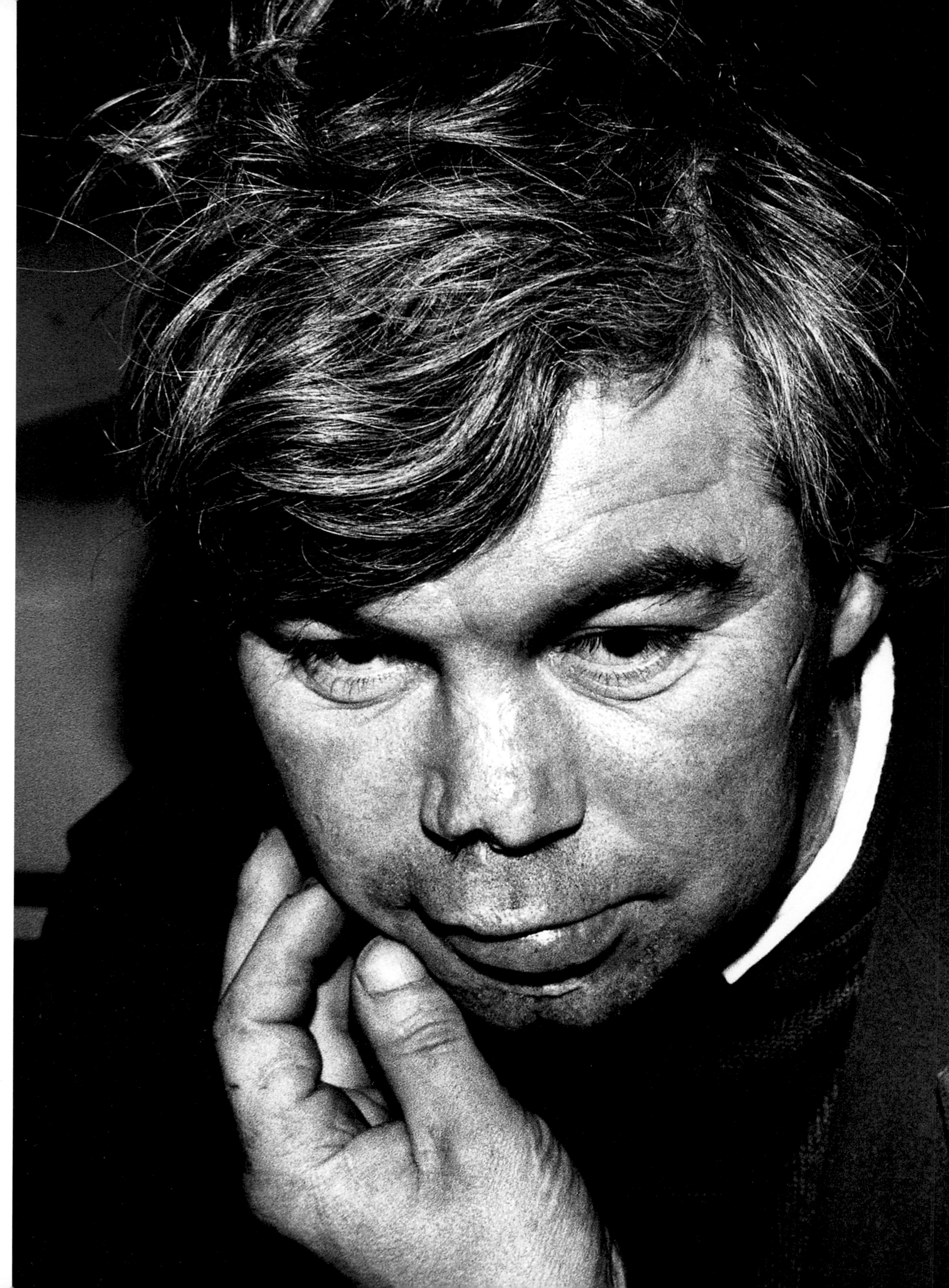

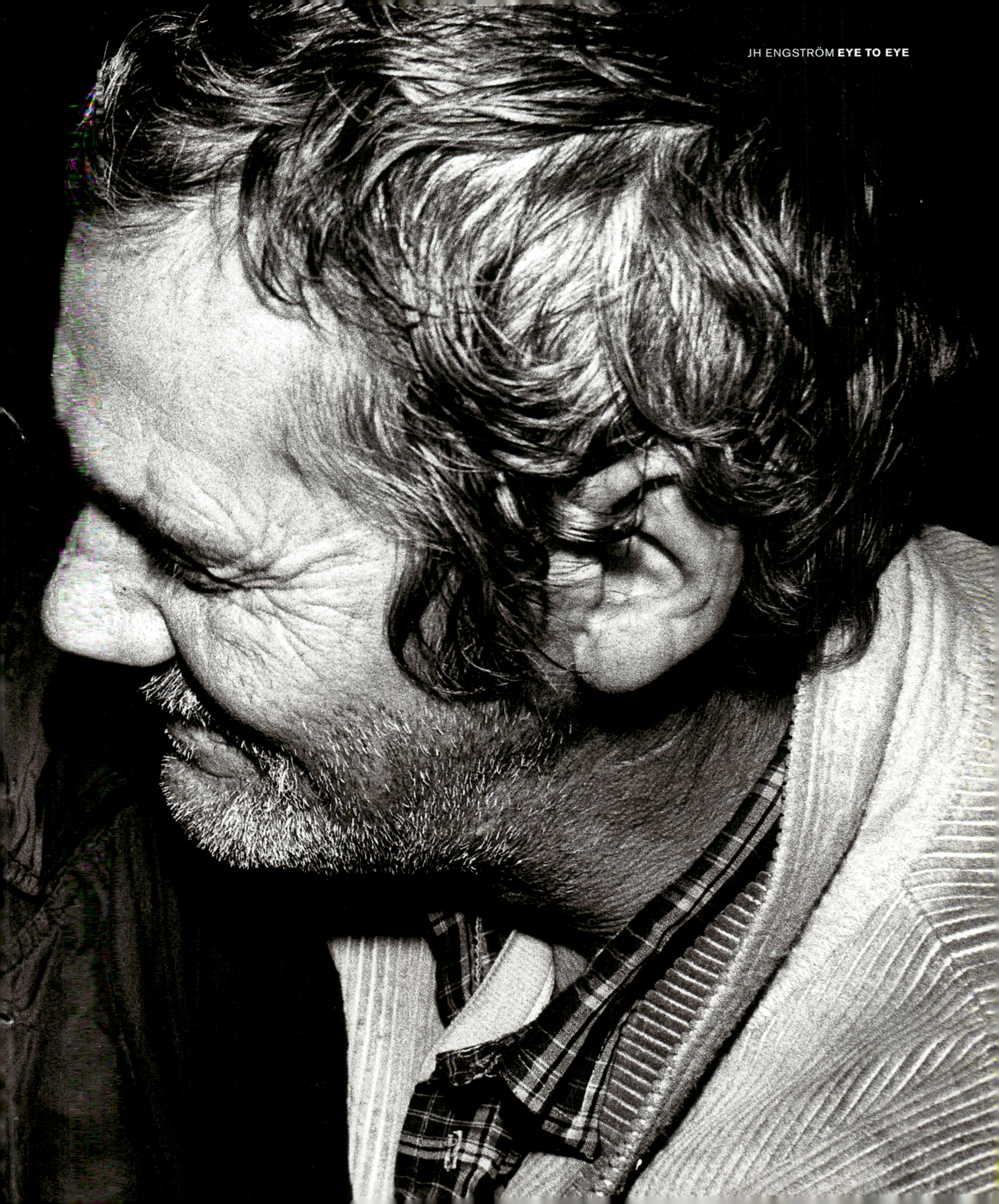

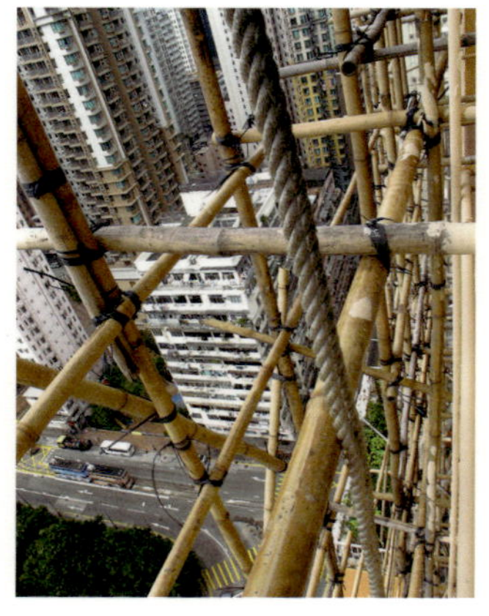
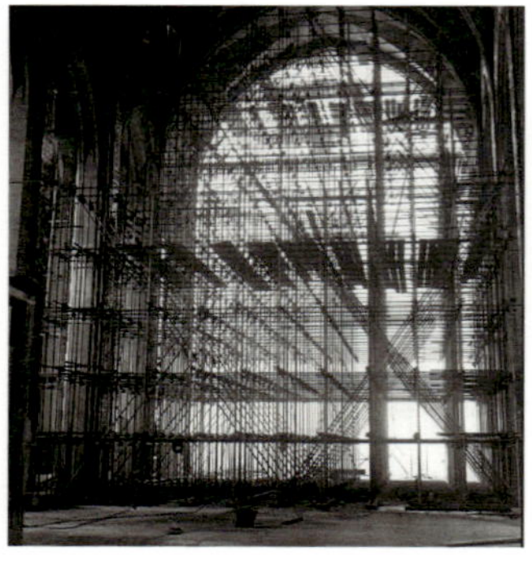
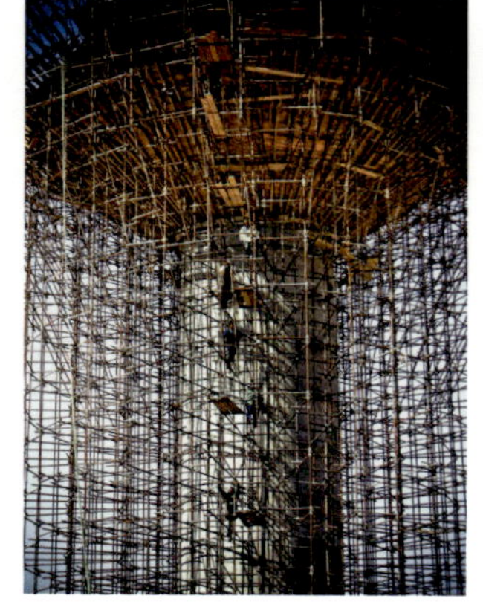
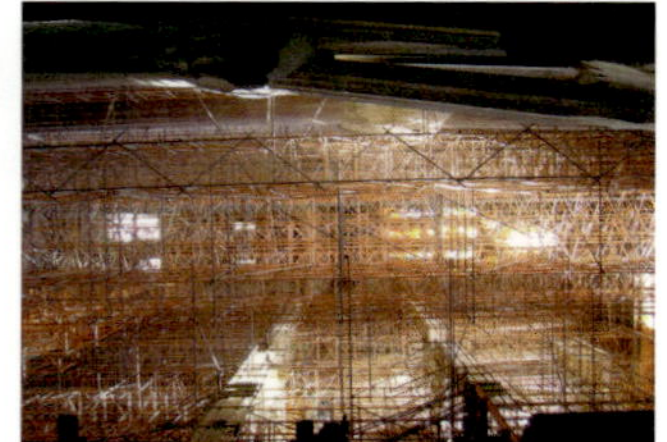
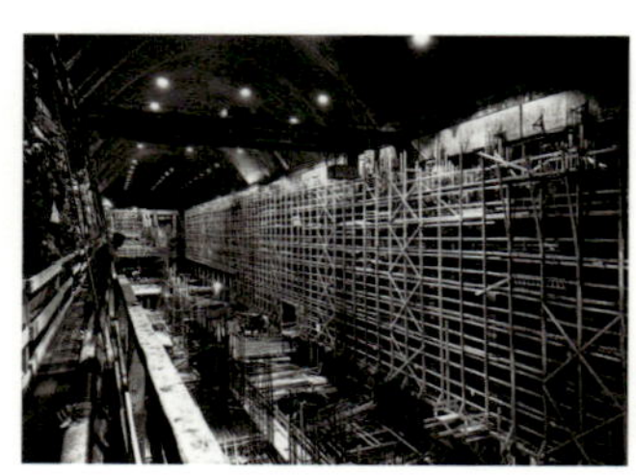
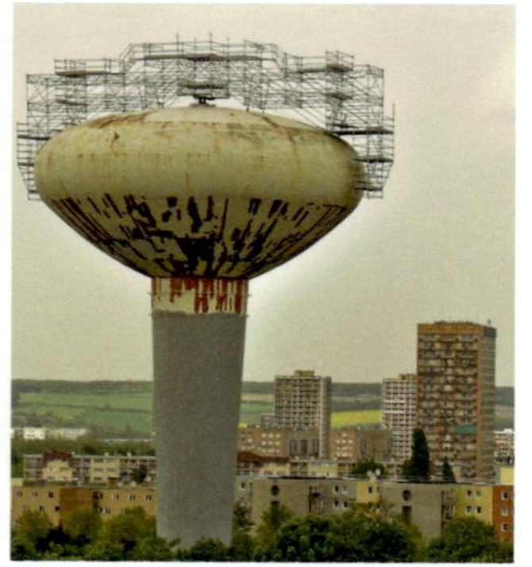
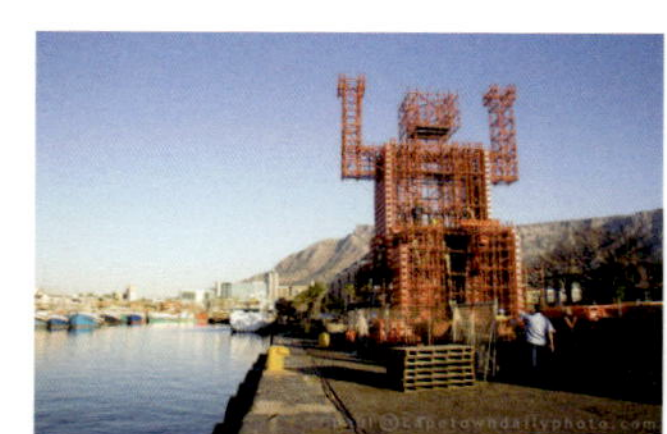
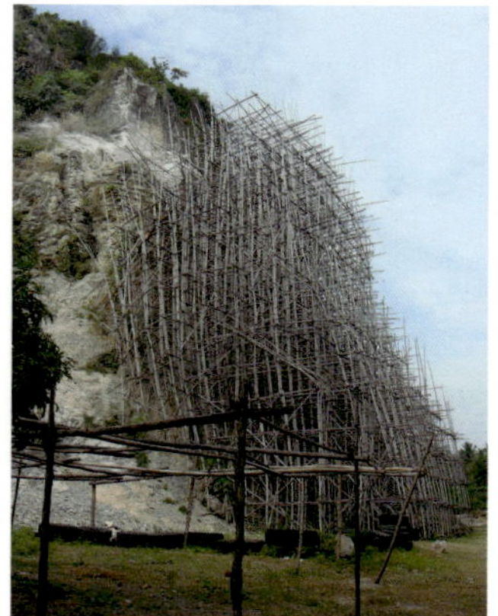
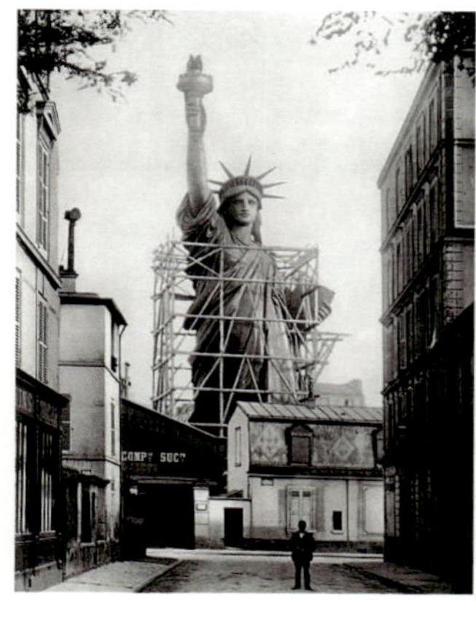
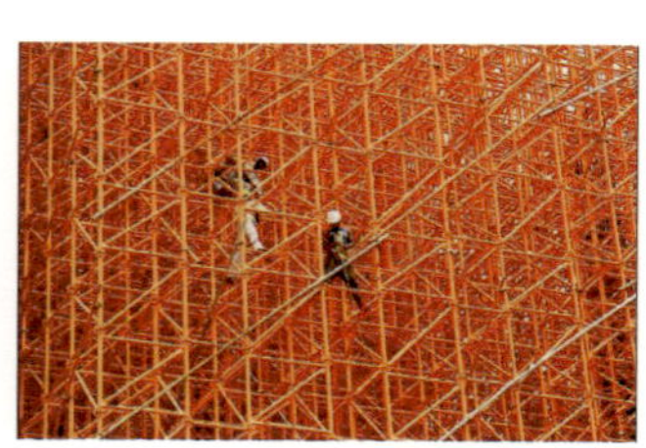
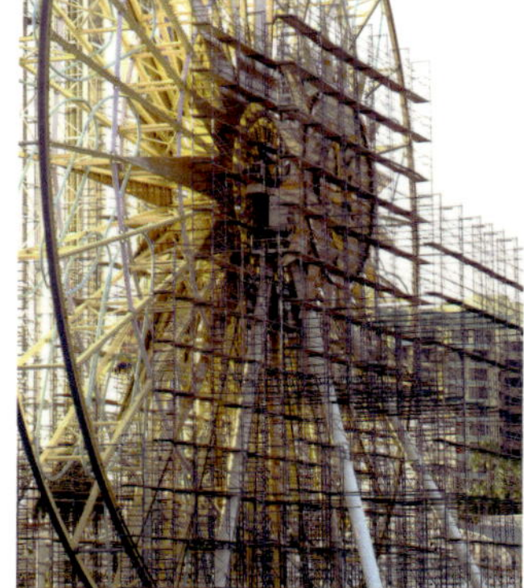
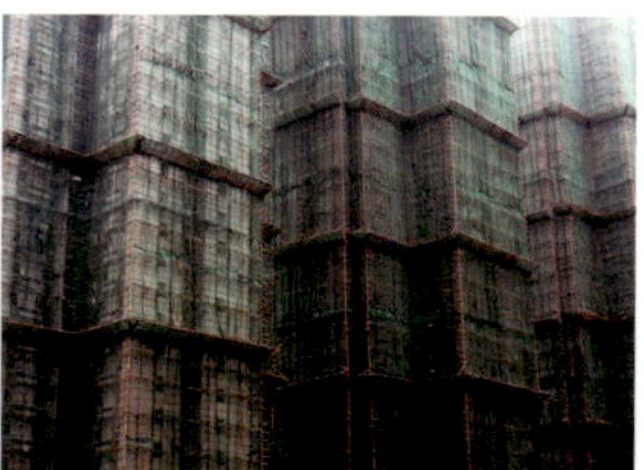

SCAFFOLDINGS
by Benjamin Godsill

The Internet is rife with all manner of idiosyncratic and distinct archives; the network's very DNA proves fertile soil for seemingly infinite collections of sounds, images, texts, movies and communities organized under the most specific of metrics. These archives create a highly mediated and subjective representation of the world we live in, their very existence becoming a drawing of the classifications of our culture. Stumbling upon and then examining these collections, it becomes clear that they are basically 'Cabinets of Curiosity' for our contemporary commons, collecting disparate images and impressions and becoming encyclopedic projects that define the boundaries of categories that do not, as of yet, exist. From arcane sexual fetishes to Second World War propeller planes, these blogs, wiki's, chat rooms and message boards are just as engaged in world making as they are in gathering or describing.

Scaffoldage, a tumblr blog project by Shaun Usher comprised of nothing but photographs on the Internet depicting the uses of scaffolding in construction and reconstruction of buildings, is one such project of making by gathering a new form of categorization. Within a minimal, almost barren layout, the blog is made up of dozens and dozens of images that unfold in page after page of close-ups, long shots, historical and contemporary views of the support structures that allow the actual edifice to emerge. Though simple in concept and clean in delivery this archive manages to unpack a broad and complex understanding of the current state of our built and represented environment. *Skeletal Archiporn* is the blog's own nomenclature, a term referencing the stunning spectacle-laced photographs of buildings often designed by starchitects that foreground the glamorous and retouched over the practical and context-mined in the world of architecture and real estate media. Presumably for the creators of this blog the distorting factor, i.e. pornography, lies in the aestheticization of the functional, the queering of the normative. The photographs

Scaffoldage sources are focused on the unglamorous though often beautiful, the structures that are rendered as precognitive shadows of the buildings and objects that will eventually be left behind. Images collected range from 21st century boom towns such as Dubai, and Shanghai - its bamboo scaffolds supporting the construction of glass and metal skyscrapers - to the supports of late 19th century icons (including the Eiffel Tower), and all manner of modern and post-modern structures in between. But of course the buildings (and the sculptures, and even the airplanes) that the scaffolding serves are never the point here. It is the superstructure, the elements that act only as temporary supports for workers and materials in the process of the making of the real that this archive collects. Here the focus is on the negative space of architecture and the city - the subtractive elements that can only exist in relationship to the final form, but without which those final forms could never come to fruition.

Likewise, the very structure of *Scaffoldage*, like many of these archive projects, acts as a negative impression - a trace, a ghost - of the world of images in which we live. The blog and its minders don't take any photographs for the website themselves: they simply cull their collection from the wider web, defining their interests and our world based on that which already exists. The individual images - the nodes of the archive - only begin to have a specific meaning, the meaning of the archive, when they are gathered from the strange backwaters of the Internet and are brought together. But they can only be united by the very search terms that will then define them. And as such, *Scaffoldage* and similar projects become both the scaffolding - the finders of images, the definers of the search terms - and the building: the ultimate and only repository wherein the results of those search terms can have any true meaning.

All images are from scaffoldage.com

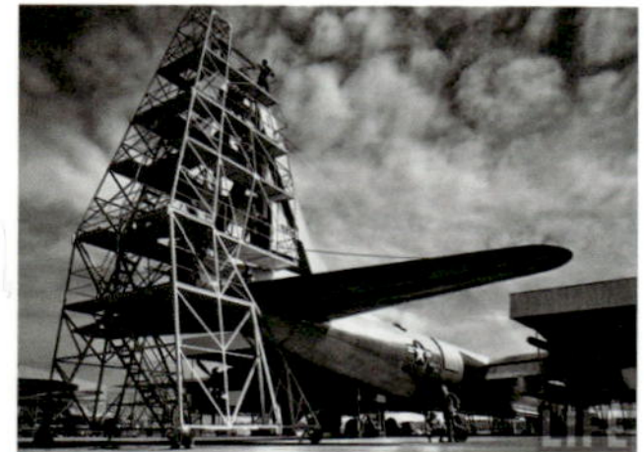
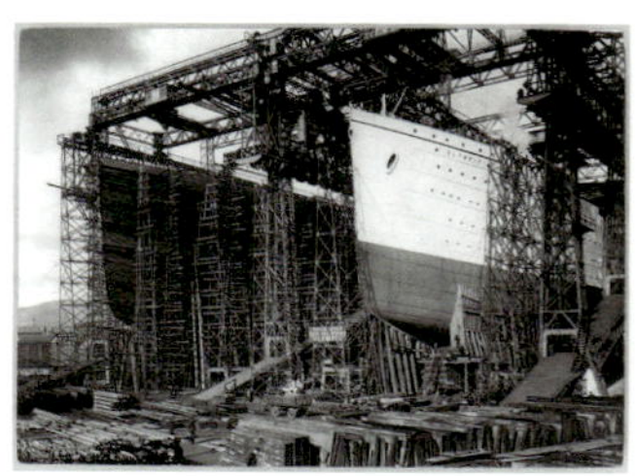
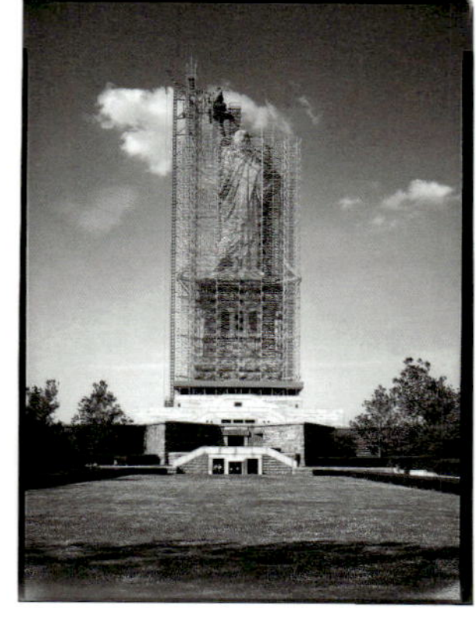
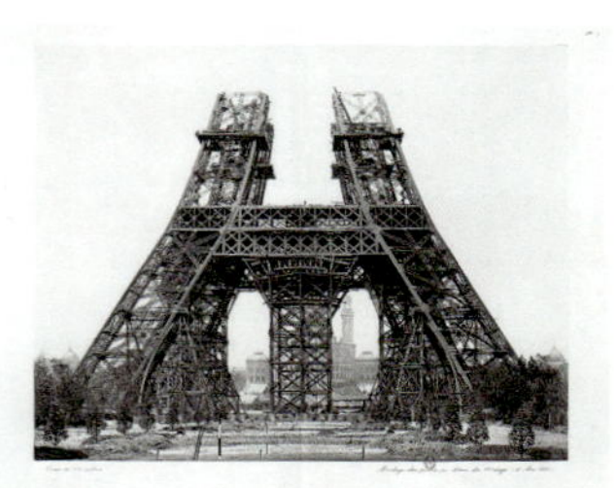
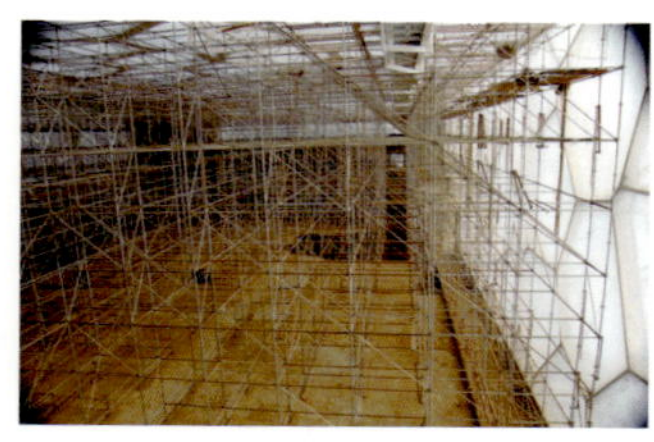
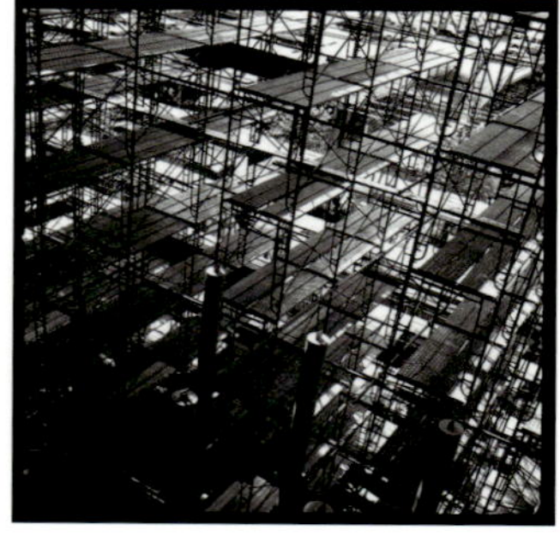
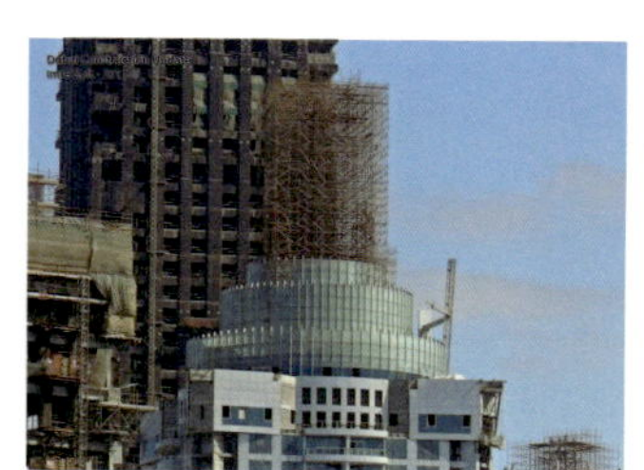
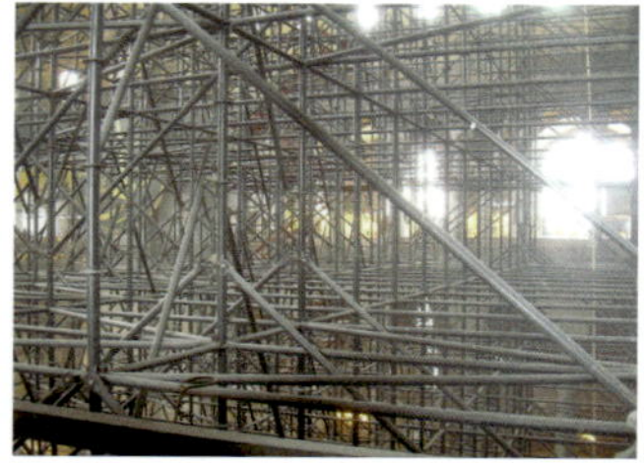
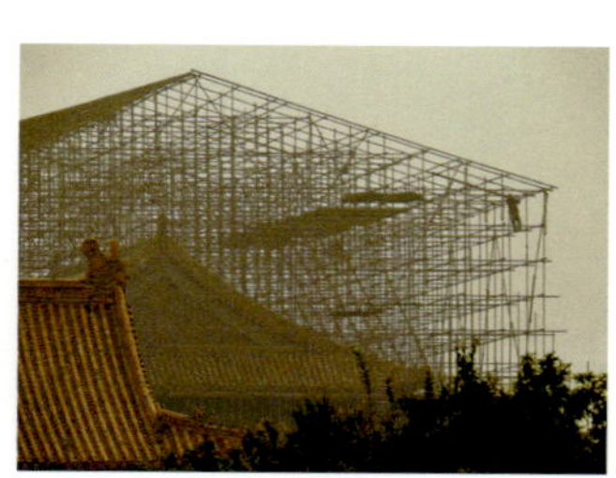
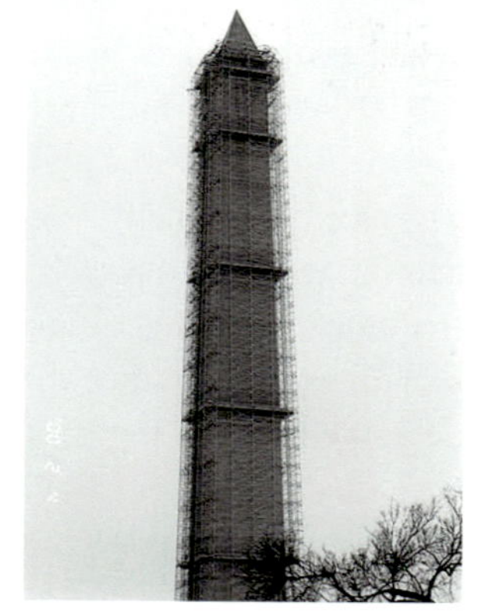
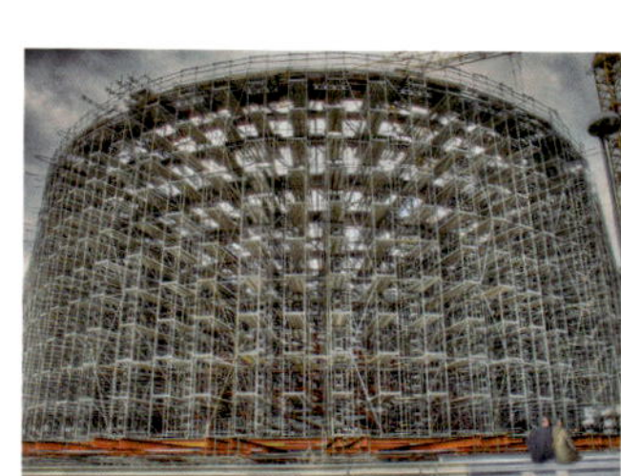
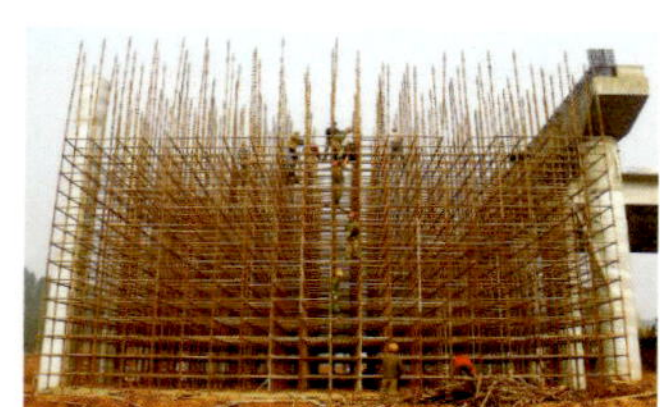

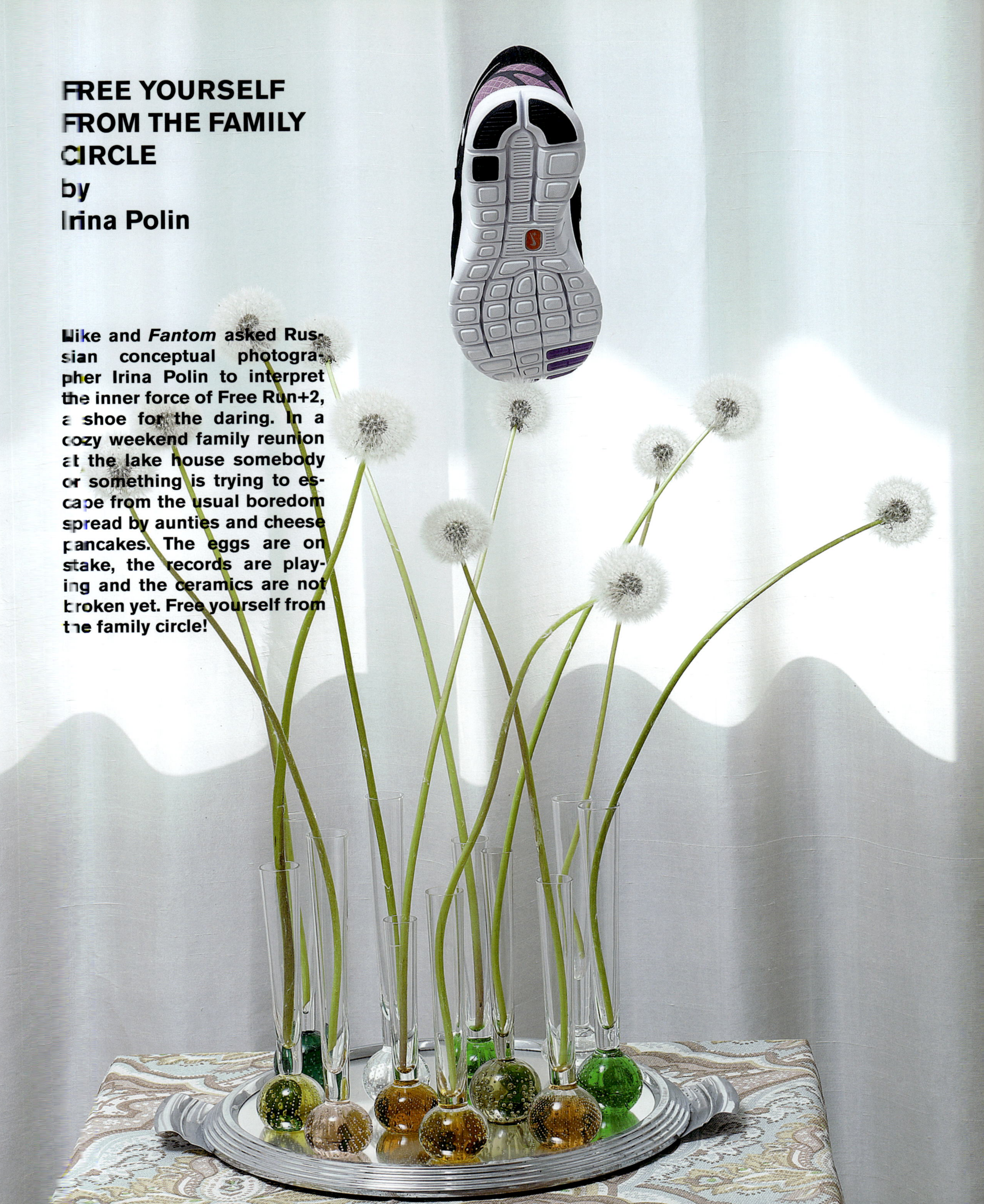

FREE YOURSELF FROM THE FAMILY CIRCLE
by
Irina Polin

Nike and *Fantom* asked Russian conceptual photographer Irina Polin to interpret the inner force of Free Run+2, a shoe for the daring. In a cozy weekend family reunion at the lake house somebody or something is trying to escape from the usual boredom spread by aunties and cheese pancakes. The eggs are on stake, the records are playing and the ceramics are not broken yet. Free yourself from the family circle!

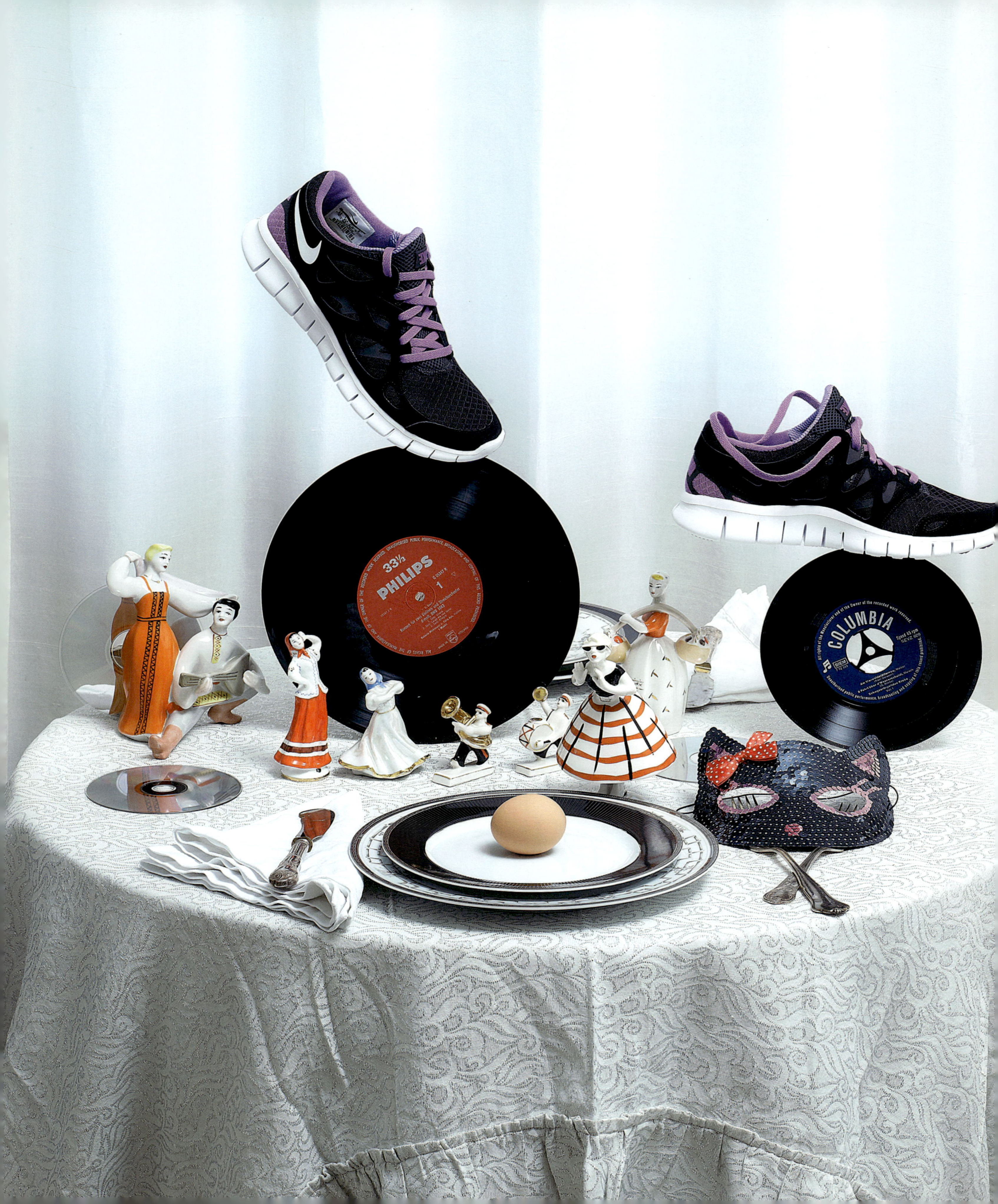

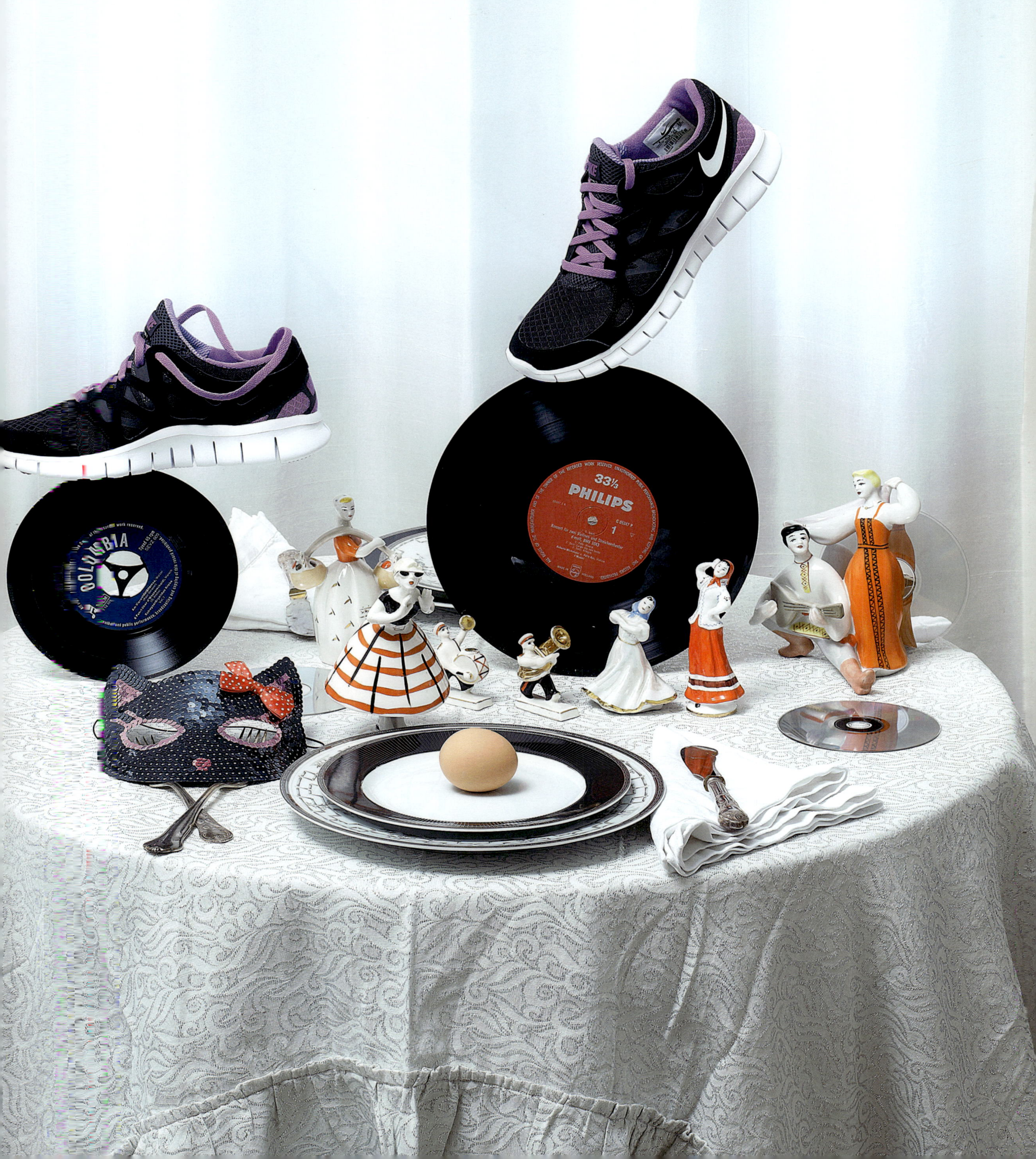

FREE

FRANCESCO ZANOT
VISITS THE COLLECTION OF GUIDO GIUDICI

Fotografia Oltre was the first gallery entirely devoted to photography to open in the Swiss Canton of Ticino. In the early 1980s every authority or devotee of this art who happened to be in the vicinity (Helmut Gernsheim lived a short distance away after he left England) would, without fail, drop by to see what was hanging on its walls. The exhibition planner was Guido Giudici who, subsequently and in partnership with his wife Danie-la, opened his own gallery in the town of Chiasso (Cons Arc *consarc-ch. com*). It was *Visioni d'Oriente*, an exhibition held in their gallery in 2000, consisting of photographs from a private collection dating from between 1860 and 1890, which sparked Guido Giudici's interest in early Japanese photography. Indeed, a few years later, he began to concentrate on the extraordinary Japanese tradition of small hand painted albumen prints, gathering over 150 of them for a collection, which continues to grow and grow. "After a lifelong love affair with photography and a sort of rejection of the historical counterpoised by a perpetual quest for the contemporary," he says, "I discovered a great deal of modernity in certain images which appear not to have aged. Moreover, a scrutiny of these prints reveals exceptional technique as regards to the shot as well as dexterity in terms of coloring. It is important to know where we come from (with respect to the history of photography) and perhaps sometimes discover that there is little new in current output." Photography is an art and it is a language: as such it develops, changes and it has roots.

1. Woman combing her hair - The Mirror What was there before photography? There are various answers to this question, depending on the specific sphere of reference. Pencils or engravings in the case of art; notebooks, tape measures or telescopes in the case of science; memory in the case of sociologists and psychologists. The mirror is another possible answer. Indeed, like a mirror, the camera is a device used for observing and whose activation depends on a point of view. Neither provide the duplicate of what you find in front of you, but only an image of it. Seeing them separately, who would say that the woman reflected in the mirror is the same woman combing her hair in front of the photographer? Photography is a medium for knowing, not for recognizing.

Hand-colored albumen print, cm 15.1 x 10.3

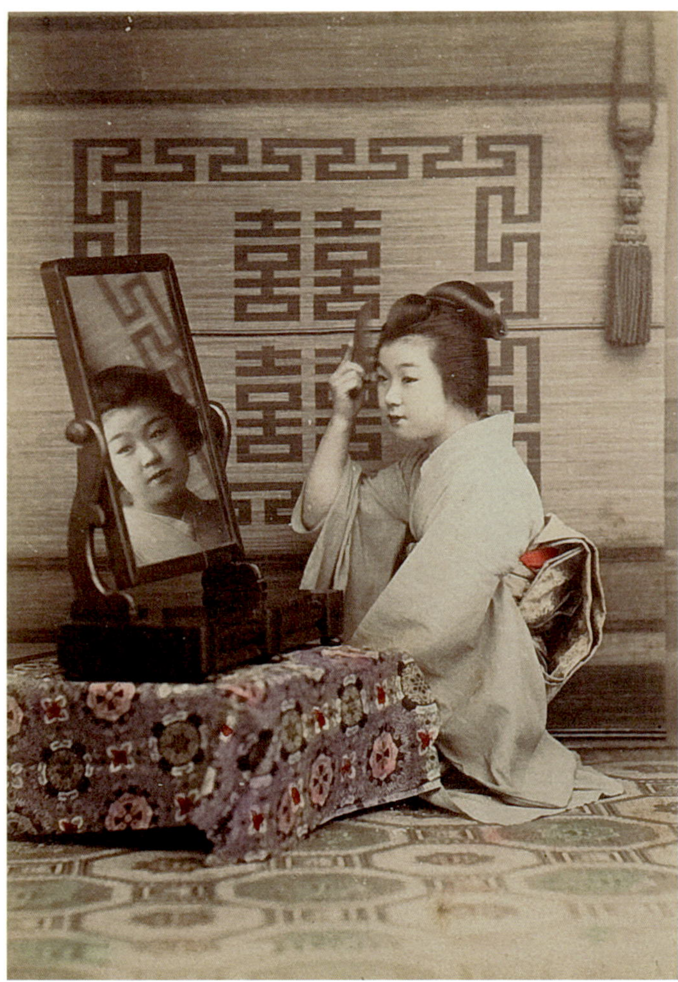

2. Fishermen's Dance - Balance Every photograph is a perfect balancing act. Even things that are unstable will look perfectly and permanently balanced in a photograph. This is what leads to the grace and safety of the photograph, in which nothing can fall.

Hand-colored albumen print, cm 20.5 x 26.2

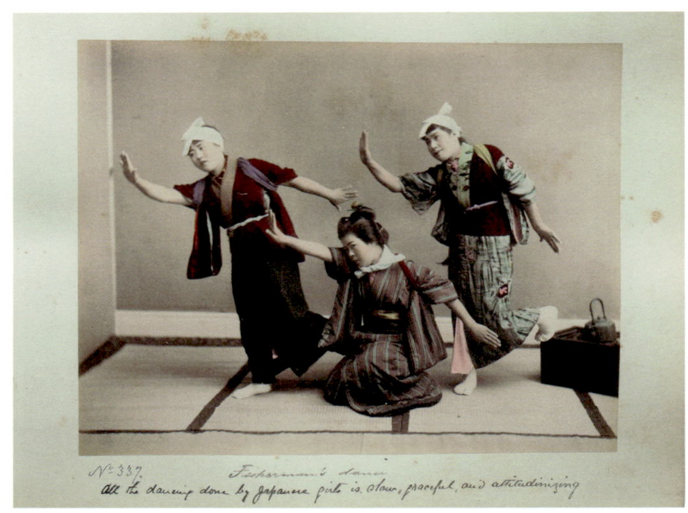

3. The presentation of a gift - The Void In his *Empire of Signs*, Roland Barthes pens some notes next to the reproduction of a Japanese print portraying two women in the act of exchanging gifts:

'The gift is alone:
it isn't touched
by either generosity
or gratitude,
the soul doesn't taint it."

That is what we see in this photograph. It isn't easy to find a picture that is as abundant in points of interest and details as it is focused on a single subject: a white box fastened by a single strand of ribbon. The giver and the recipient are bowing low, sinking into and flattening themselves on the rug at their feet, in order to leave room for it alone. Thus the gift conquers the surrounding space, makes the air perceptible, to the point of remaining suspended in the void.

Hand-colored albumen print, cm 18.5 x 26.5

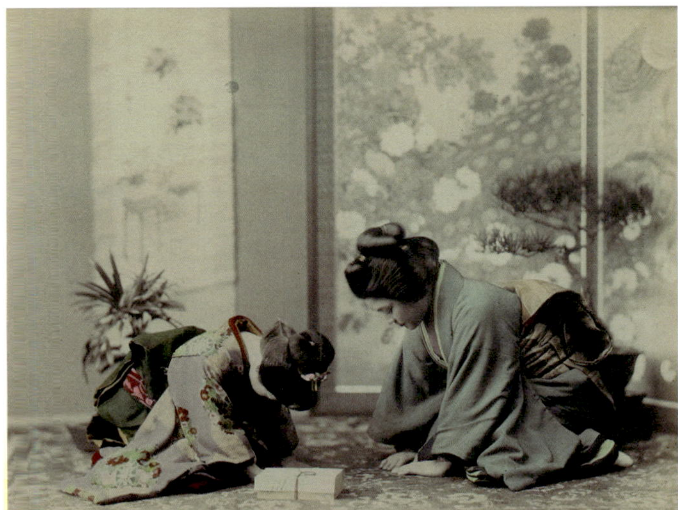

4. Basket Maker - The Archive The medium of photography is a hoarding device. It enables us to gather an exceptional quantity of information within a single frame and generates the production of negatives, prints, digital files and other image supports, which tend to be selected and stored. The result is the archive or, in other words, a drawer, a server, a room where, like the workshop of this Japanese basket maker, many typologies of the same object are collected. It is a way of ordering the complexity of the world and, above all, a relief from its hard to pin down diversity.

Hand-colored albumen print, cm 20.6 x 25.8

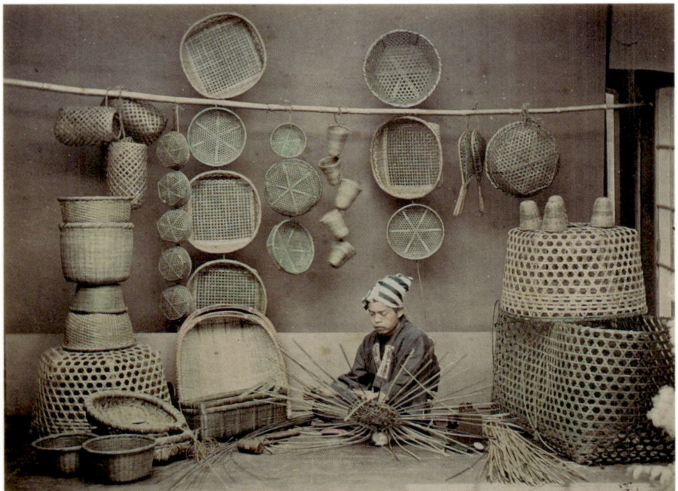

5. The Doctor - Touch Looking at a photograph can pro-
voke an enormous sense of frustration. The fact is that of the
five senses only one is satisfied: sight. However, the meticu-
lousness with which it is able to describe each detail enables
us to approach subjects to the point that we can almost touch
them. This precision in producing the surface of things may
even result in a kind of "simulation of tactility." We can rest
not only our eyes but also our hands on the woman lying in
the center of this picture and feel, like the man behind her,
the thin stripes on the blanket that envelops her body.
Hand-colored albumen print, cm 19.9 x 26.1

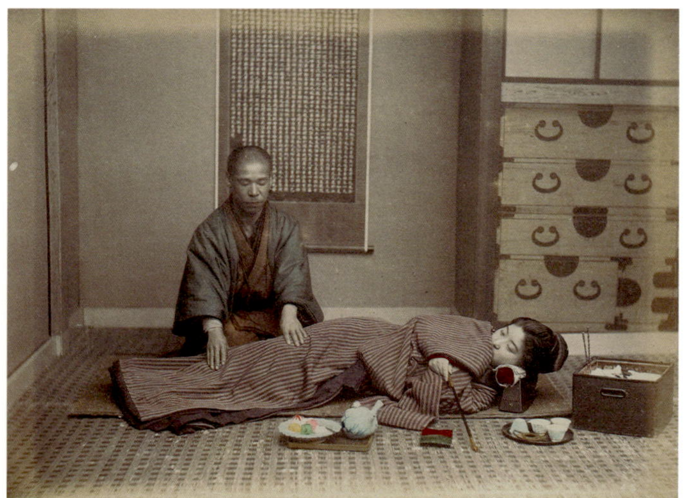

6. Lake Nikko - The World Photography enjoys a relationship with the world it represents that may be defined in
various ways: interpretation, translation, transposition, editing. What marks it is the impossibility to introduce a term
that, in addition to these, can be used instead to describe the
creative process of other figurative arts, such as drawing and
painting: invention. In order to show this, all you have to do
is to place the photograph reproduced here alongside any
of the most celebrated paintings by Caspar David Friedrich
(beginning, naturally, with his *Monk by the Sea* of 1808-1810.)
There, the subject, despite being enveloped by the grandeur
of the space surrounding him, can always take comfort from
the line of the horizon, traced by the artist within the four
walls of his studio (Friedrich only produced some sketches *en
plein air*, which he then assembled, modified and reworked
in his atelier.) The protagonist of this photograph, equally
captured in the act of contemplating the landscape, appears
to be overwhelmed by the height of the mountain. His gaze,
like ours, collides with an insurmountable wall of rock and
vegetation. The paintbrush would have been able to demol-
ish it. The lens, on the contrary, immortalizes it.
Hand-colored albumen print, cm 20 x 25.8

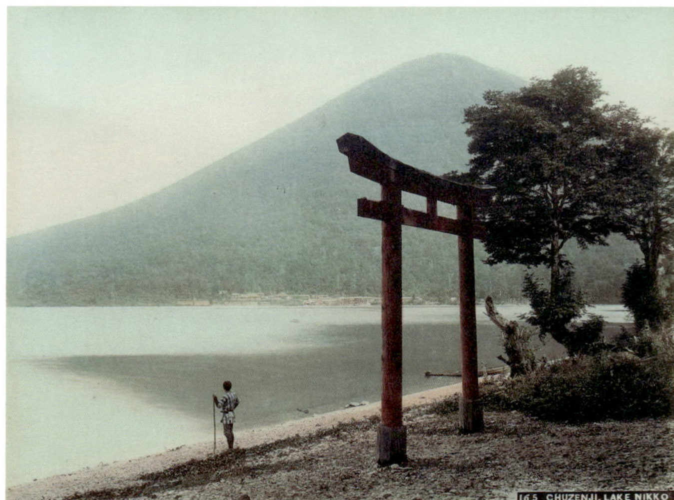

7. Konkonchiki - The Shift The act of taking a photograph implies a shift. It means transporting everything that lies beyond the lens to the other side, where the photographer is. It is an act of delicacy, so much so that often the transfer only works by shrewdly choosing the right moment to do it. This is what happens in *konkonchiki*, a popular game with women in the Meiji period, which consisted in taking a glass of tea or sake through a ring of fabric before it was tightened around the arm with a sharp tug.

Hand-colored albumen print, cm 20.5 x 26.5

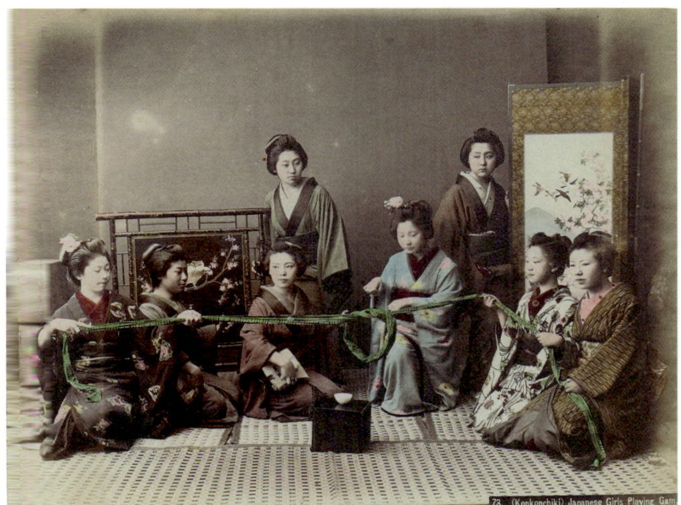

8. Dancing of Shinto priests to offer to a false God - The Mask Any photograph is a mask. It overlays reality and transforms its face into an image. It is simultaneously an act of concealment and of ostentation.

Hand-colored albumen print, cm 20.4 x 26

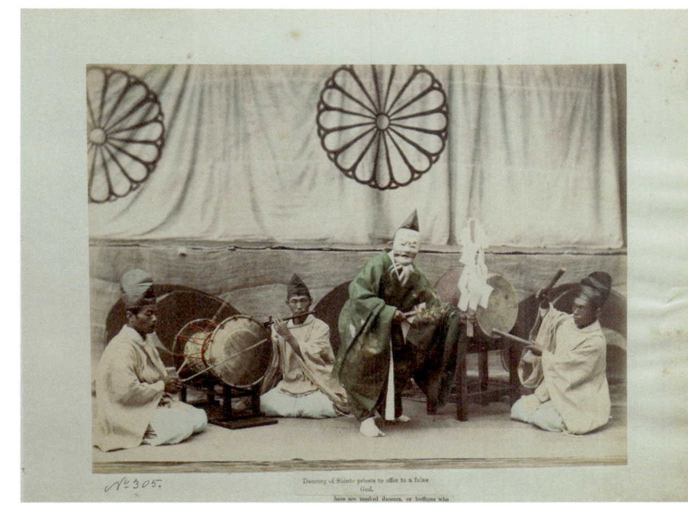

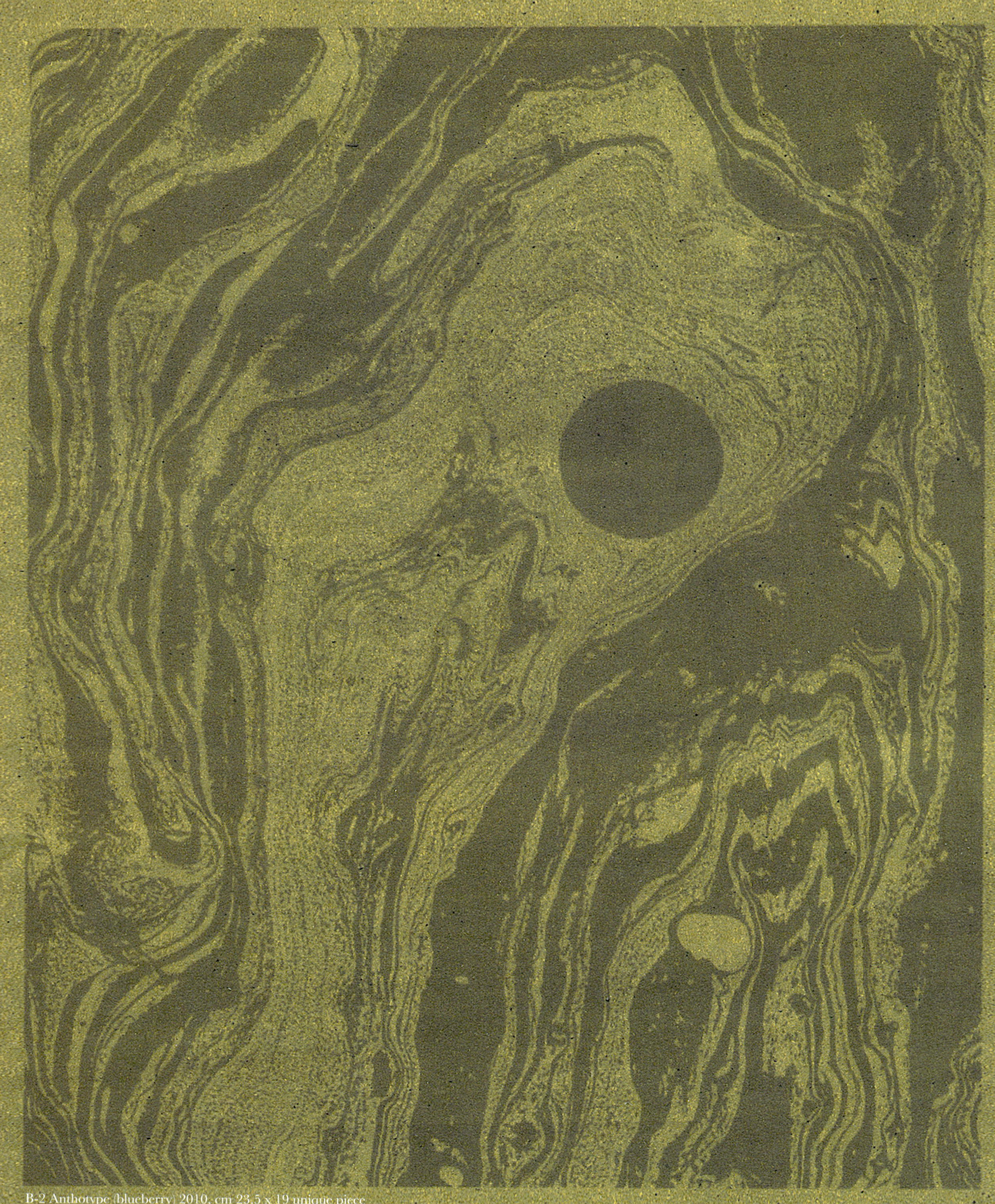

B-2 Anthotype (blueberry) 2010, cm 23,5 x 19 unique piece

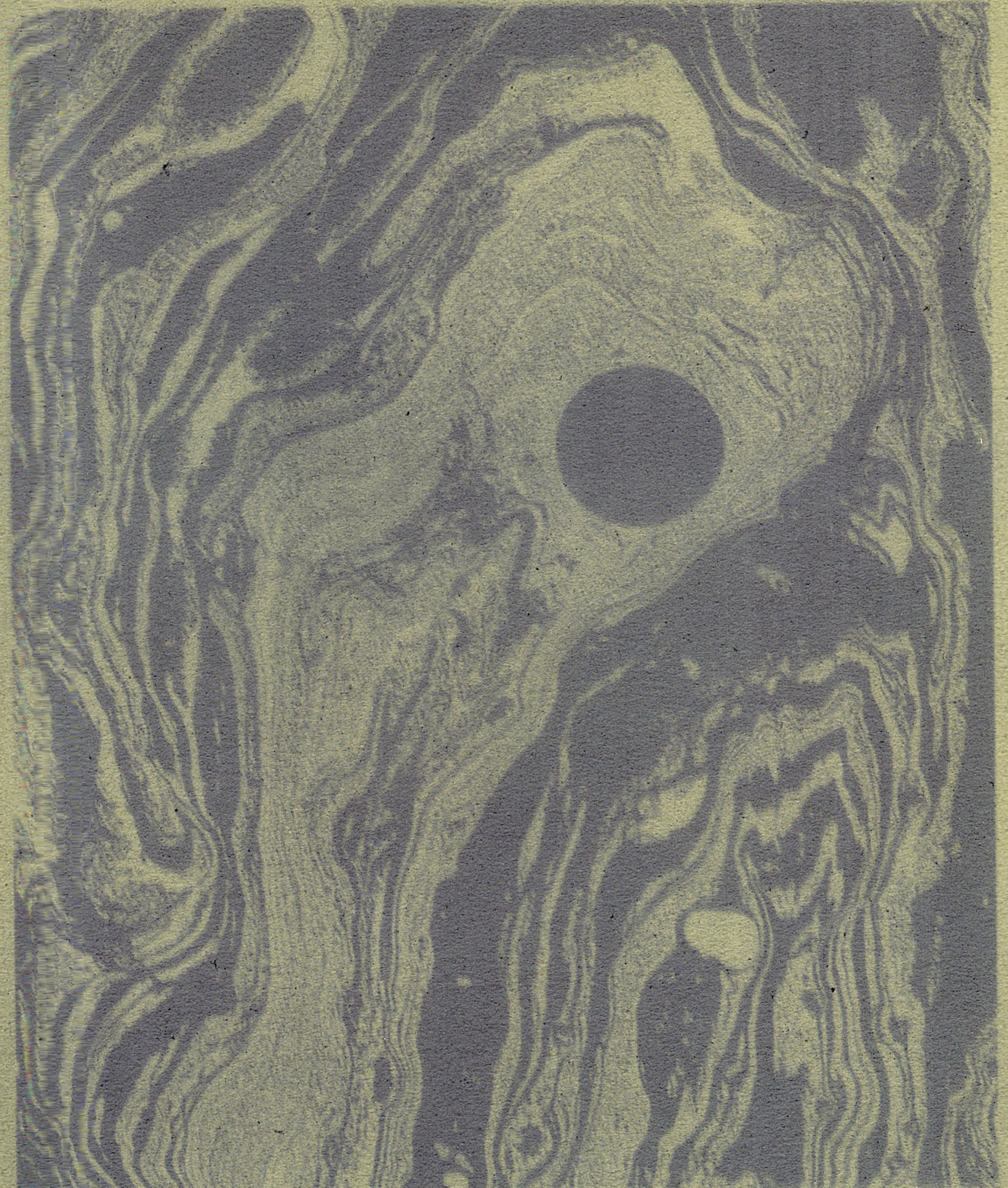

B-4 Anthotype (blueberry) 2010, cm 23.5 x 19 unique piece

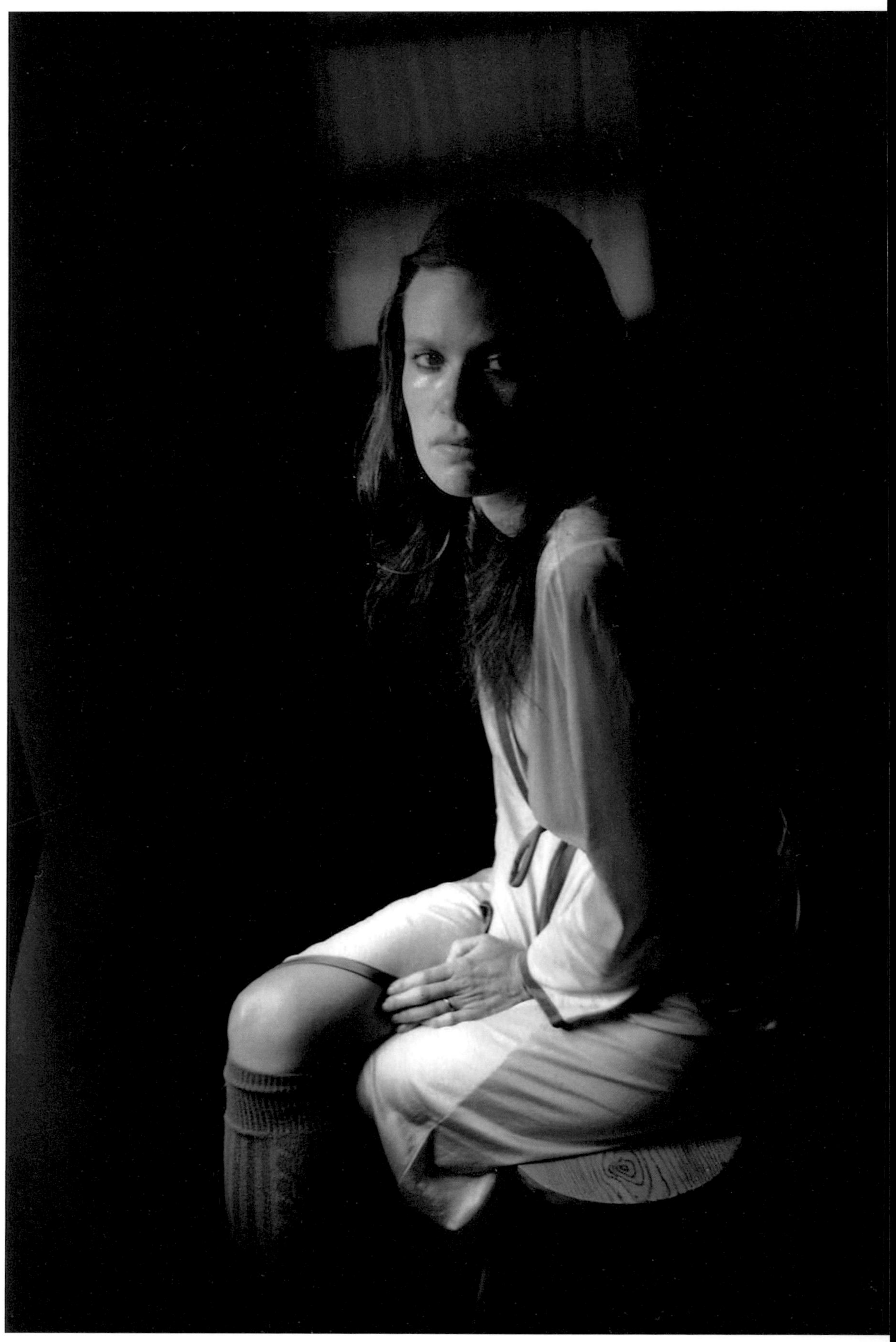

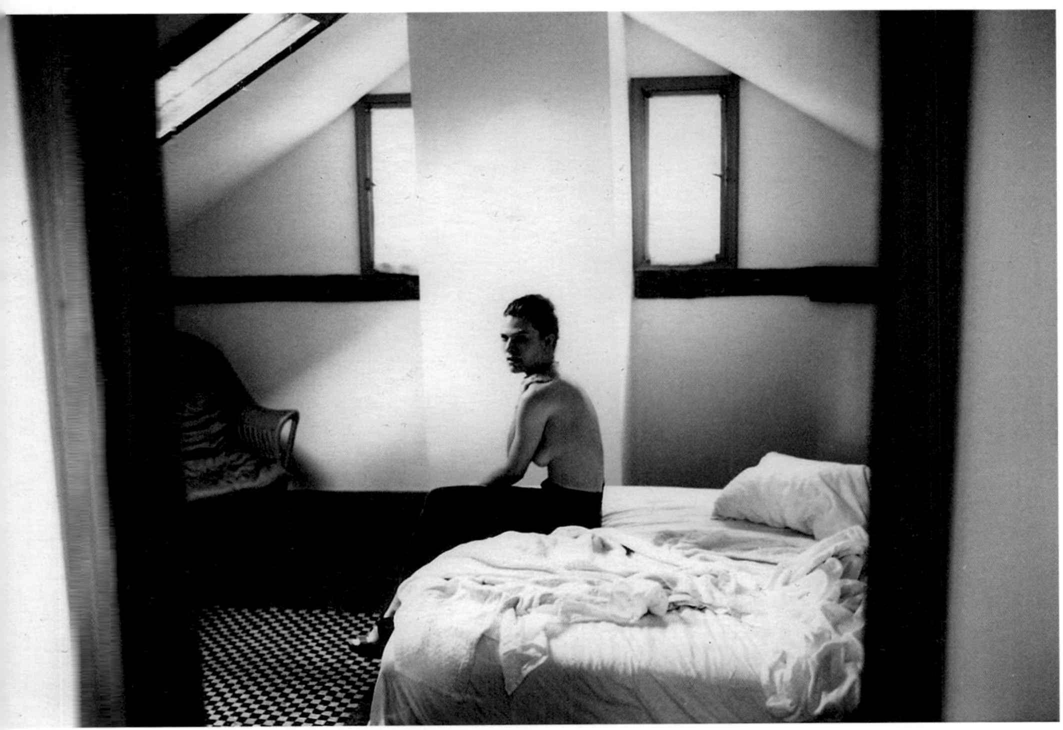

Double Bind
LEIGH LEDARE
by
Shelley Fox Aarons

Ledare, a name that means leader in Swedish, is the family name that Leigh Peterson and Meghan Hague both took when they married each other ten years ago. In English it is a *nom de plume* that brings to mind someone who dares. Five years ago, the Ledares divorced, and Meghan Hague subsequently married a photographer named Adam Fedderly. She is now called Meghan Ledare Fedderly. Although the marriage of Meghan and Leigh has expired, this conceptual artist, Leigh Ledare, who often works in photography, daringly folds both his former wife and her new husband into his artistic practice with his new work entitled *Double Bind*. Peterson remains Ledare, as he leads viewers into territory that many might just as soon leave unexplored. If you do choose to follow, you will be rewarded.

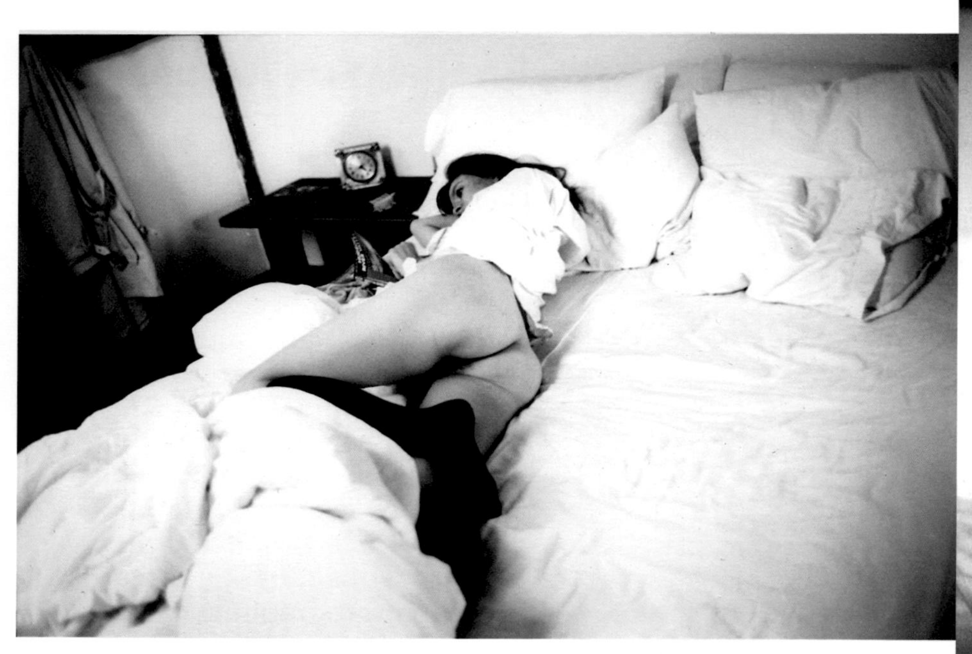
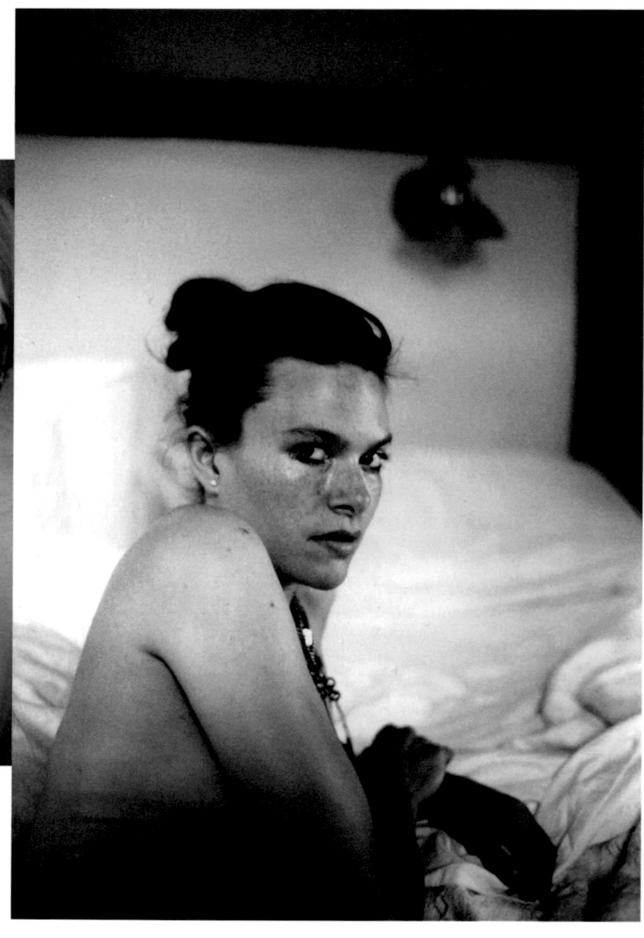

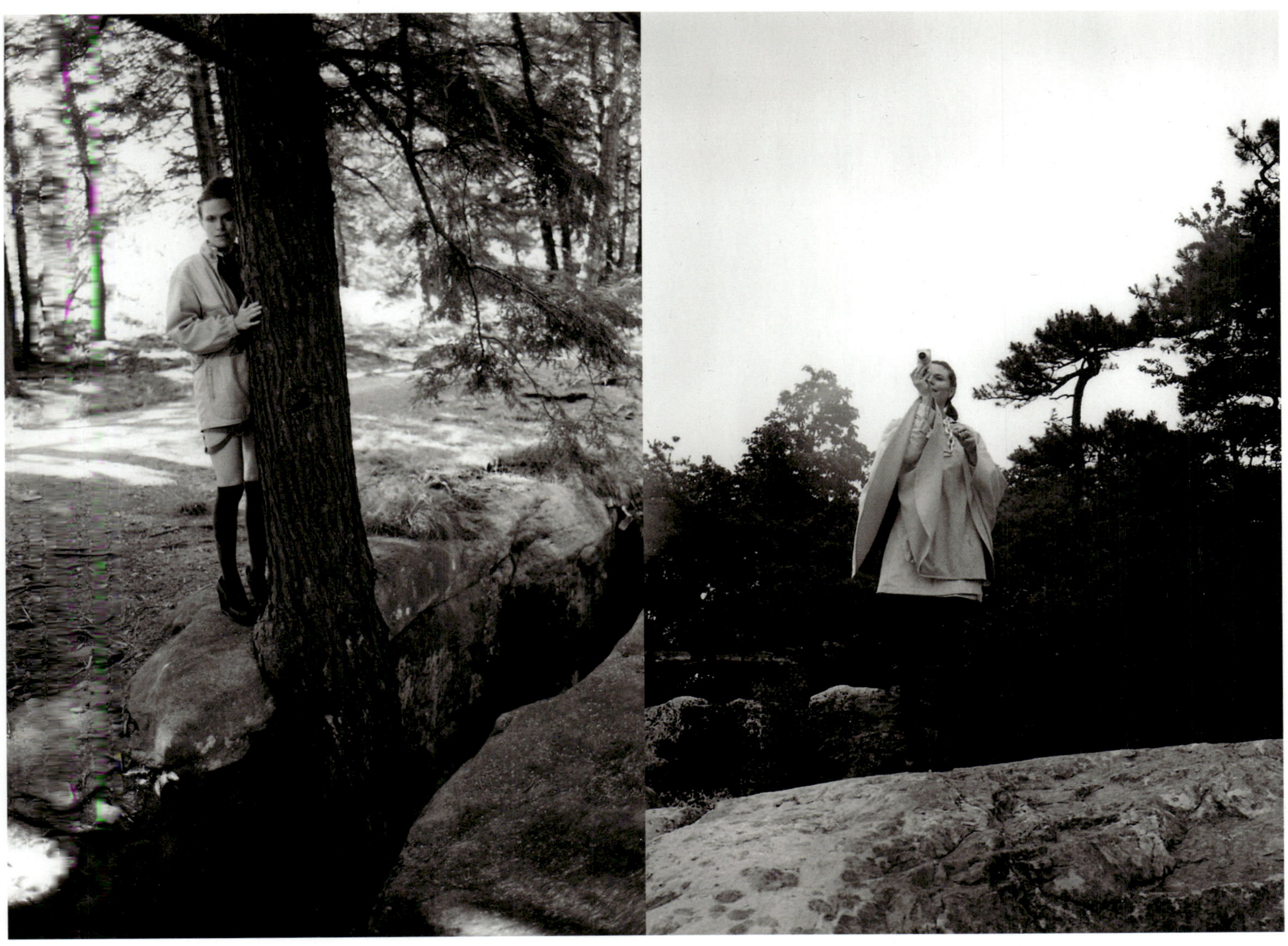

Page 86 Double Bind (Meghan Ledare-Fedderly photographed by Adam Fedderly). *Page 87* Double Bind (Meghan Ledare-Fedderly photographed by Leigh Ledare). *Page 88 left* Double Bind (Meghan Ledare-Fedderly photographed by Adam Fedderly); *right* Double Bind (Meghan Ledare-Fedderly photographed by Leigh Ledare). *Above left* Double Bind (Meghan Ledare-Fedderly photographed by Adam Fedderly); *right* Double Bind (Meghan Ledare-Fedderly photographed by Leigh Ledare)

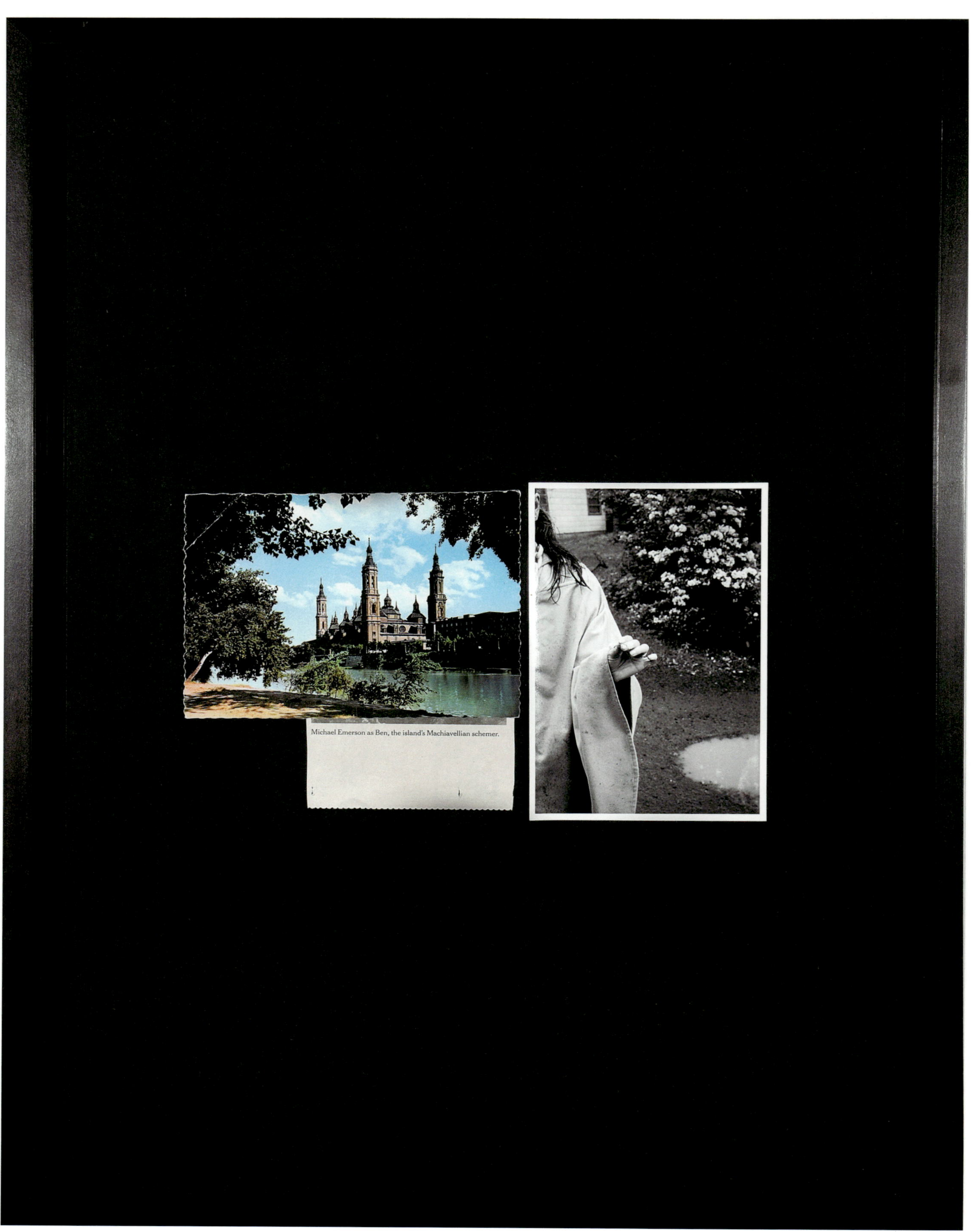

Above and right Double Bind (Diptych #6/25)

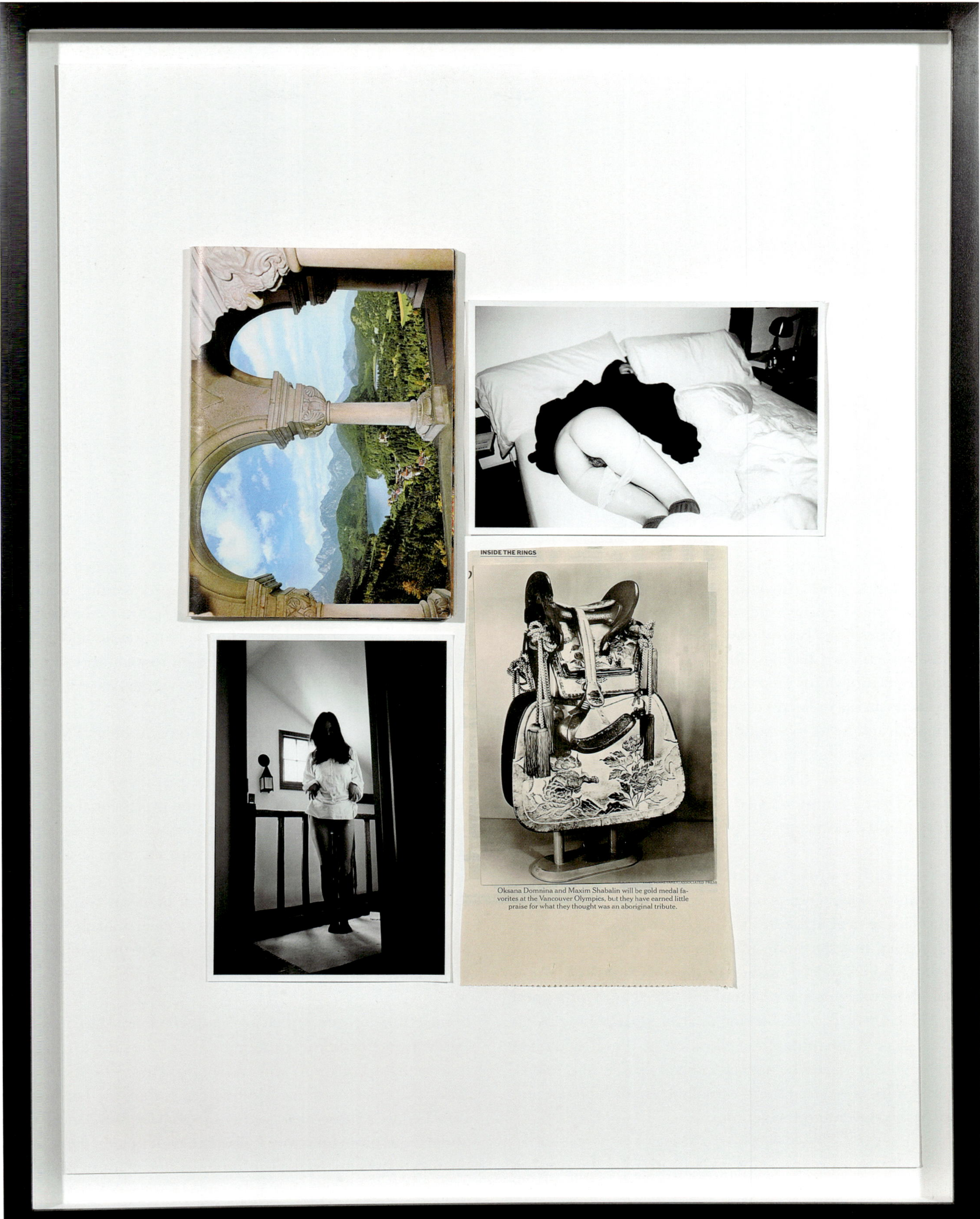
INSIDE THE RINGS
Oksana Domnina and Maxim Shabalin will be gold medal fa-
vorites at the Vancouver Olympics, but they have earned little
praise for what they thought was an aboriginal tribute.

Ledare does not only cross boundaries (bending social norms, codes, and conventions), or violate boundaries (breaking social norms and codes); more interestingly he actually repositions boundaries as he forces viewers to re-evaluate their own feelings about what may take place in intimate relationships. To produce *Double Bind,* Ledare spent a weekend in an isolated cottage with Ms. Ledare Fedderly to photograph her. One month later, the same scenario was re-enacted, but this time the photographer was Meghan Fedderly's current husband, Adam Fedderly, who had agreed to give his undeveloped film over to Leigh Ledare for selection and processing.

Just as in earlier works by Ledare, *Double Bind*'s objective is much more than mere provocation. There is a theoretical and philosophical armature to this piece built on the ideas of Gregory Bateson and Gilles Deleuze. These structural reference points indeed include the 'double bind', as well as ideas about difference, repetition, and alterity, self, other and intersubjectivity. But the beating heart and throbbing pelvis of this piece is the in-depth exploration of power dynamics in relationships, issues of agency, control (of self and other), shifting roles of exploiter and exploited, enabler, victim and perpetrator, lover and tormentor.

Specifically the way consent is granted and consent is revoked transfers an awareness of instability to every party involved, even - and in some cases, especially - the viewer. In an earlier

and somewhat lesser known series, Ledare engaged specific viewers, namely, his collectors into the production, similarly exploring power dynamics in the artist/patron relationship. Here too, with the possibilities for exploitation on both sides, it makes sense that Ledare would want to include, examine, and maybe even expose his collectors/viewers as well.

When Ledare inquired about photographing Phil (my husband) and me in our home, at first, I was resistant; boundaries, privacy, respect for the privacy of others and myself had been so much a part of my professional training as a psychiatrist. While I did not want to impose those conventions onto my relationship with an artist, I also did not want to be cast as a victim, or a perpetrator for that matter. Ledare himself has stated that he never wants to be considered a victim, just as he is very clear that the use of autobiography in his work is a means, not the goal of his investigative (analytical) art practice.

Some critics have described an Oedipal relationship between the artist and his mother in their reviews of the still earlier work that brought Ledare to wide attention, *Pretend You're Actually Alive*, his project with his Mother. But it took my encounter with Ledare's subsequent works - especially *Double Bind* - to understand more fully why I disagree with that analysis. The relational dynamic staged in these earlier pictures, such as those of Ledare's mother with splayed legs or vamping in garter belt, or even giving a blow job to a young lover or

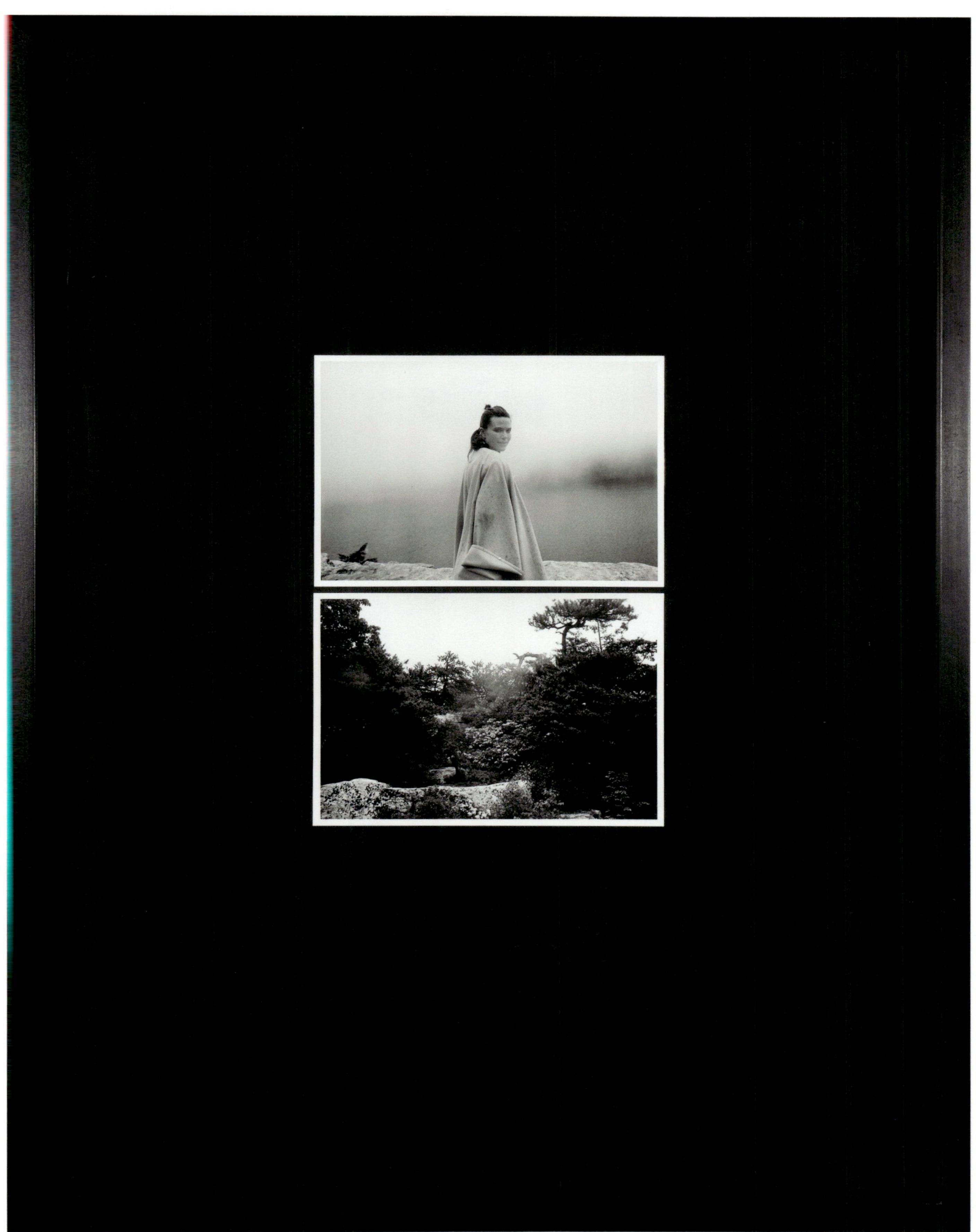

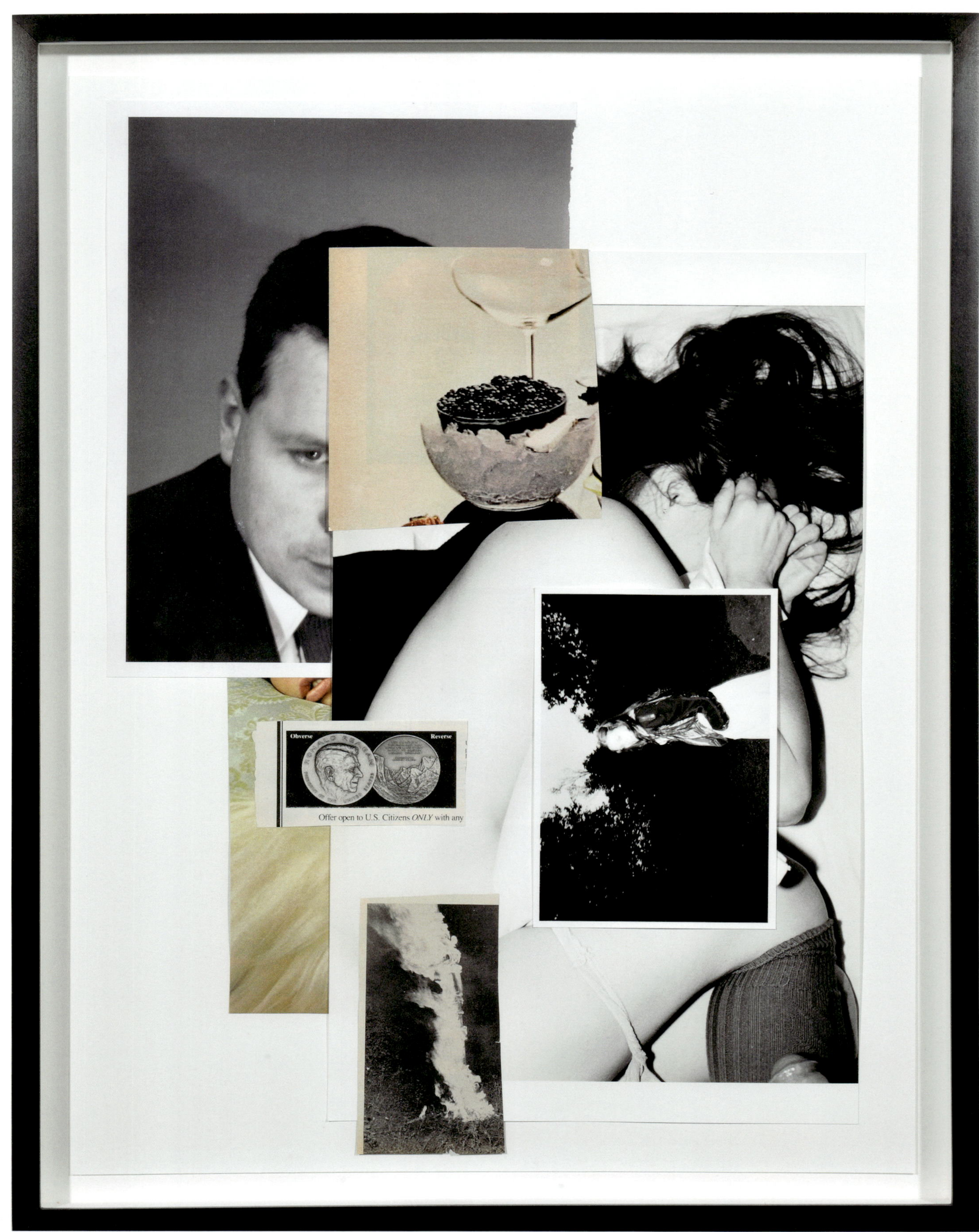

Above and previous page Double Bind (Diptych #15/25)

where he tries to calm her recurrent tears, maintain a binary structure. In these photographs there is no important male figure, which would be required to make the relationship configured therein an Oedipal triangle. That work was more about pre-oedipal issues such as abandonment and self/ other separation: all binary conditions.

In this new work, Ledare has indeed created a triangular formal structure through which he explores inter-subjectivity. And at the risk of indulging in a bit of jargon, one might safely go so far to describe this *Double Bind* as a partly shared but partially divergent understanding between competing realities.

Ledare seems to borrow from Bateson's *Double Bind*: wherein the first injunction is that one must or must not do something specific and the second injunction is more general, or more 'abstract', more implicit than explicit, but inevitably the second always conflicts with the first. He also invokes Deleuze's interest in repetition, difference and alterity by generating a triangular configuration, which is repeated with a shift in the dyadic base of the triangle; Meghan/Leigh, with Adam as the outsider, Meghan/Adam with Leigh as the outsider.
In addition to the photos of Meghan taken by Ledare and Fedderly, presented in 25 diptychs, the installation contains vitrines filled with photographic outtakes from the two photo shoots, and ephemeral materials of importance to the artist, picturing disparate subjects: stacks of photographic prints and collages (with Levi Strauss), portraits (of Meghan) and advertising portfolios (of milk) presenting the product seductively (advertising porn), pornography (including homosexual and heterosexual imagery) and poetry (Bataille) and much, much more. Since it remains inevitable that one will be forced as a viewer, and a collector, and now a collaborator, into Ledare's *Double Bind*, I dare - or maybe I am forced - to return to my inevitable engagement about triangles.

The third triangle explores power plays between the two men including a scenario in which the woman becomes a lesser concern, almost irrelevant despite being the ostensible focal point, as the two men compete in a power struggle through which there is an element of collaboration and bonding creating possible homoerotic undertones.

Despite the autobiographical nature of the material, Ledare engages the viewer with the universality of the material's concerns. In exploring the unraveling of his own marriage to someone he obviously cared for profoundly, he raises a question that many grappled with - how does one fall in or out of love? His intermixing of advert porn, enticing products with built in expiration dates, reflect his speculation that relationships too may have expiration dates built in. Mr. Ledare doesn't claim to have the answers, but his work boldly explores the questions and leaves the viewer with a lot to think about.

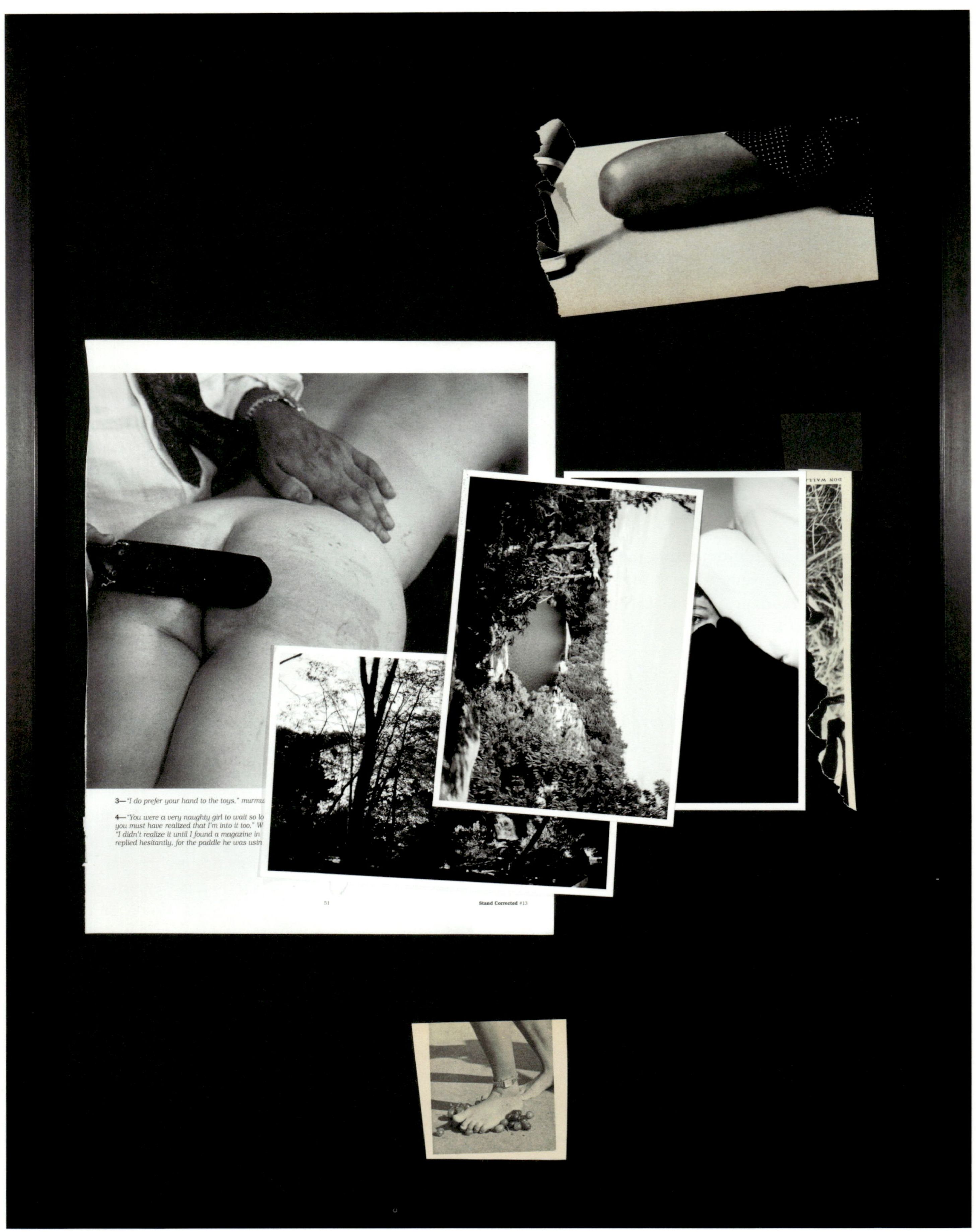

Above and right Double Bind (Diptych #20/25). *All images 2010 © and courtesy the artist and Pilar Corrias Gallery, London*

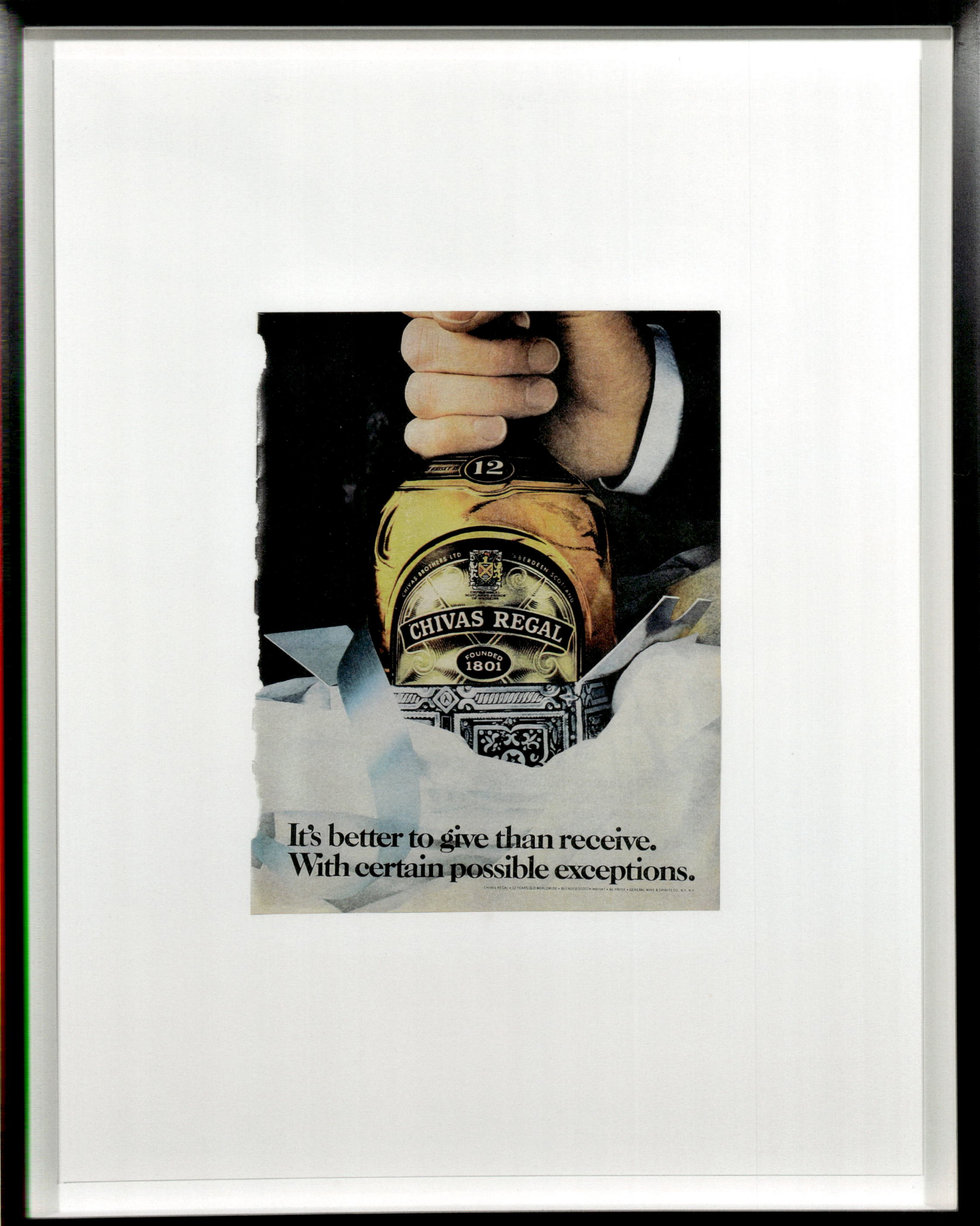
12
CHIVAS REGAL
FOUNDED
1801
It's better to give than receive.
With certain possible exceptions.

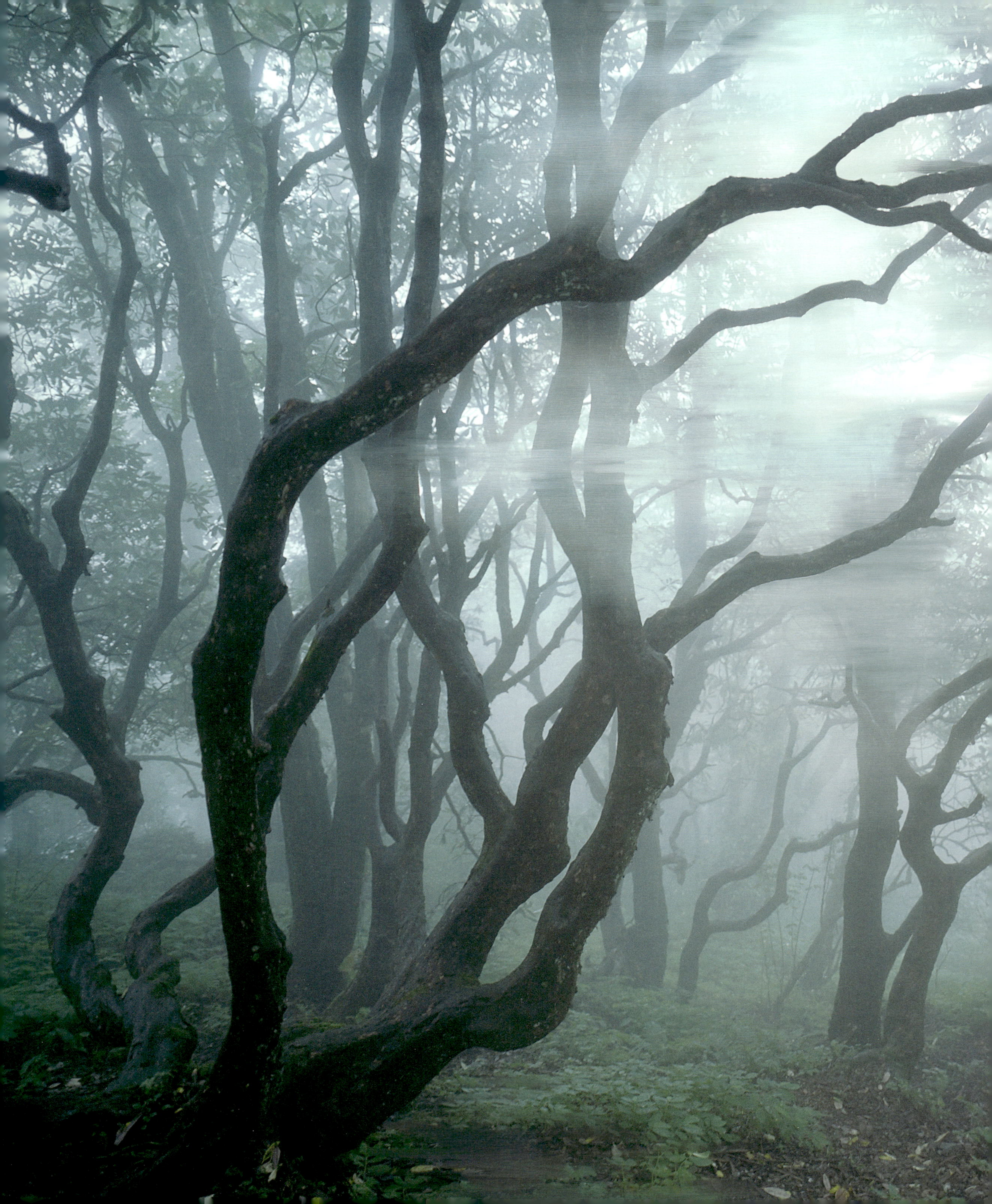

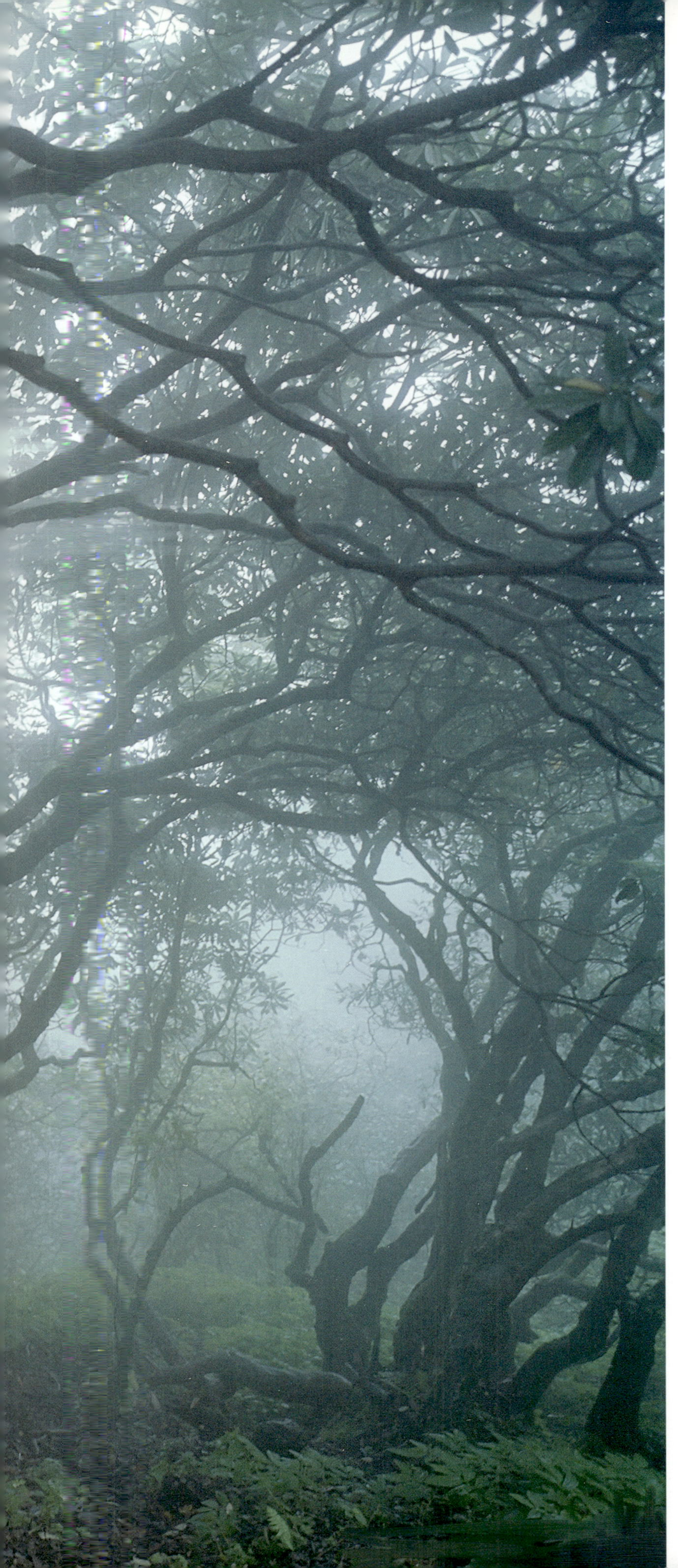

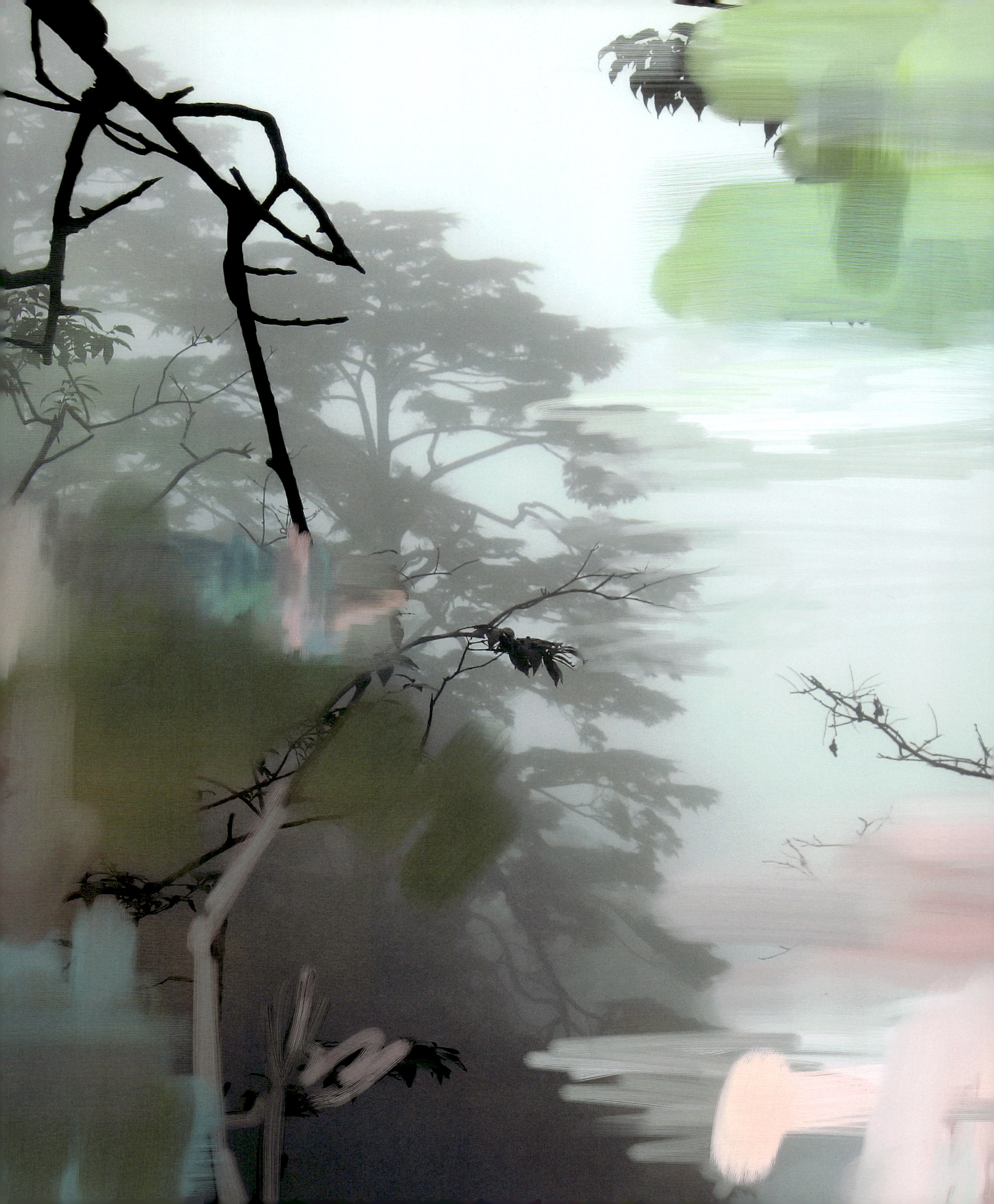

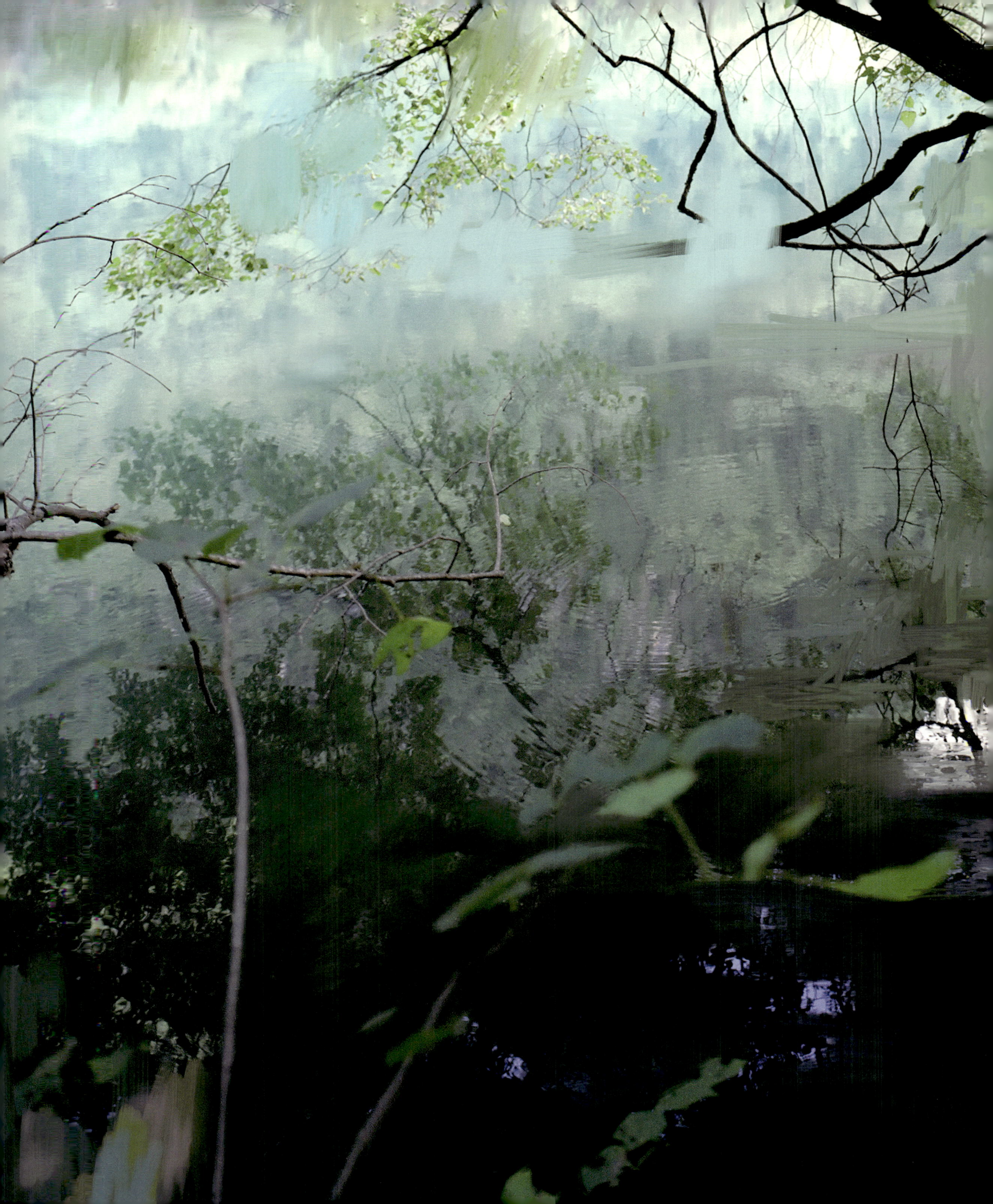

SANDRA KANTANEN Shadow Images

Referencing Chinese and Japanese landscape painting, *Shadow Images*, Kantanen's latest series, evolves from the Platonic philosophy that all perceived visions are a shadow of their reality. Here, the objects or landscapes photographed are of secondary importance; rather, they serve as a basis for finding and sensing the ideas that lie behind the immediate world, chromatic reverberations, movement and passage, with a meticulous focus on the superhuman and the supernatural in everydayness. Kantanen writes, "I work within certain traditions of image just to have a starting point for viewing. I try to state, 'visibility begins here.' I have been greatly inspired by artists like Timo Kelaranta and Hiroshi Sugimoto, to name a few. They have all traced photography back to its own materiality. This is what interests me too." By taking photographic expression to the edge of its technical boundaries, by experimenting, for instance, with light, exposure time and mixed media, with plates, scanners and printers, Kantanen attempts to convey something about the fundamentals of photography itself. Shot in China, Tibet, Japan, and Finland, the layered and lyrical tonal gestures in *Shadow Images* demonstrate a Romantic search for a chimeric landscape, one that embodies an idealized representation of the natural world, and reaffirms the doubleness, the silhouettes, that is inherent in all. Sandra Kantanen was born 1974 in Helsinki, Finland, and studied at the Central Academy of Beijing, 2001, and at the University of Art and Design, Helsinki, graduating in 2003. She has been shown in international group and solo exhibitions, and she is a member of the Helsinki School, the same city in which she lives and works.

Opening spread Untitled (Woods 1) 2010, cm 108 x 128. *Page 101* Untitled (Mountain 5) 2010, cm 65 x 50. *Page 102* Untitled (Lake 4) 2010, cm 65 x 50. *Right* Untitled (Sakura 2) 2009, cm 128 x 108. *Page 104* Untitled (Mountain 1) 2009, cm 128 x 108. *Page 105* Untitled (Sakura 3) 2009, cm 128 x 108. *Pages 106 - 107* Untitled (Sakura 1) 2009, cm 108 x 128. *All images pigment print on paper © and courtesy the artist and Gallery Taik, Berlin*

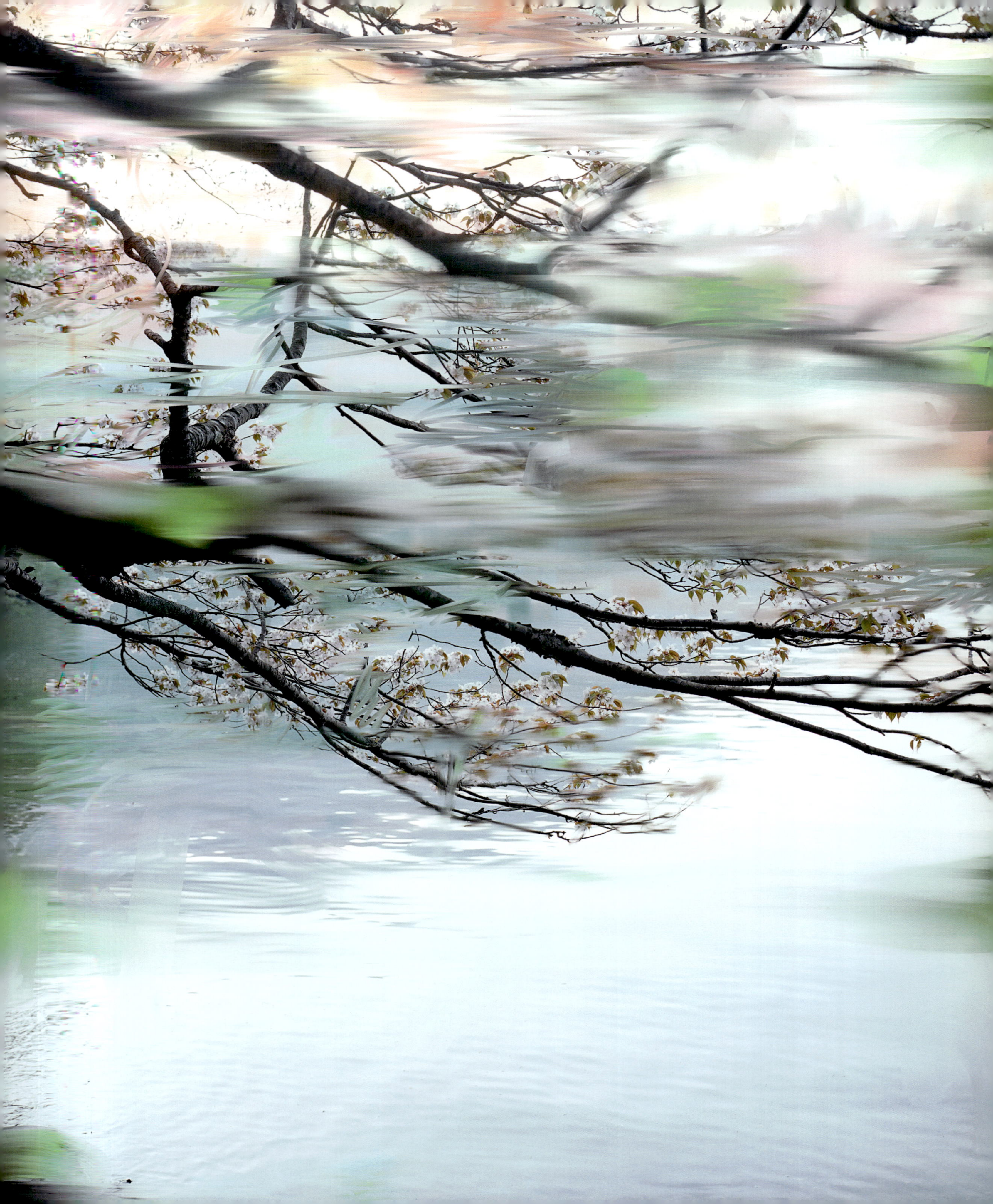

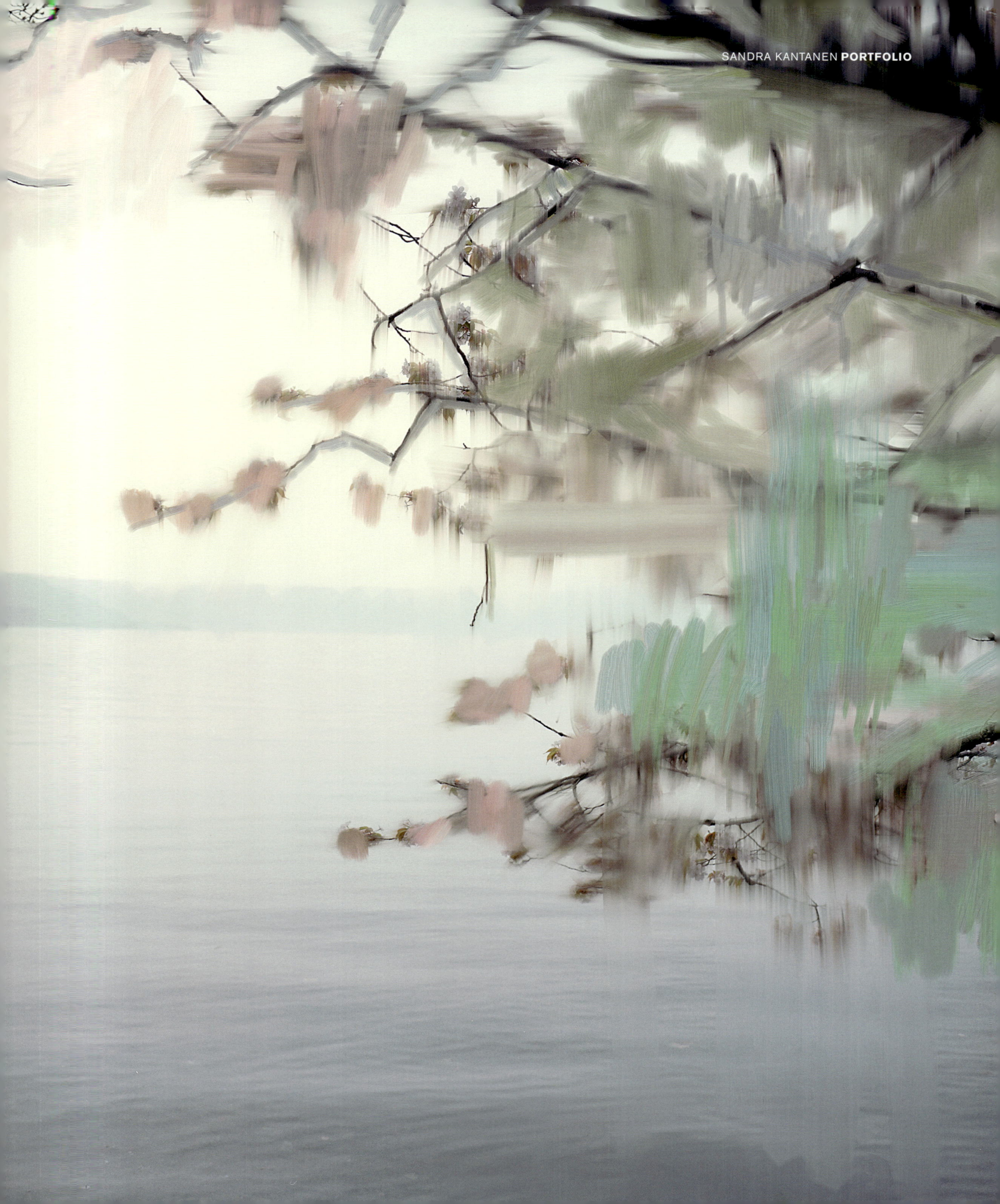
SANDRA KANTANEN PORTFOLIO

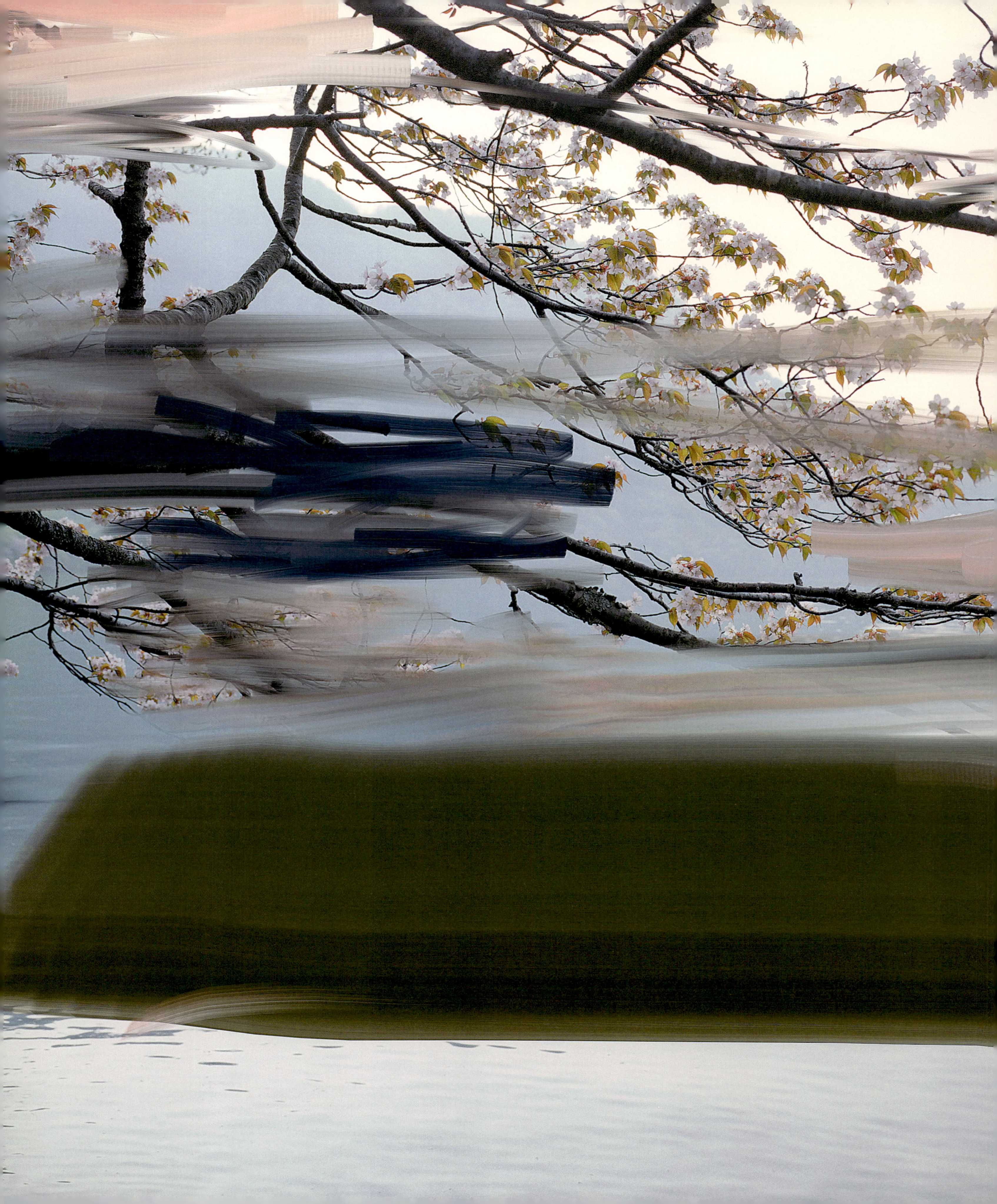

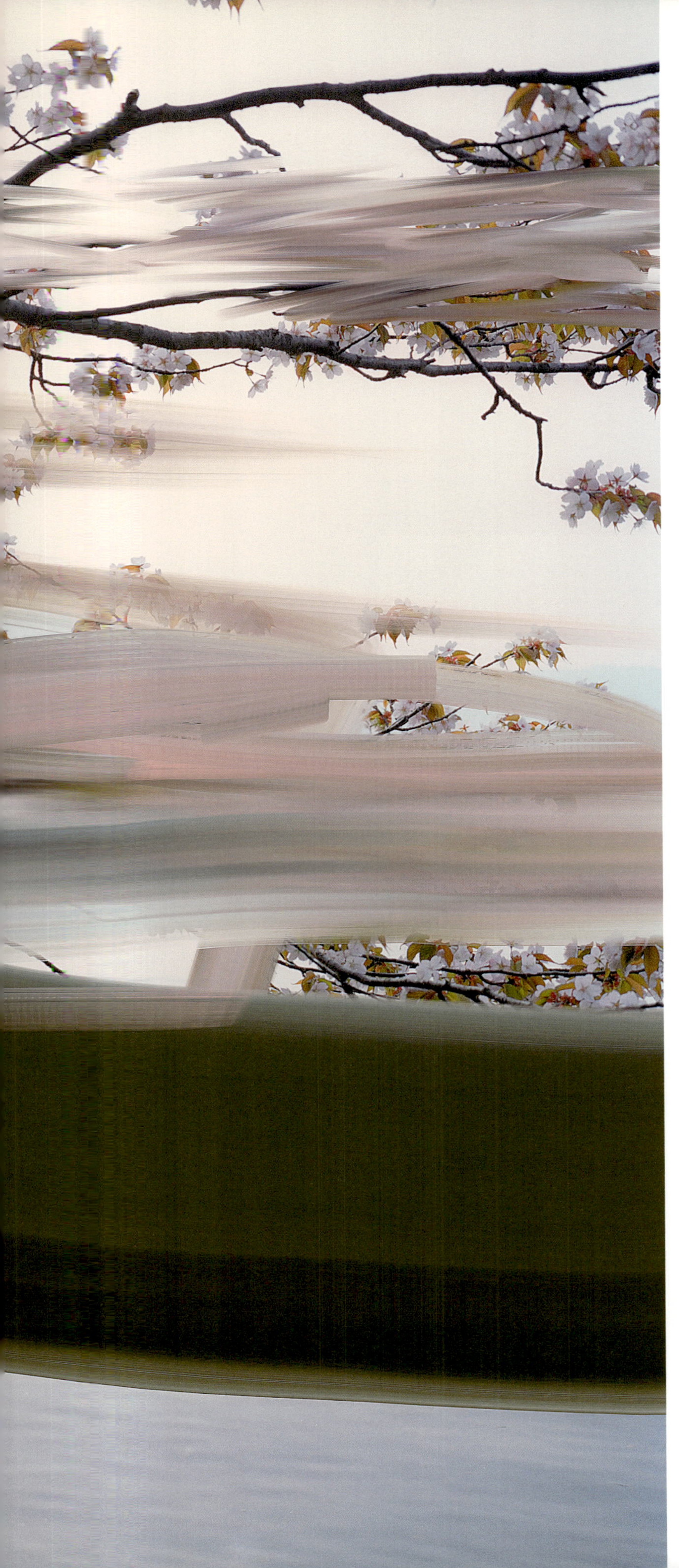

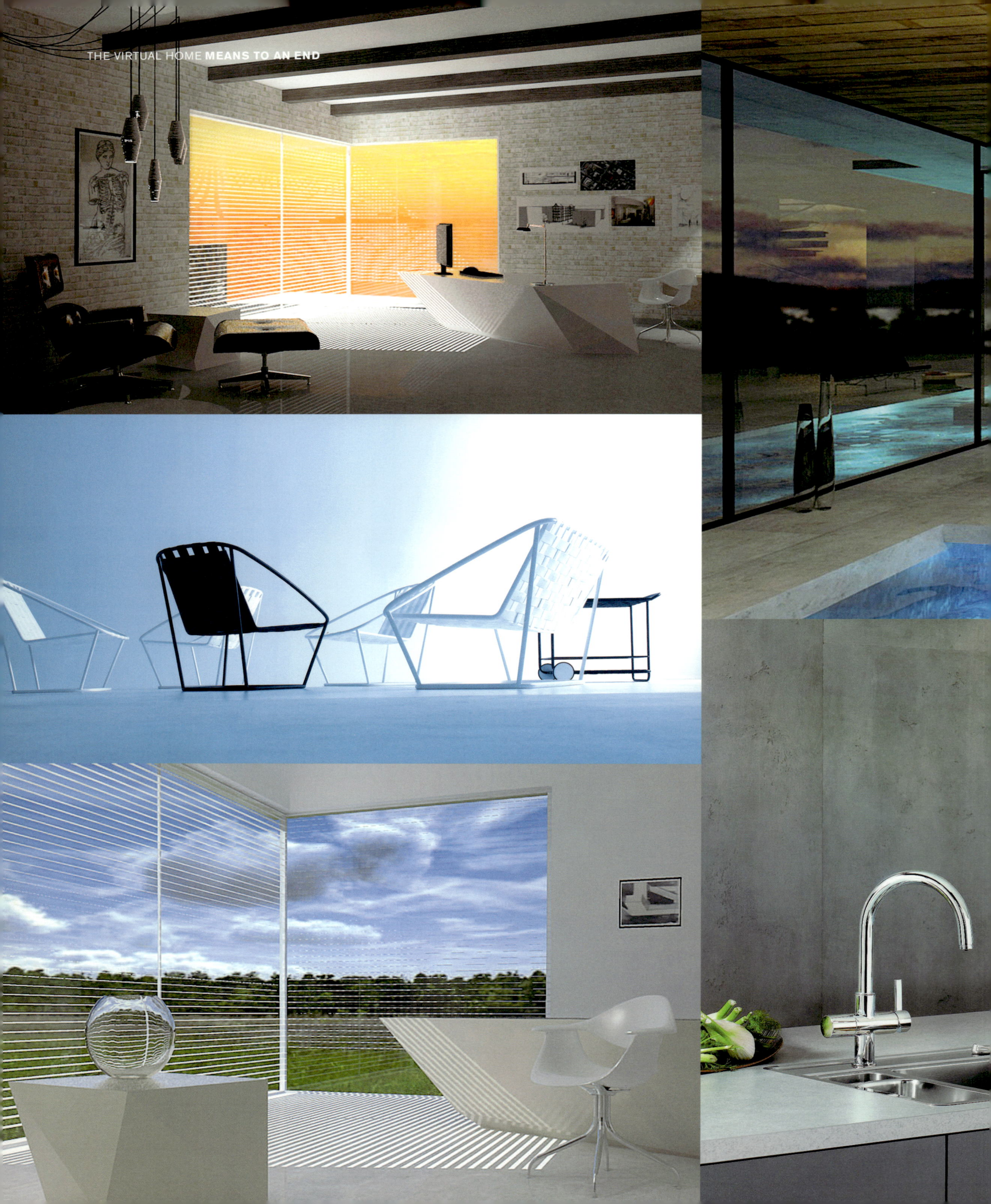

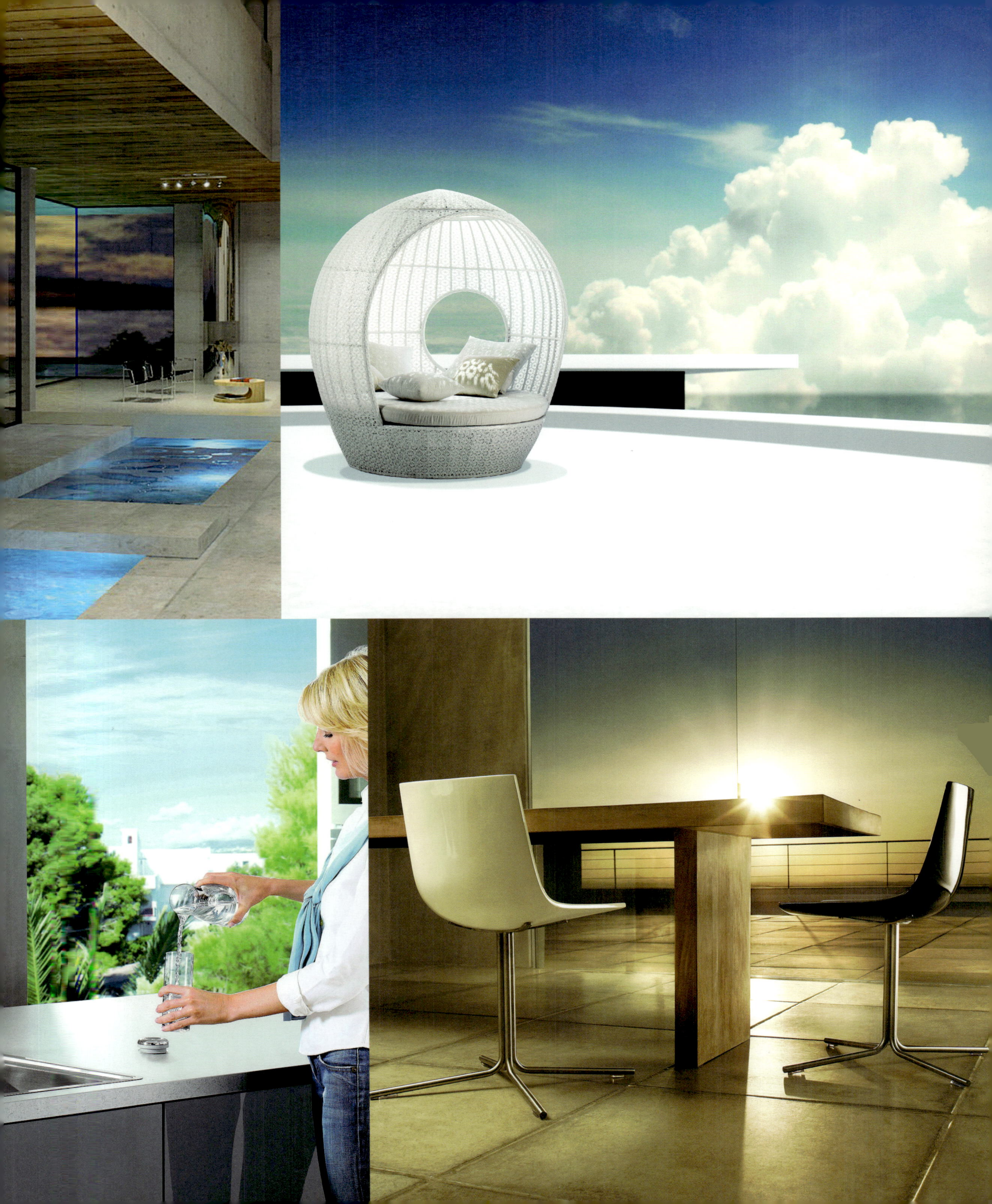

THE VIRTUAL HOME
by Tim Mills

Using the language of photography to present the 'real' through a simulation that is distinctly virtual, these visualizations, associated with and commonly used by architects and designers, function to provide a sense of scale, shape, and form with respect to the environments in which these products could or should be situated. However, these spaces and objects reside in another world, a space that does not physically exist, but one that might in a utopia or a lifestyle fantasy.

Illusion is integral to the vending of these commodities: sunshine, a lush garden, a terrace with white fluffy clouds. If these products were placed in an unexceptional or 'normal' environment, would they function as successfully in selling the dream?

It is commonplace to see such visualizations; they suggest scenarios and environments that are yet to be discovered or realized, an aspirational sense of wonder and intrigue, and a way to project our idealized notions of status and self. These same elements are both the aesthetic and ideological foundations that drive the website Second Life, where players are encouraged to personify and live as anyone they wish to be.

The following images of residential interiors and exteriors move us into a hyperreal photographic realm that is burdened by its lack of reality. In some sense they are so modern that reality hasn't yet caught up.

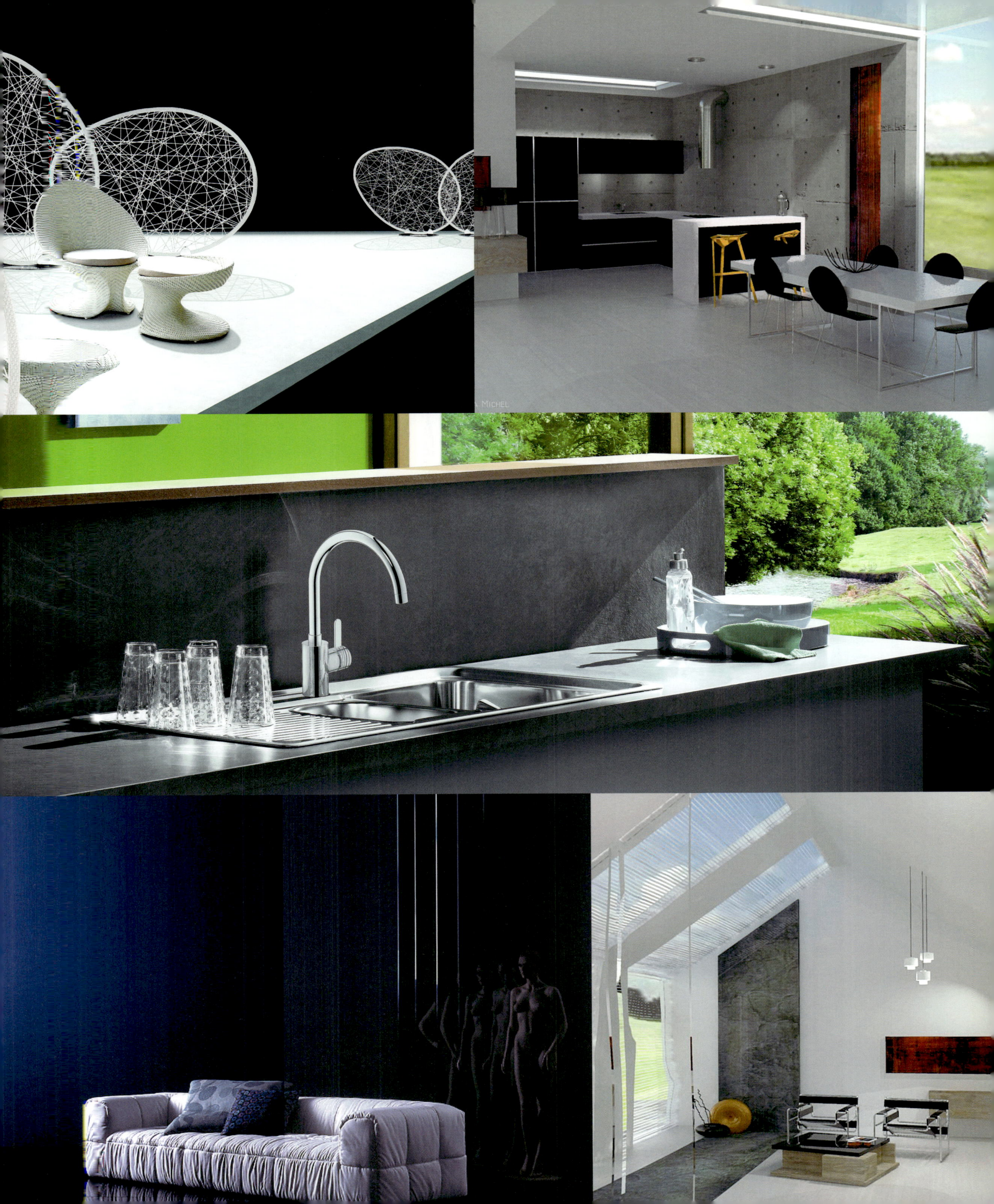

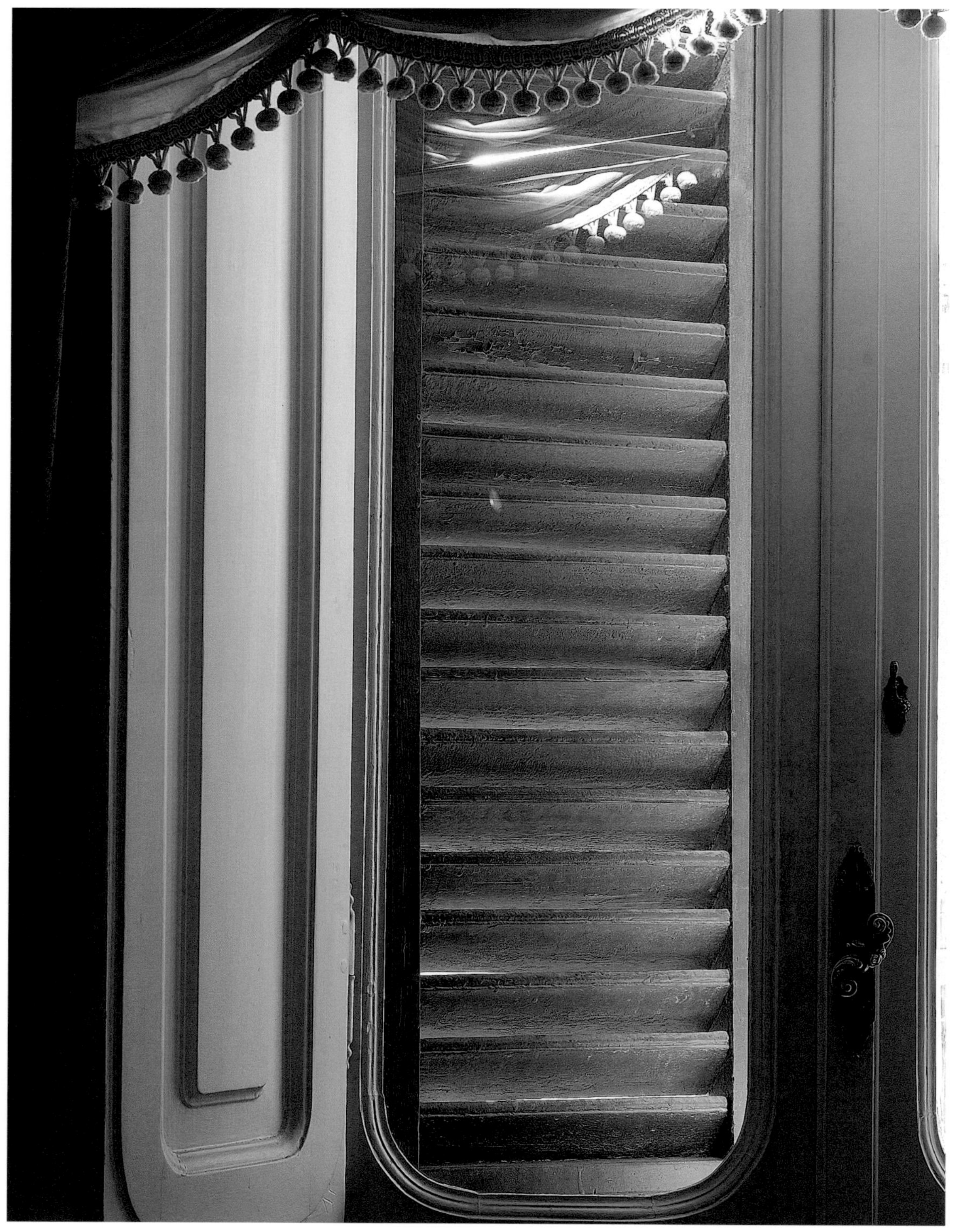

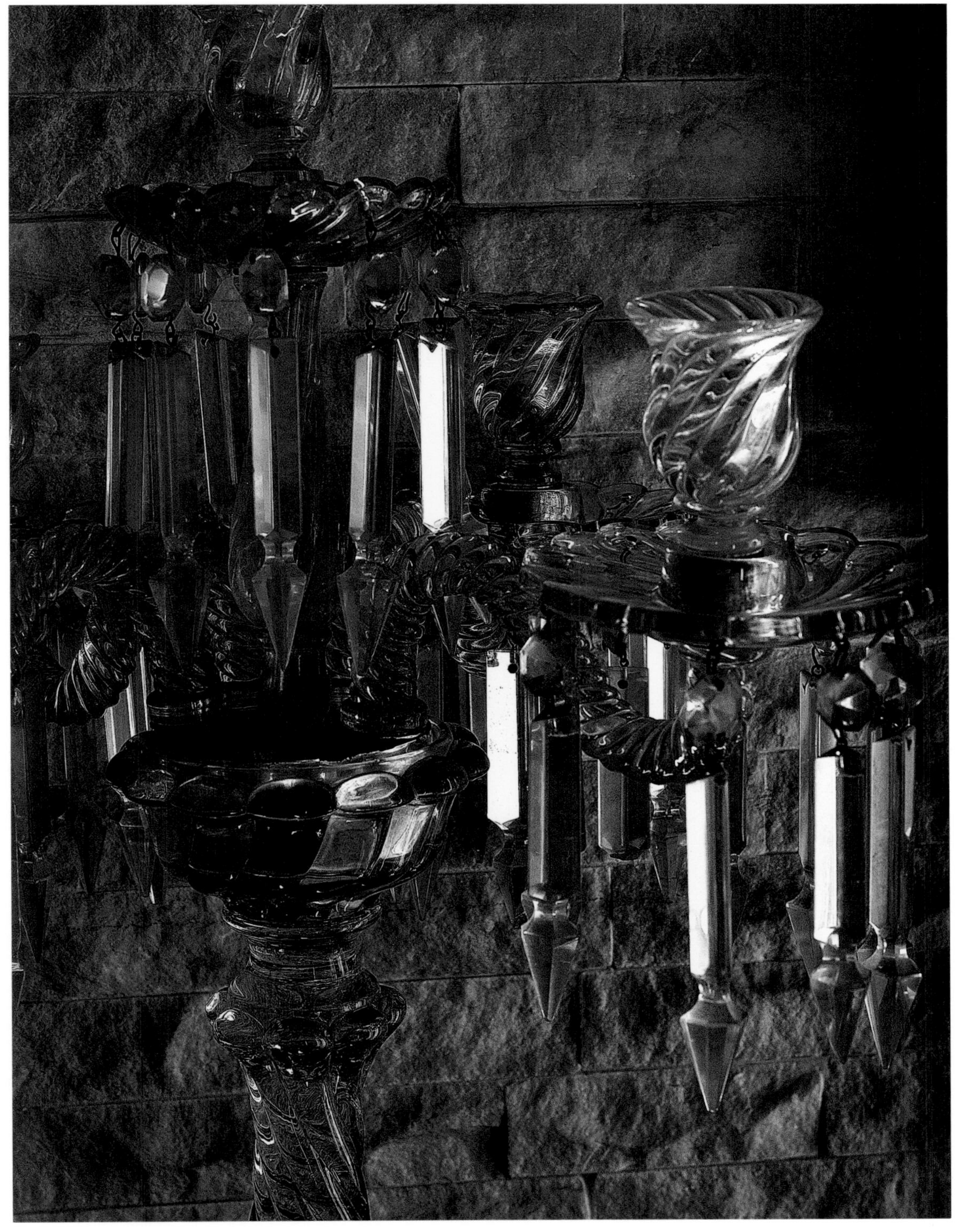

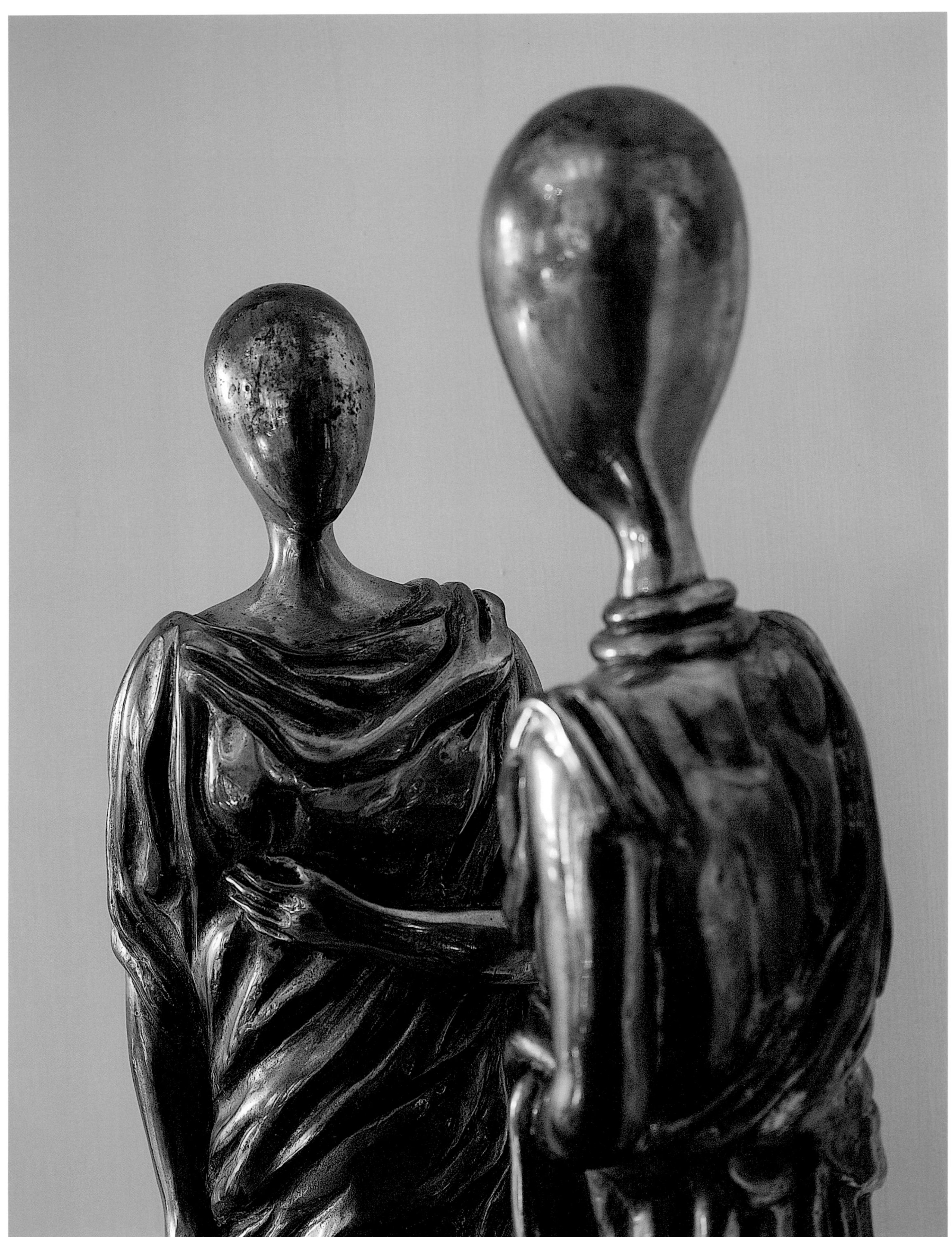

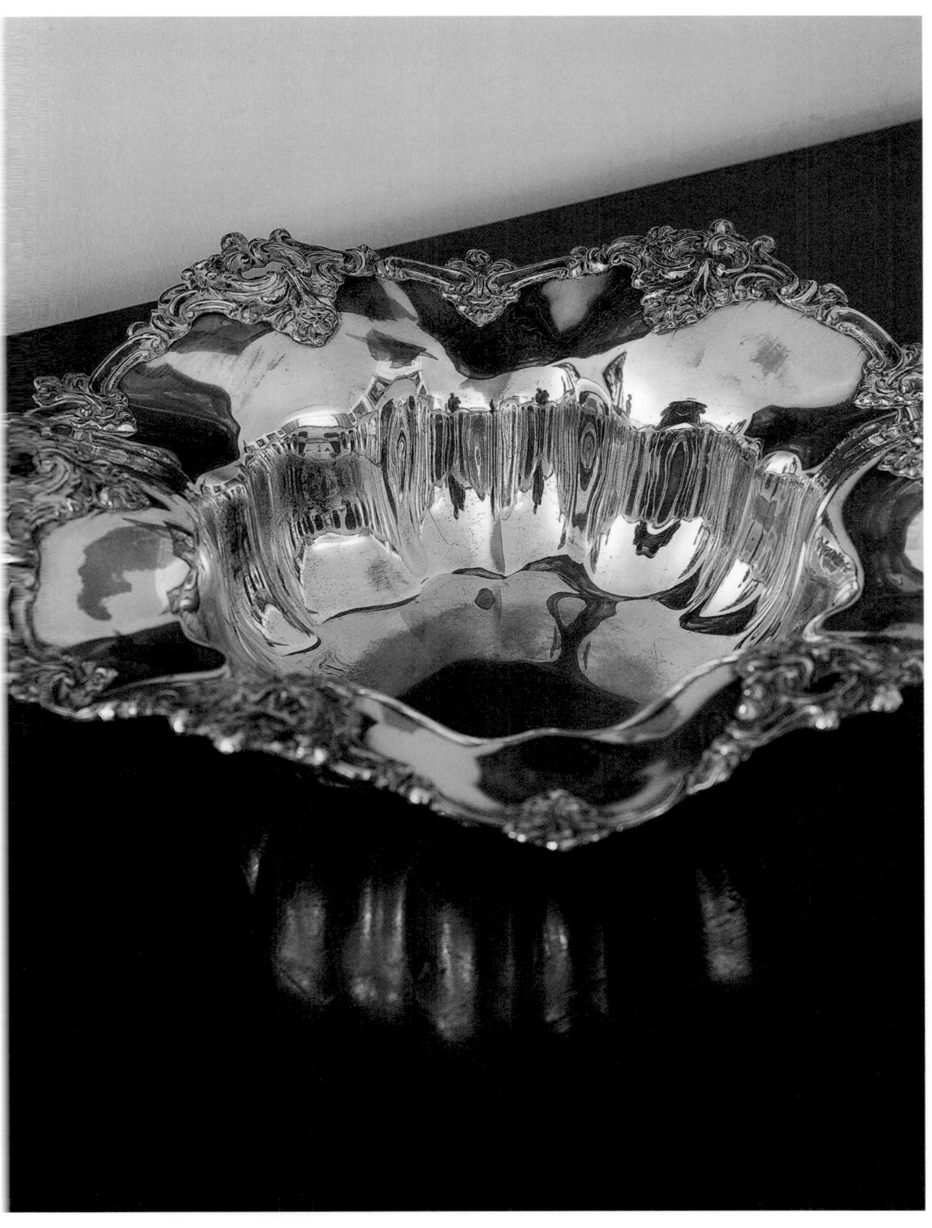

Termini
HEIDI SPECKER
by
Walter Guadagnini

"Bangkok ist eine Quelle", Bangkok is a source of inspiration. So ends the imaginary letter that Heidi Specker writes to Germaine Krull at the close of the volume *Bangkok*, which contains work by both photographers. One source is the Thai capital, and the other is the German photographer, with whom Specker establishes a long distance dialogue, seeking her presence in the words of those who knew her in that far-off land and period, tying up the loose threads of memory not with iconographies but with the very practice of photograph; by focusing the eye on the world and on things, an eye which is able to transform reality using the details of its forms. The first inspiration is therefore symbolized by the journey, by movement, by the desire to be somewhere that is other than home: Thailand, Australia, Italy, destinations on a journey that are both physical and intellectual.

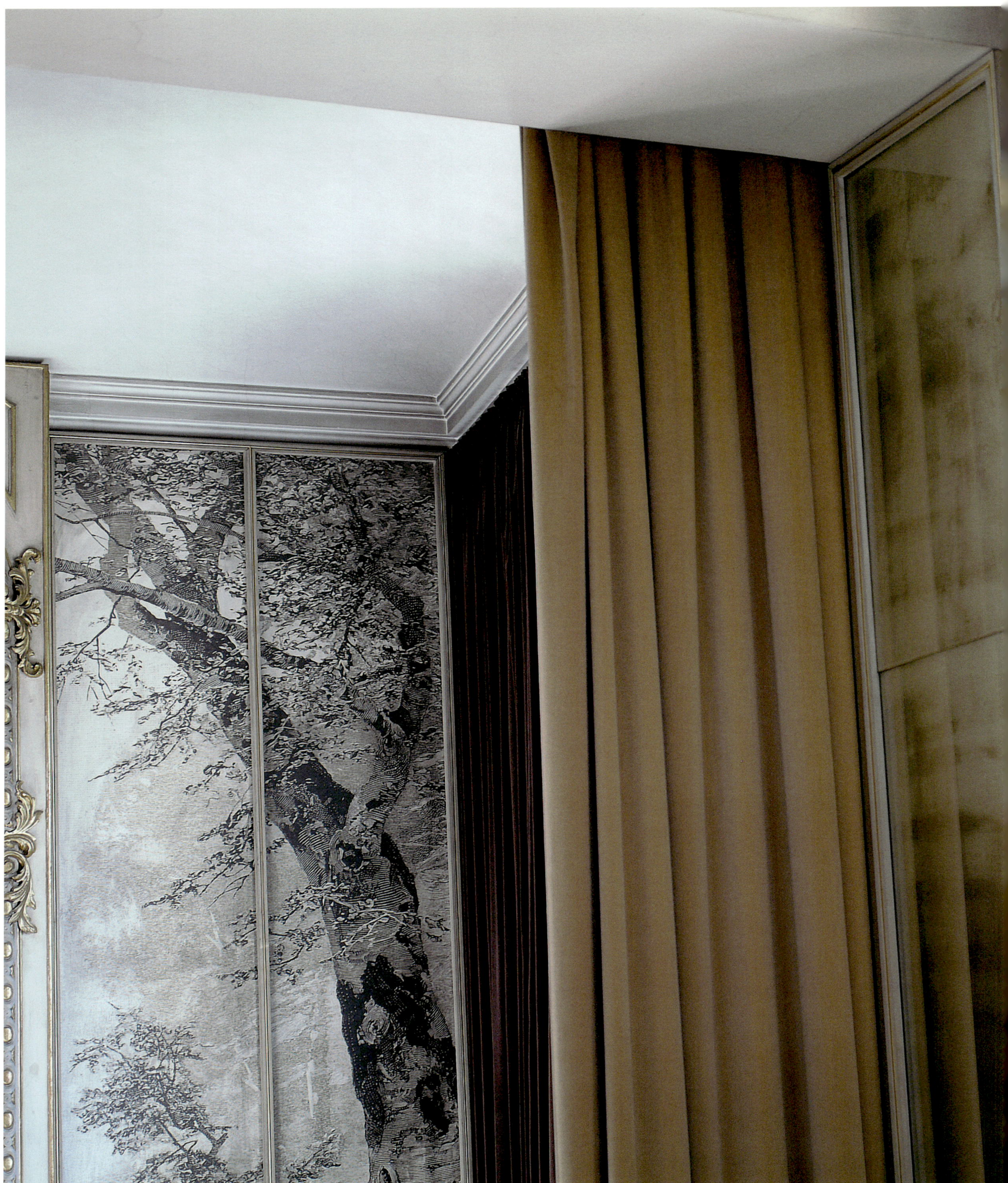

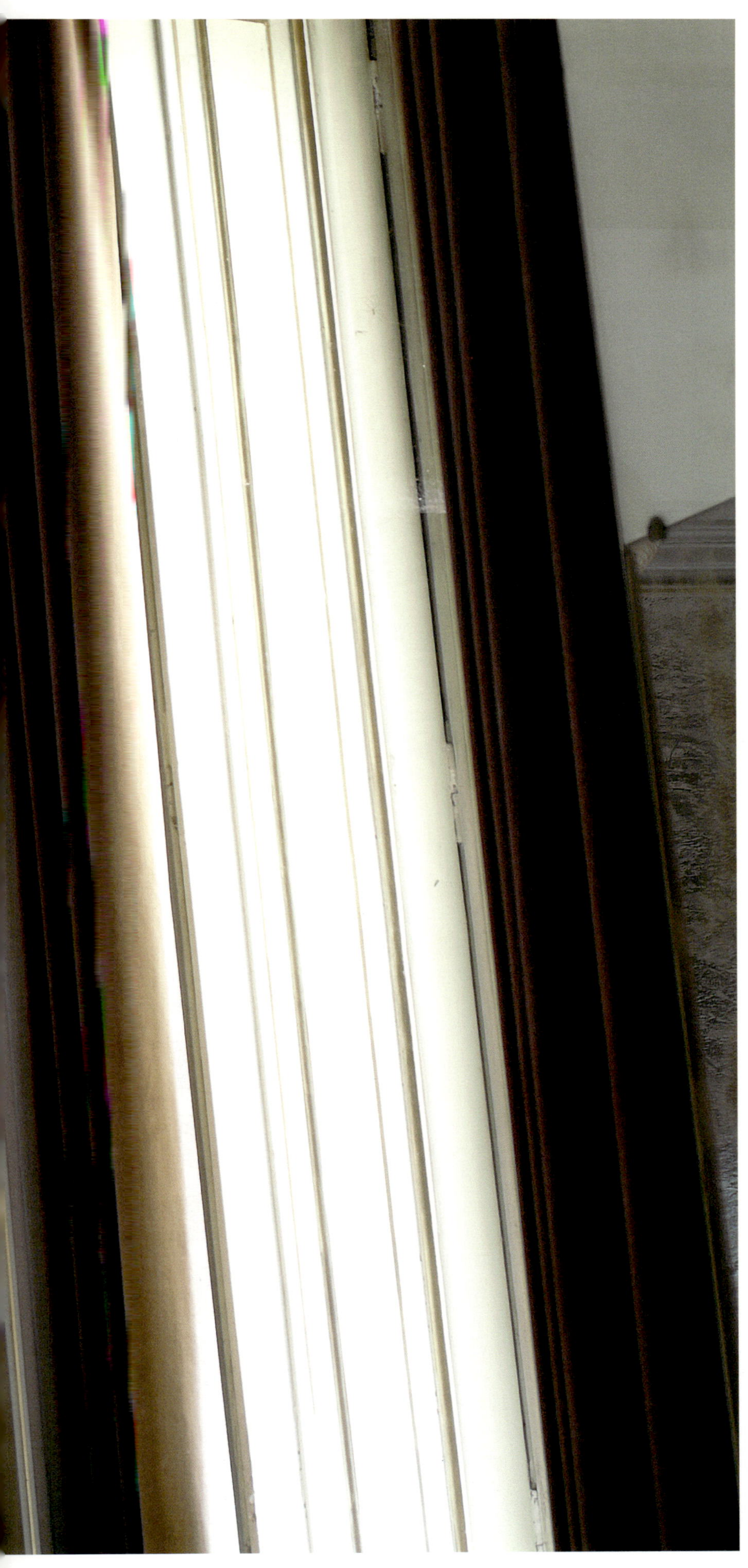

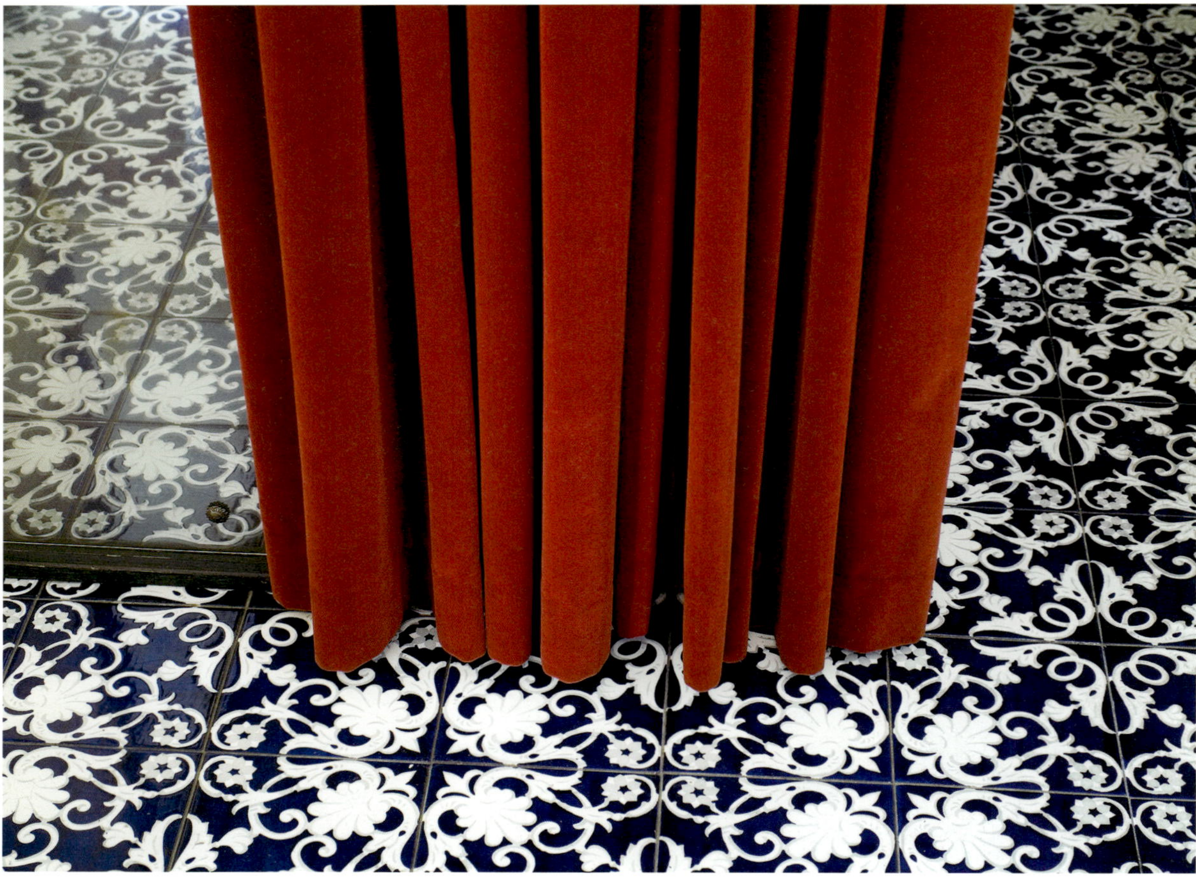

Destinations that are, at first sight, exotic and rich in potential images that tell of difference, surprise, as in the best (or worst) tradition of travel photography. But the images that Specker brings back from these journeys are in a completely different style and belong to a whole other discourse. It is no coincidence that *Bangkok* begins with two photographs of trunks and branches which might easily belong to the twin volume, *Im Garten*, published simultaneously. In the same way, *Im Garten* begins with three city views, weaving together motifs and images in a short circuit. This process magnifies the ability to suspend the image in an undefined time and place, by means of its extreme adherence to the datum of reality.

Five years after the Thai experience, the German photographer is in Italy, thanks to a grant from the Accademia Tedesca of Villa Massimo in Rome. It is certainly a less exotic destination, and yet it too is full of suggestiveness and memories linked to the history and architecture of the city and, even more so, to the relationship between two cultures that have, since at least the time of Goethe, been extremely fruitful. In Rome as well, Specker finds her interlocutor, she even goes to visit him at home; Piazza Spagna 31 is the address and the inhabitants are mannequins. It is the last studio of 'Pictor Classicus', another piece of the mosaic in the construction of her map of cultural affections, and the other well. Giorgio de Chirico, a Greek from Volos, dazzled by Nietzsche and Arnold Böcklin in a Turin square. And in Turin, Specker retraces the steps of Carlo Mollino, another eccentric exponent of Italian culture between the two wars, a designer and architect who did not fit the mold, a lover of photography, an art to which he would dedicate himself and *Il messaggio dalla camera oscura*, a large and curious volume that appeared in 1949. Another home-studio; some photographs are taken outside in the city in search of Mollino's traces, mirroring the search for Krull in Bangkok.

They are both sources and pretexts: Specker does not cite de Chirico or Mollino (and she does not cite Krull either), nor does she describe them; and this is one of the cruxes of the artist's relationship with her sources of inspiration, which bolster intellect and trigger poetics to develop both coherently and independently. Of no less

Page 112 Piazza di Spagna 31 - I, 2010. *Page 113* Piazza di Spagna 31 - VI,
2010. *Page 114* Piazza di Spagna 31 - II, 2010. *Page 115* Piazza di Spagna
31 - V, 2010. *Pages 116 - 117* Via Napione 2 - II, 2010. *Left* Via Napione
2 - I, 2010. *Below* Via Napione 2 - VI, 2010. *Page 120* Cavour - II, 2010.
Page 121 Torino - I, 2010. *Page 122 left* Piazza C.L.N. - III, 2010; *right*
Piazza C.L.N. - IV, 2010. *Page 123* Piazza C.L.N. - V, 2010. *All images from
the project* Termini, © *the artist, courtesy Brancolini Grimaldi, London*

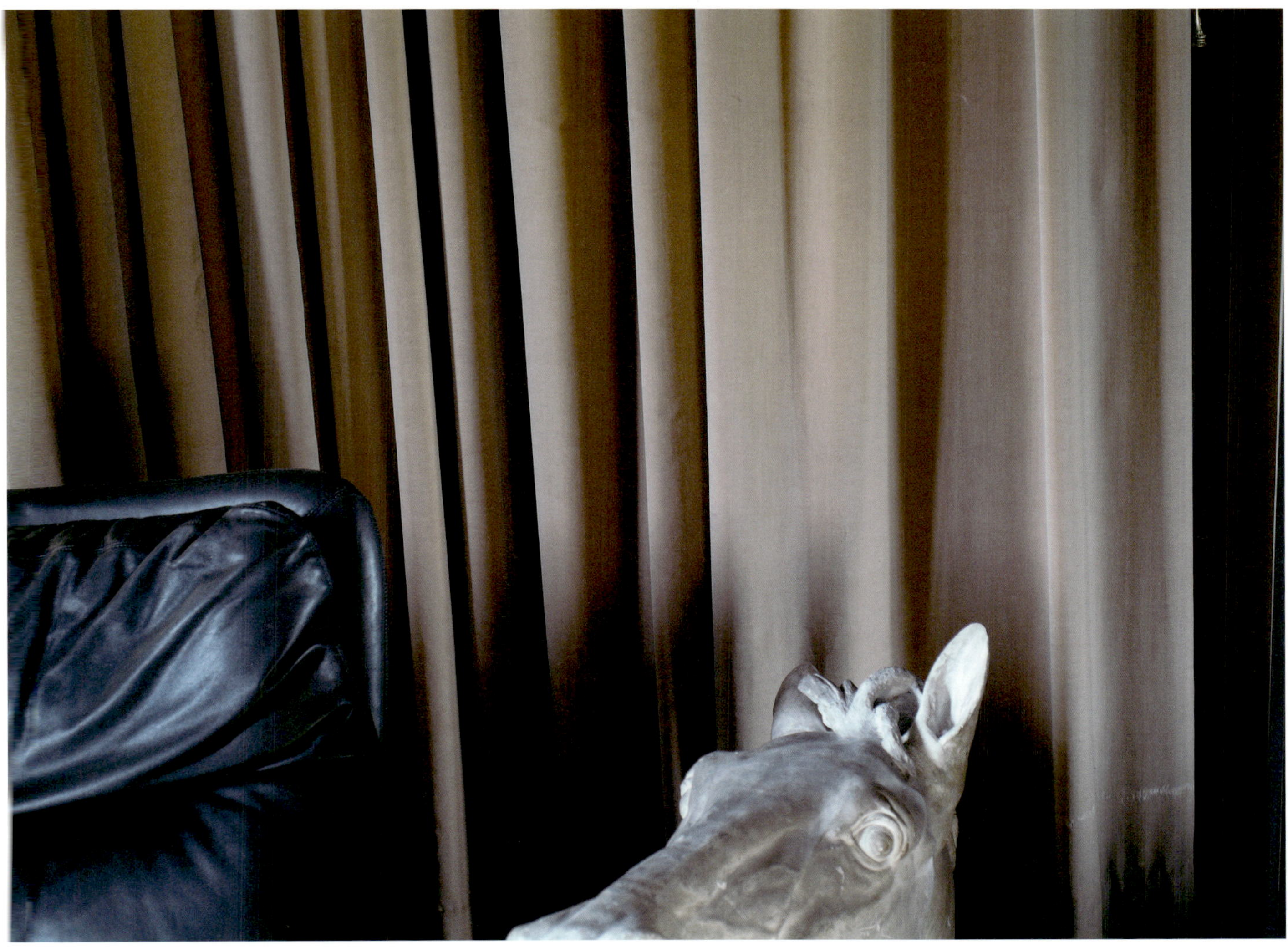

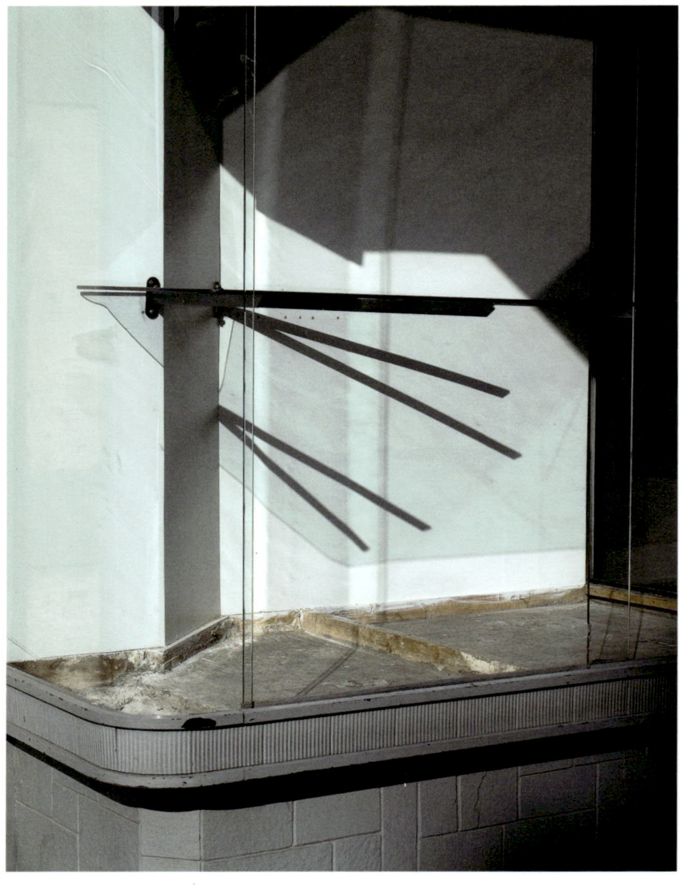

importance is the theme of memory and of intellectual legacy, which is absolutely central to the poetics of Heidi Specker, and so it is appropriate to exit from an overview of her work in order to enter into the language, in the constituent elements of this photography. Guided once more by the artists whom the images explicitly recall, it is easy to pinpoint in that complex period between the two wars the primary source of inspiration, a mixture of New Objectivity and Metaphysics. Trees, buildings and objects are transfigured, starting with the precision with which they are photographed; the mystery of things is in the things themselves and in the point of view of those who observe them. The shot, which is often a close-up, modifies spaces and proportions, isolating the subjects from the context and making them absolutes. The use of light contributes in a defining manner. It literally produces the forms and creates the spaces, each time accentuating the two dimensional or three dimensional aspect of the image. Specker's decision to use stark black and white for these series is certainly not random; it removes objects even further from the everyday and leads them into a timeless dimension, just

as the interiors where the photographs are taken are timeless. And the choice of the small format, in clear contrast with the blow-ups of much of contemporary photography, is also deliberate. It is as though Specker wished to reinforce the classical character of her work with its dimensions, as though she were demanding total concentration from the observer, paralleling the concentration she uses in constructing the image. Because, ultimately, if there is a constant feature in the language of this heir to the finest tradition of modernist photography, it is precisely that desire to create her own story beginning with the forms of things, the point where they meet and the spatial possibilities which emerge from them. Whether it be the shape of a trunk or the decoration on a façade, or windows which frame a portion of outside space, or the half-closed shutters as a play of light and shadow, it is, in any case, the dialogue between these impressions of the world that creates the unexpected forms of a new reality. Abstract forms which originate from extremely concrete objects such as the structures of the Tour Eiffel by Germaine Krull or the porticos of a Piazza d'Italia by de Chirico.

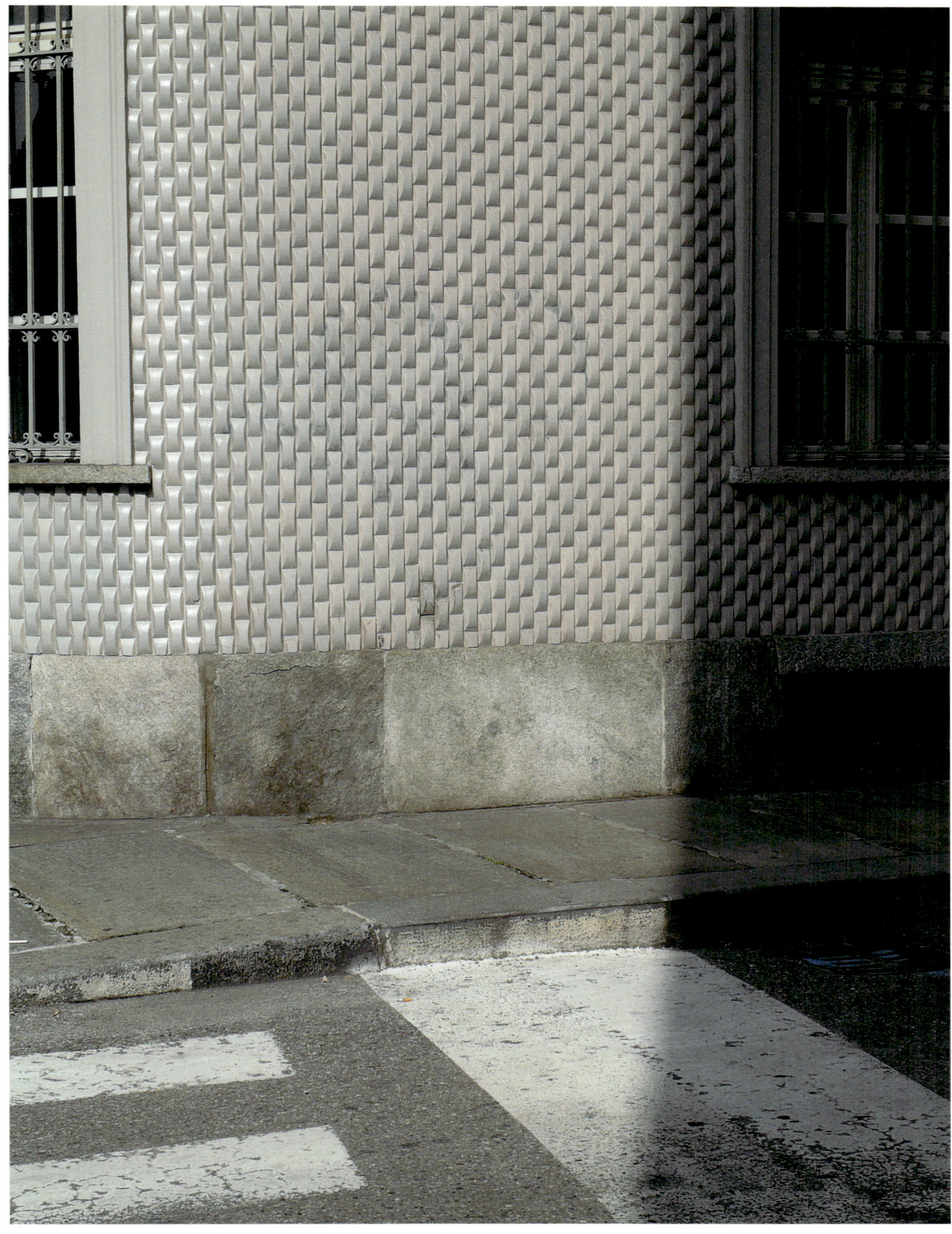

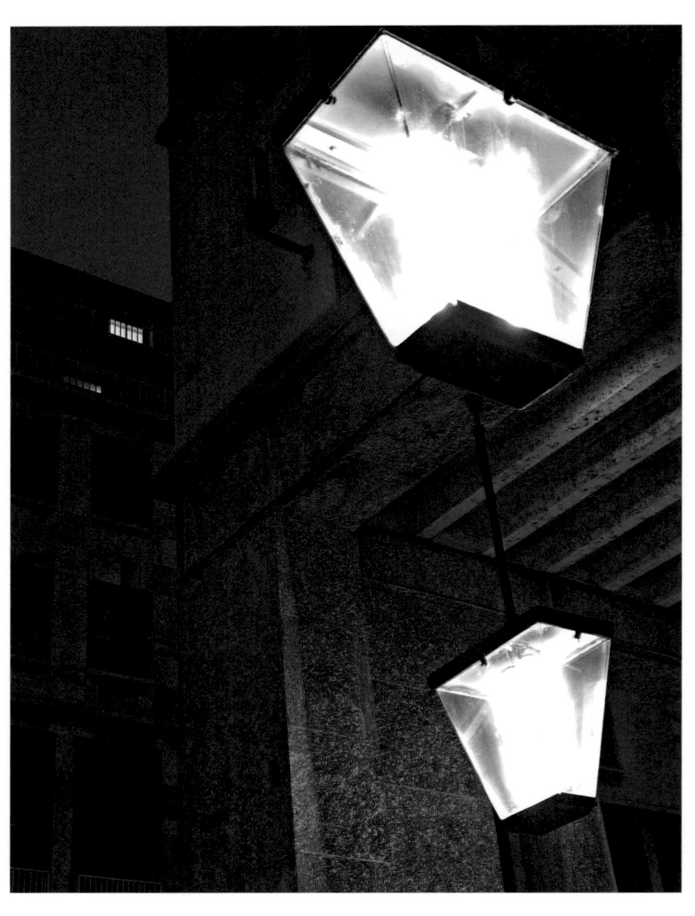
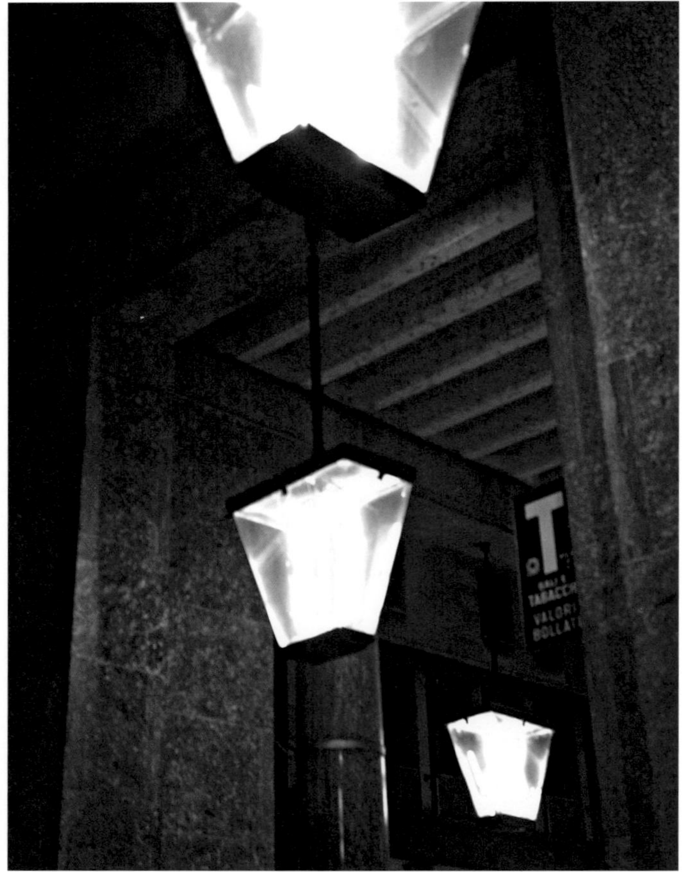T
TABACCHI
VALORI
BOLLATI

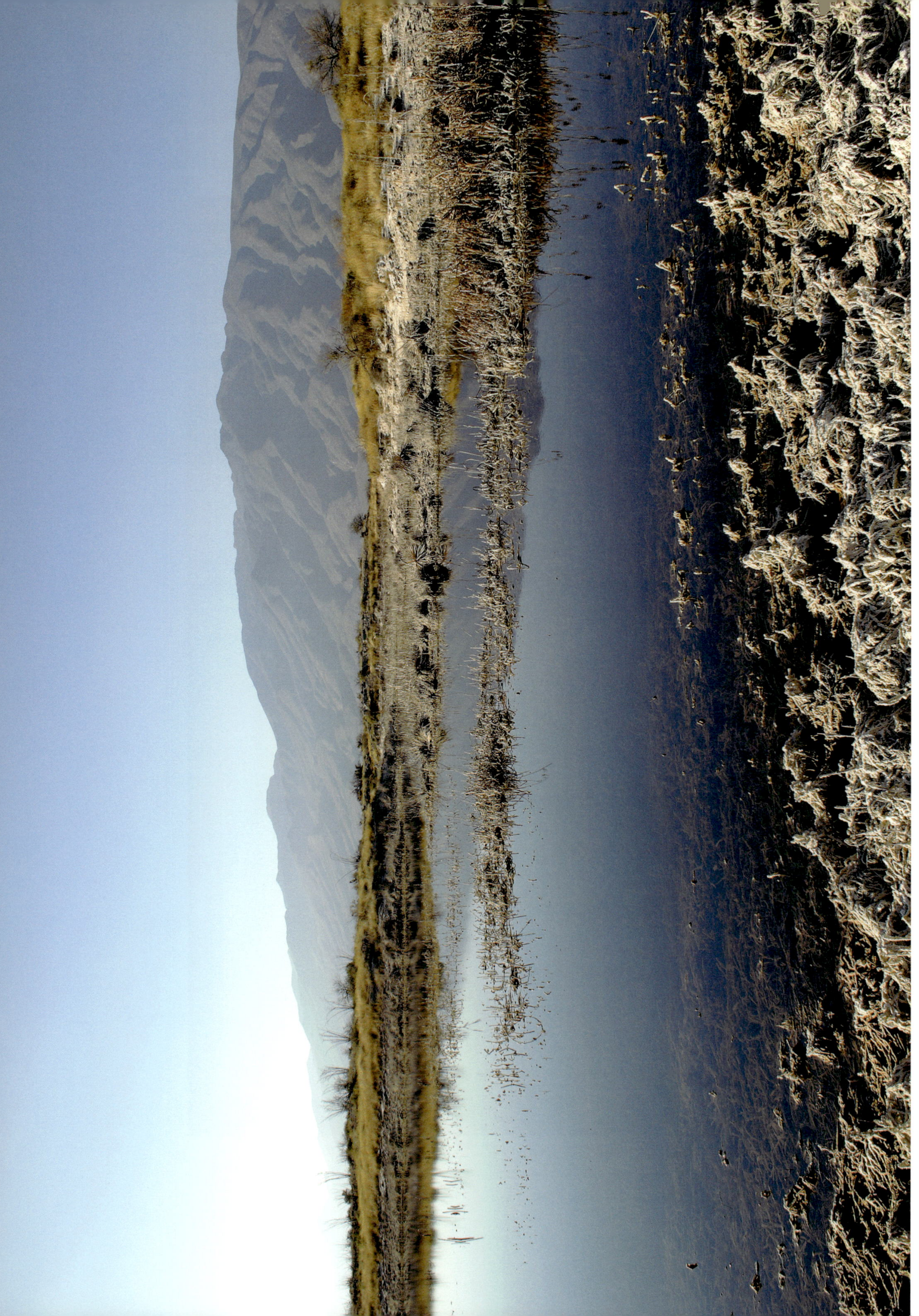

CAROLINA FUENTES
CUATRO CIÉNEGAS

A place of infinite possibilities, small details and contrast, the valley of Cuatro Ciénegas is ranked among the world's most unique ecosystems, surrounded by sand dunes and eventually mountains that rise up to 3,000 meters. It is located on the banks of the Sierra Madre Oriental in Coahuila, Mexico, a desert region with very arid weather, blistering daytime temperatures and below-freezing temperatures at night. In 1994 most of the valley was declared a Natural Protected Area by the federal government, because of the uniqueness and fragility of its ecosystems.

The diversity of terrain, textures and colors, reveals itself in different situations and seasons, multitudinous matter and color. The waters of the Cuatro Ciénegas wetlands, in Mexico's Chihuahuan Desert, come from aquifers deep underground and therefore remain crystal clear. It is carved by a system of underground rivers, springs, swamps, lakes and canals, with a total of around 200 bodies of water, habitats are now threatened by a diversity of factors. The 1,295-square-kilometer region has been isolated from other water systems for millions of years, allowing dozens of endemic species to evolve. It houses more than a thousand species of living beings. Of those, at least 56 are unique: there are 23 types of plants, nine types of snails, three types of turtles and various additional species of frogs, snakes, scorpions and shrimp.

Poza Juan Diego. Thick patches of submerged aquatic vegetation cover approximately half of the bottom, the remaining areas are bare, revealing grayish sediment

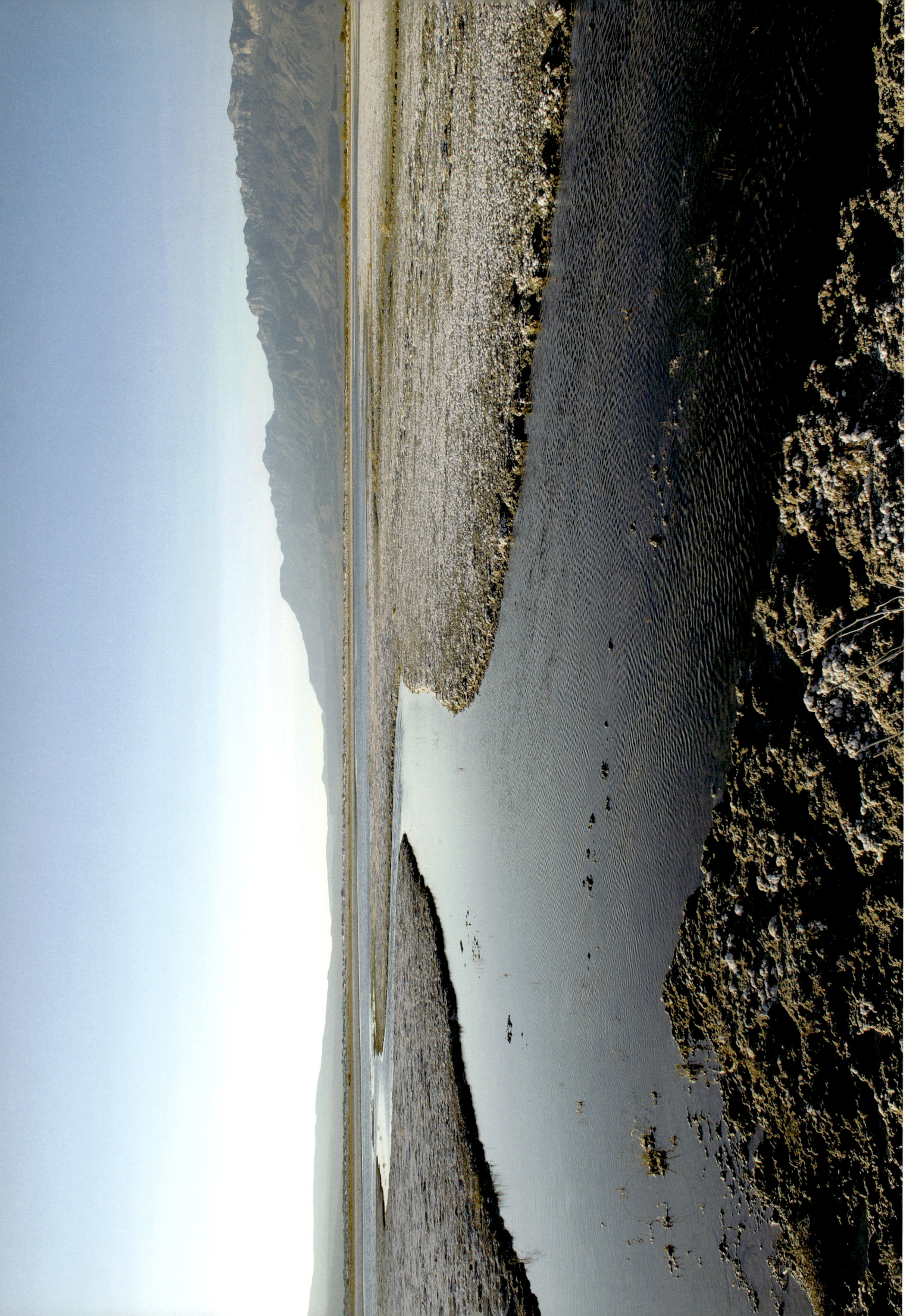

Laguna El Churince. With recently rain falls, it now contains water, after being dry for a couple of years

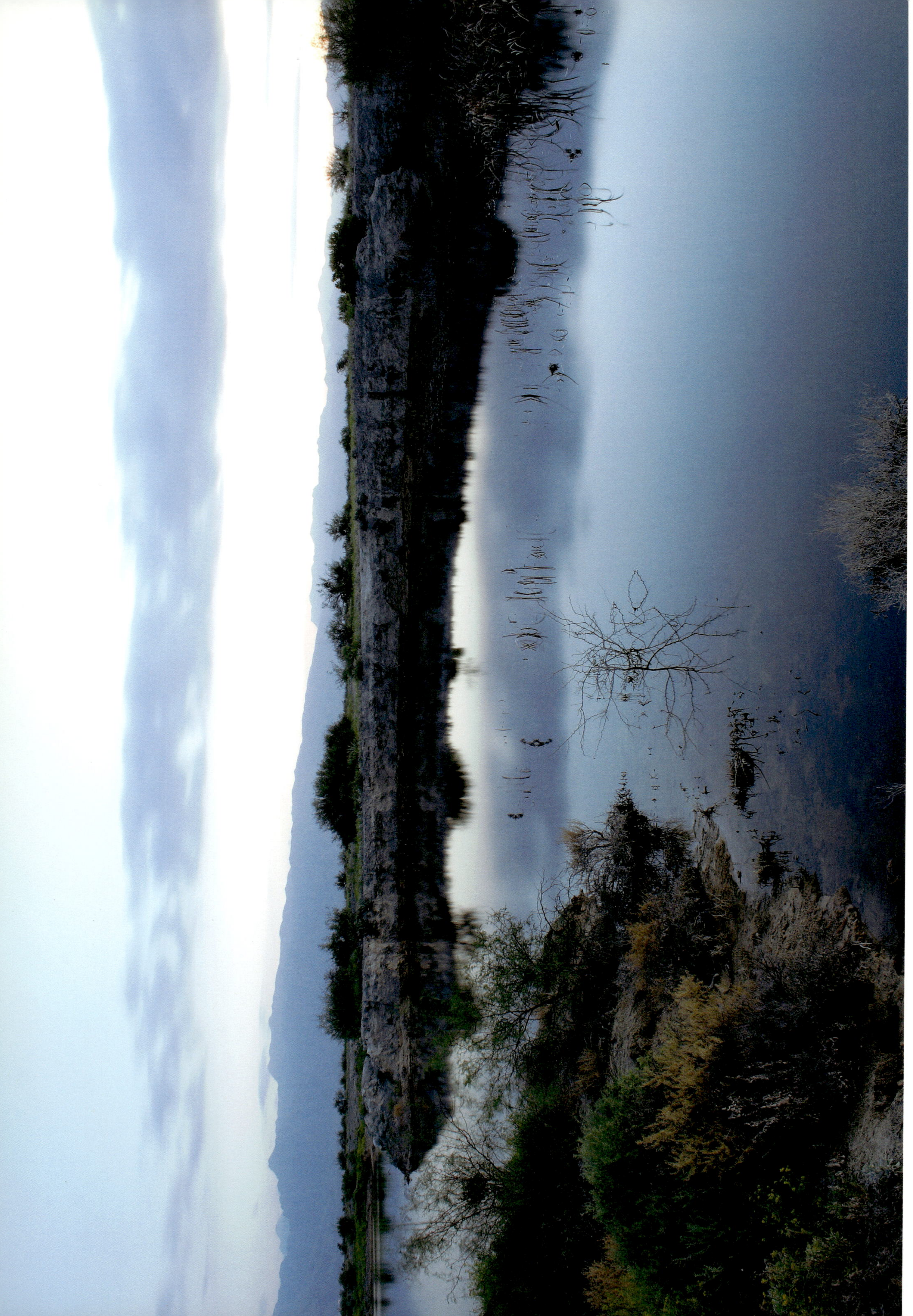

Poza Los Hundidos

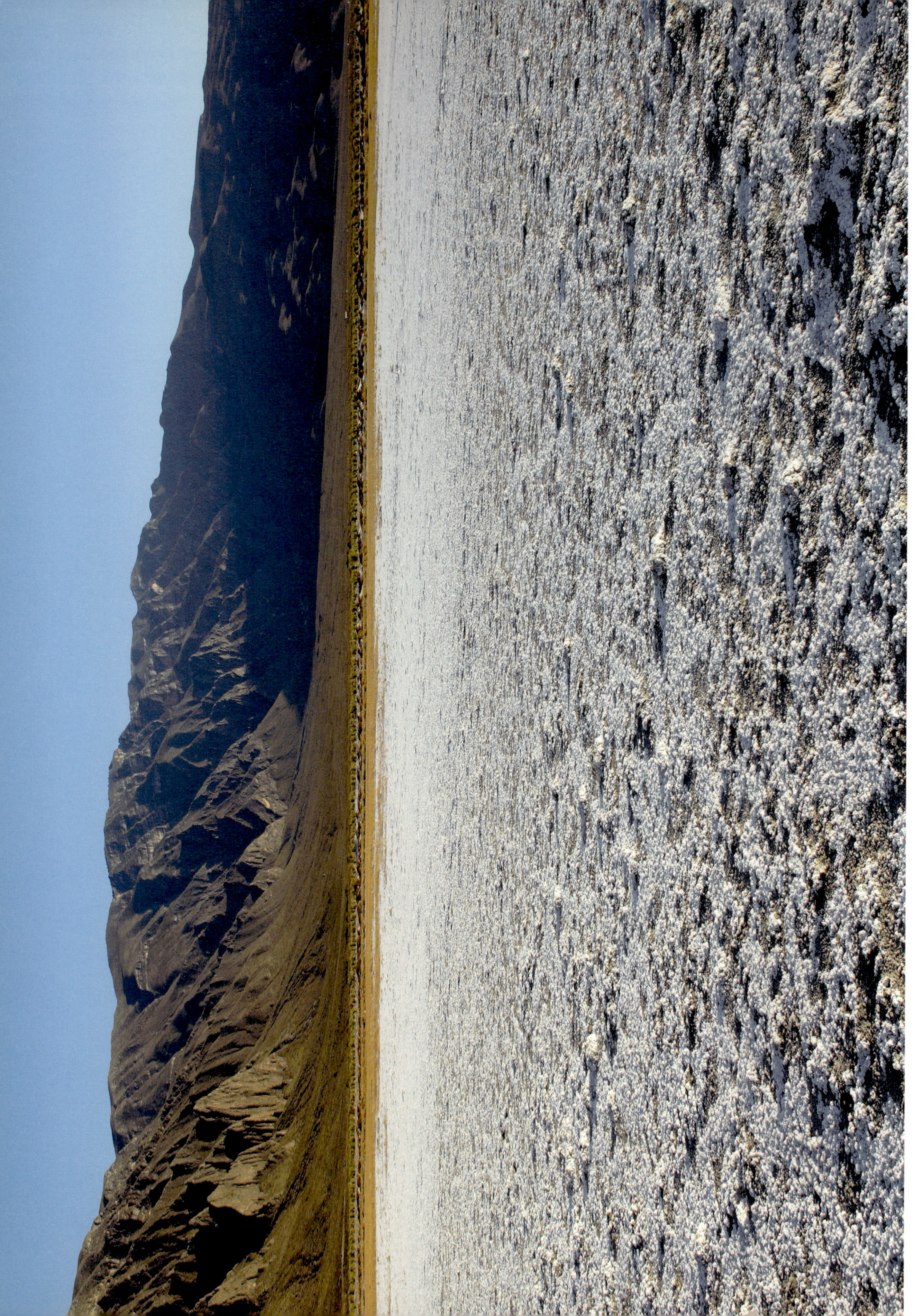

Laguna Churince. A lake formed from the outflow of water from Poza
Churince. It has been dry for a couple of years
All images © and cortesy the artist

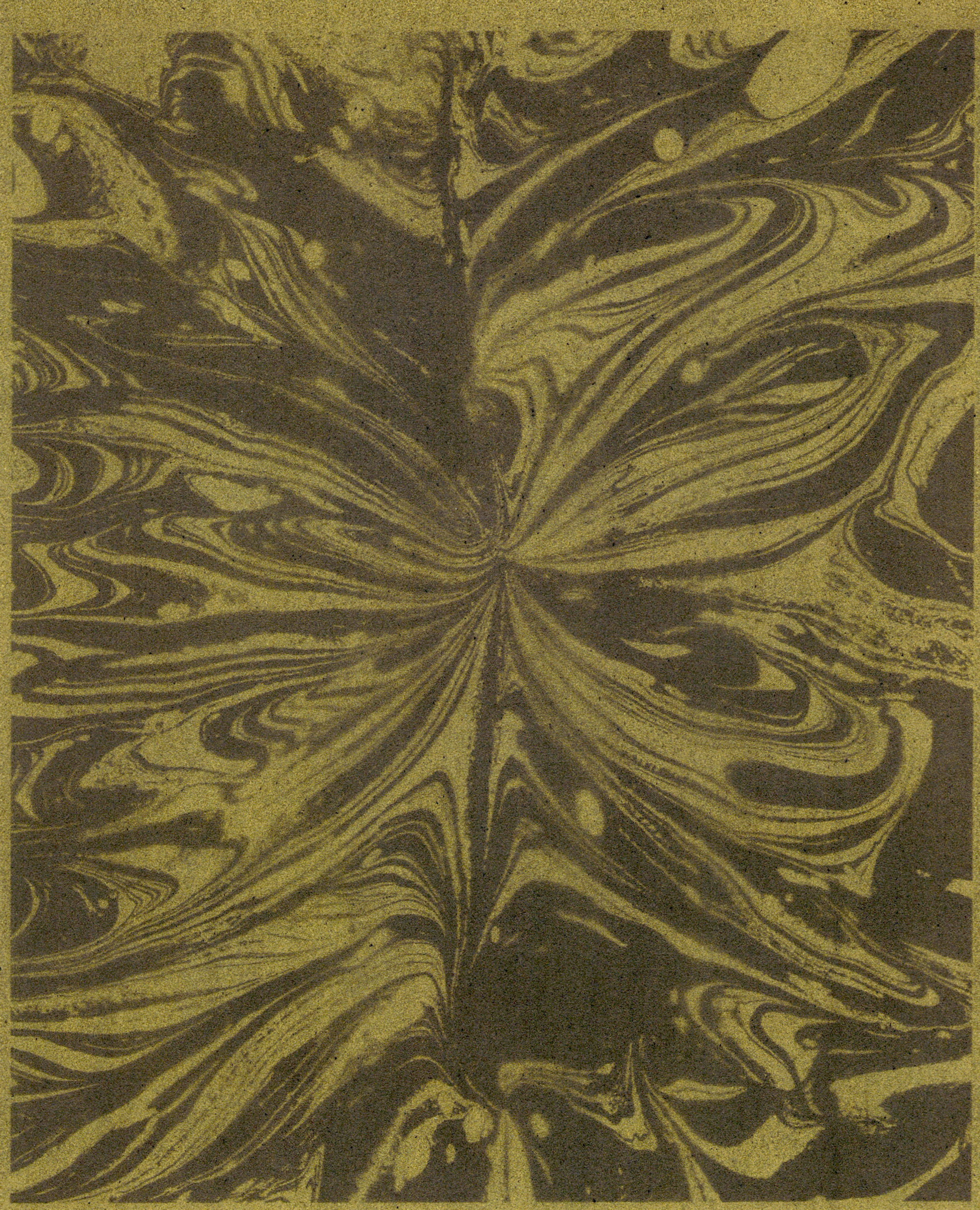

H-3 Anthotype (bleuberry) 2010, cm 23.5 x 19 unique piece

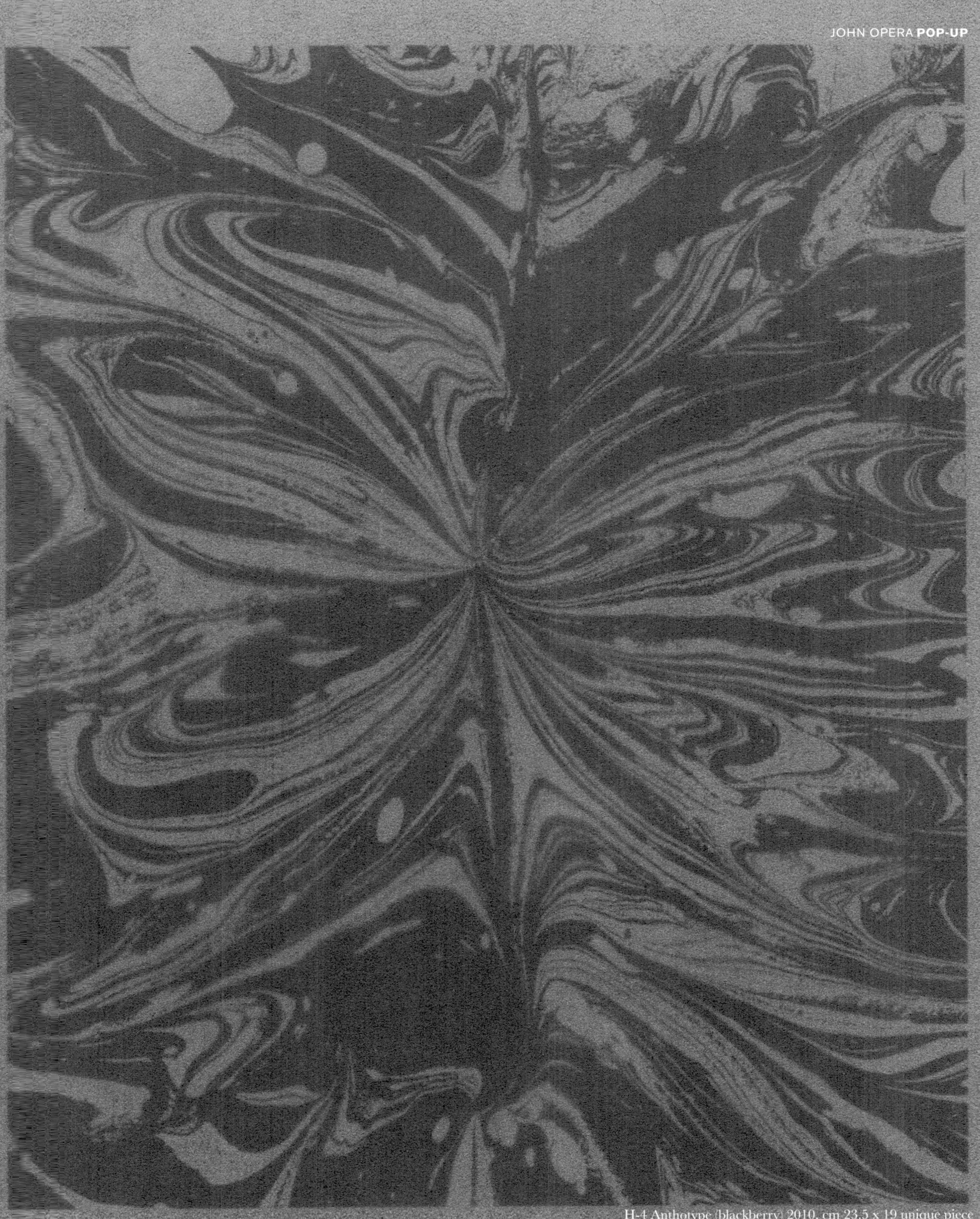

H-4 Anthotype (blackberry) 2010, cm 23.5 x 19 unique piece

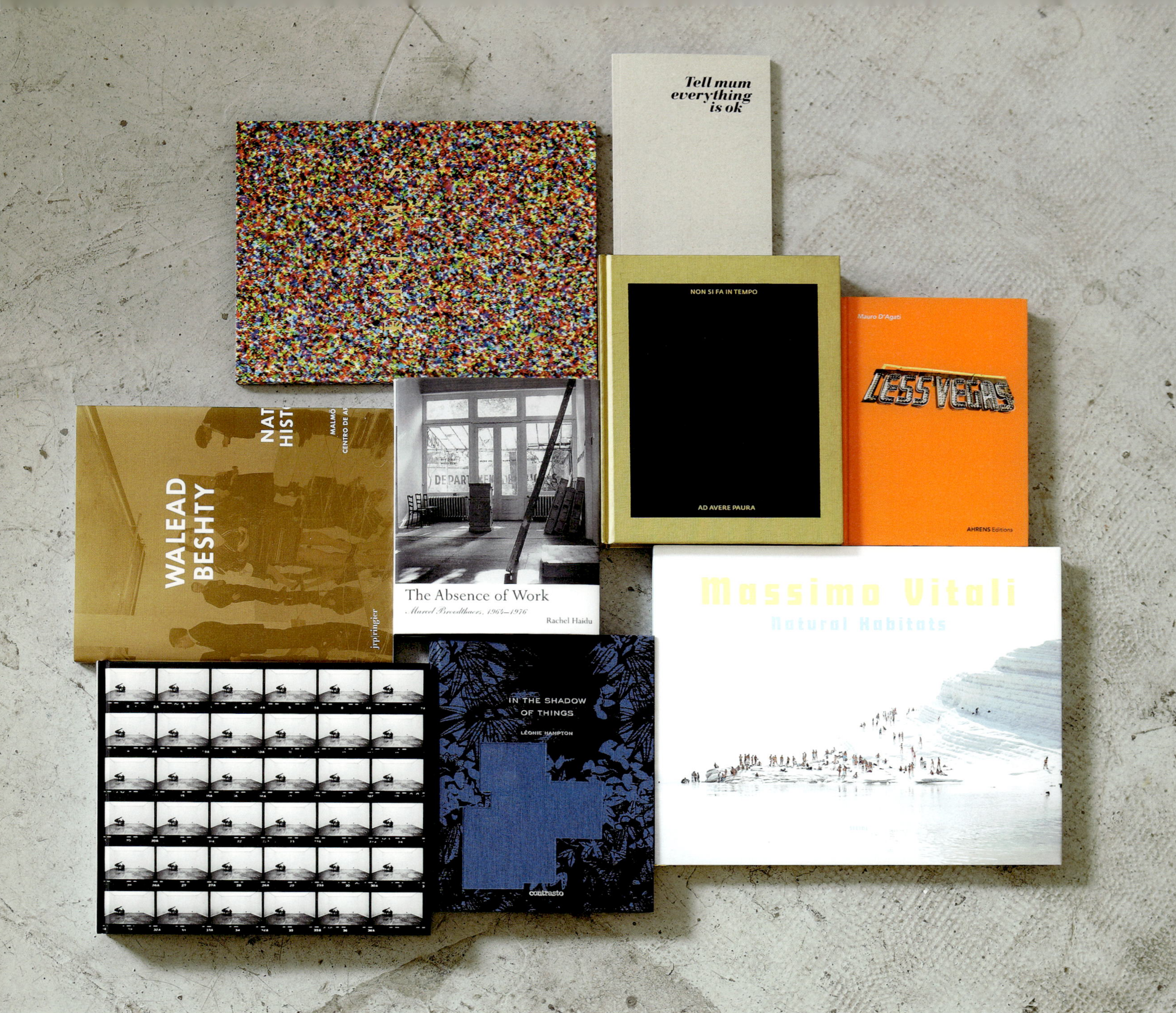

ON OUR SHELVES *From top left:* Paul Graham *Films*, 64 pp., MACK, *mackbooks.co.uk*; *Tell Mum Everything is Ok #4*, 80 pp., Editions FP&CF, *editionsfpcf.com*; Walead Beshty *Natural Histories*, texts by Nicolas Bourriaud, Suzanne Hudson and Bob Nickas, 160 pp., JRP-Ringier, *jrp-ringier.com*; Rachel Haidu *The Absence of Work - Marcel Broodthaers, 1964-1976*, 392 pp., The MIT Press, *mitpress.mit.edu*; Luca Andreoni *Non si fa in tempo ad avere paura*, curated by Francesco Zanot, texts by Francesca Lazzarini, Francesca Mila Nemni, Francesco Zanot, 192 pp., Musumeci Editore, *musumecispa.it*; Mauro D'Agati *Less Vegas, A Vacation Photo Album Of The Fabulous Las Vegas*, 168 pp., Ahrens Editions, *ahrens-editions.com*; Ugo Mulas *Vitalità del negativo* curated by Giuliano Segio, 208 pp., Johan and Levi Editore, *johanandlevi.com*; Léonie Hampton *In The Shadow Of Things*, 184 pp., Contrasto, *contrasto-books.com*; Massimo Vitali *Natural Habitats*, 144 pp., Steidl, *steidlville.com*

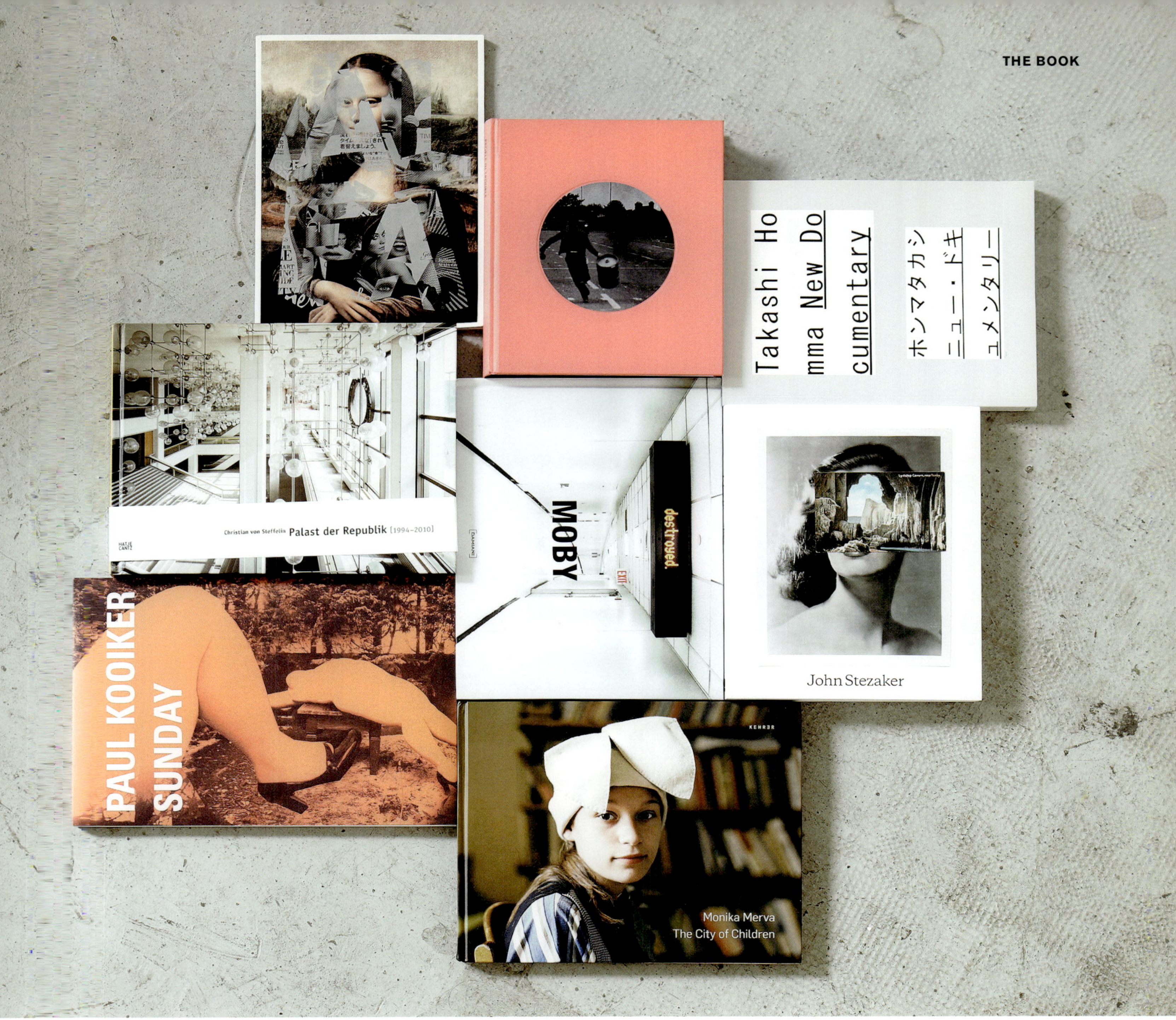

Nazareno Crea *Beauties and Beasties* ALFA Magazine, 67 pp. *artevisuale.it*; Adam Broomberg & Oliver Chanarin *People In Trouble Laughing Pushed To The Ground*, 416 pp., MACK, *mackbooks.co.uk*; *Takashi Homma New Documentary*, 240 pp., The Asahi Shimbun, *kanazawa21.jp*; Christian von Steffelin *Palast der Republik 1994-2010*, texts by Knut Ebeling, Manfred Schmalriede, Christian von Steffelin, 248 pp., Hatje Cantz, *hatjecantz.de*; Moby *Destroyed*, 128 pp., Damiani Editore, *damianieditore.it*; *John Stezaker* text by Dawn Ades, Michael Bracewell, John Stezaker in conversation with Daniel F. Herrmann and Christophe Gallois, 224 pp., Ridinghouse/Whitechapel Gallery, *ridinghouse.co.uk*; Paul Kooiker *Sunday*, 84 pp., van Zoetendaal, *vanzoetendaal.nl*; Monika Merva *The City of Children*, 112 pp., Kehrer, *kehrerverlag.com*

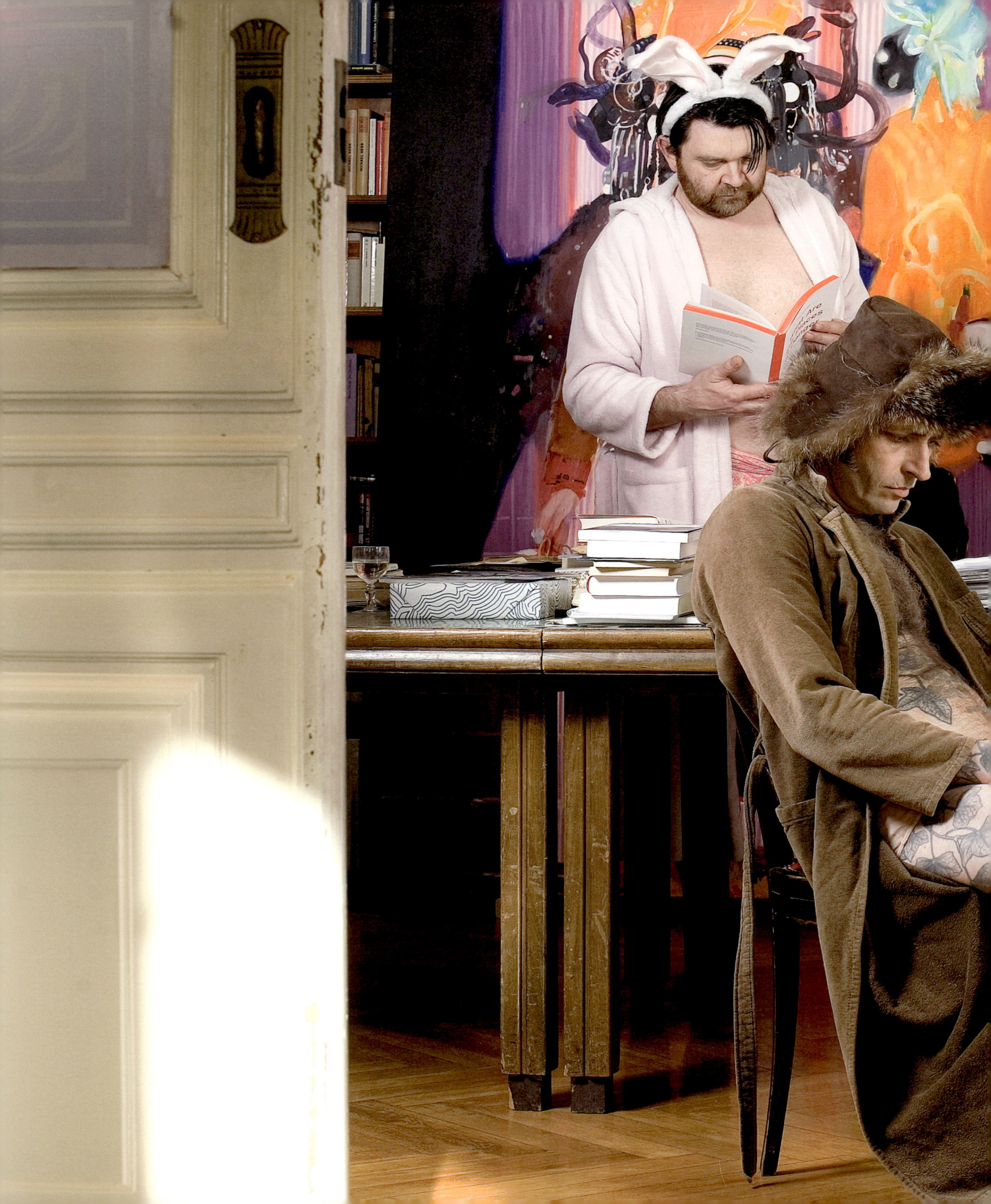

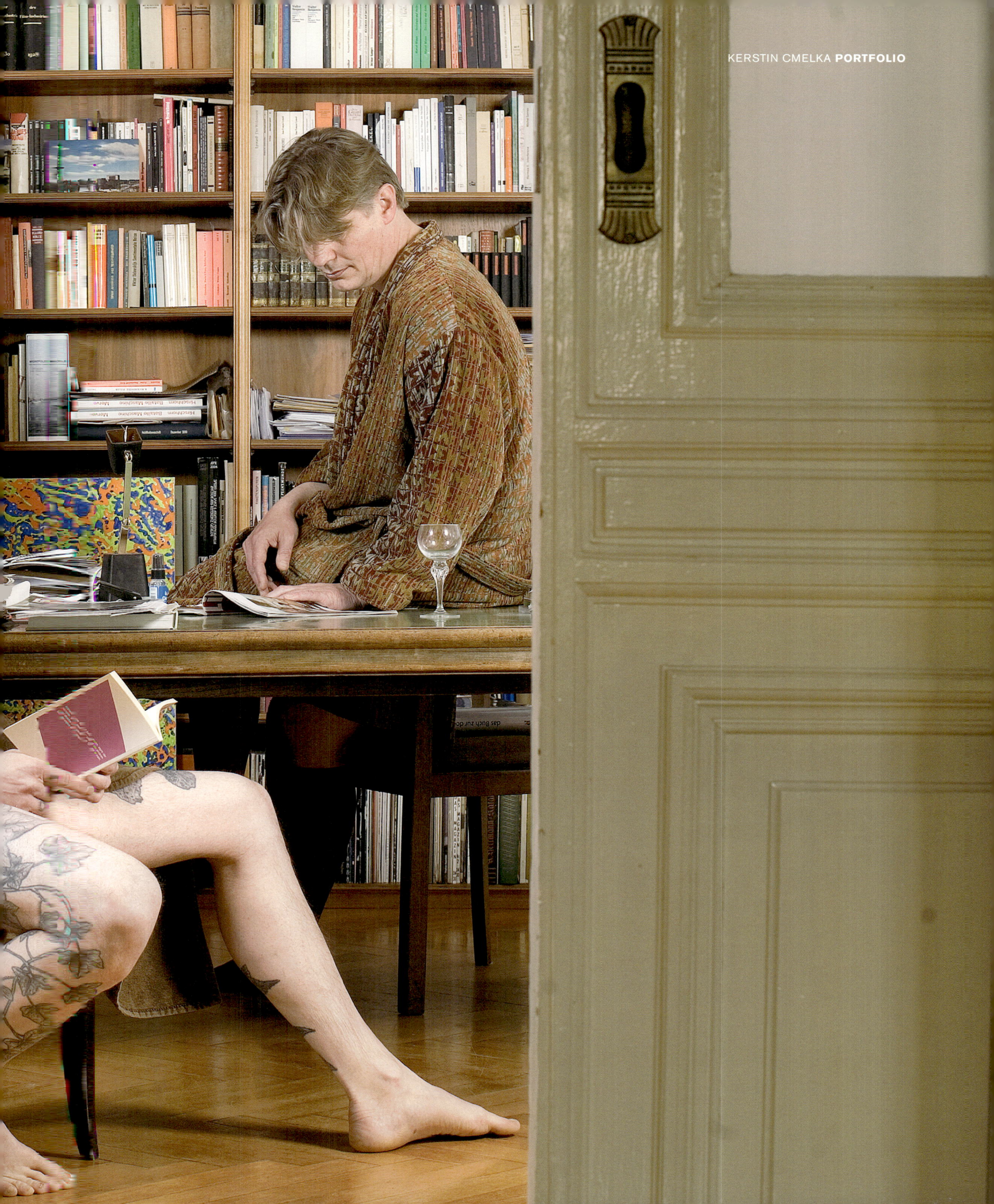
KERSTIN CMELKA PORTFOLIO

KERSTIN CMELKA Male!

"It all started when my friend Martin Hoener gave me Timothy J. Clark's essay *Jackson Pollock's Abstraction* which begins with a series of photographs that Cecil Beaton made for Vogue in 1951 featuring female mannequins, Irene and Sophie, posing in pastel evening dresses in front of Pollock's drip paintings "Number 27", *Number 28*, *Autum Rhythm* and *Lavender Mist.*"

"I often use repetition in my work as a means to find 'new habitations' for subjects, gestures and choreographies that are part of our collective knowledge. I wanted to do a photo series mimicking the format of Beaton's fashion shots with Pollock's art as 'atmospheric background'. So together with Martin I decided to do a male underwear photo shooting with the models posing in front of contemporary paintings."

Underwear models' body types generally do not go in and out of fashion so quickly as the bodies of prêt à porter models. The males often seem to have a facial expression that exists independently from their body as if to suggest: "I have my own opinion and I look sexy" or as in the new metro sexual style: "I am offering myself to you" which has been the role characteristically assigned to females.

"I wanted to do a work about this new masculinity that seems to be independent and fragile at the same time."

As in the earlier works called *Microdramas*, Cmelka cast amateur artists, and designed together with them the costumes (underwear collection), props, and choreography. This collaboration of art professionals enacting dramatic (i.e. fantastic) roles for the production of art, resulted in images that are both portraits and fashion shots.

"The title, *Male!* comes from my love for word plays: it means 'masculine' in English and 'to paint' in German… I don't have a suitable interpretation for 'male' meaning 'bad' in Italian, so I guess this series will have to be about painters being filtered through the market, and also about men and their outer representation as such."

Cmelka and Hoener have developed different versions of this *Fantom* portfolio for two forthcoming Fall shows at West Germany in Berlin and at Eva Winkeler in Cologne.

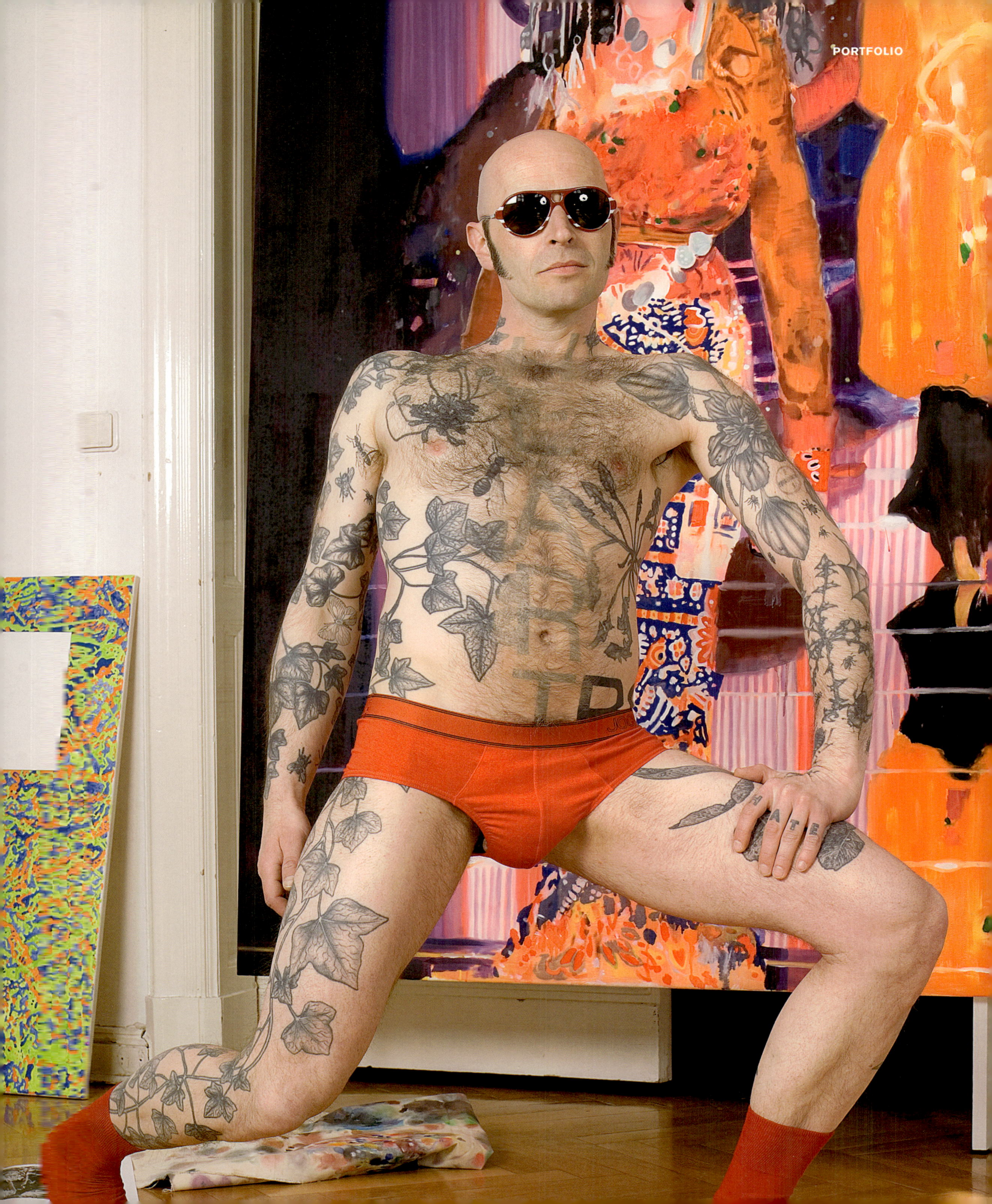

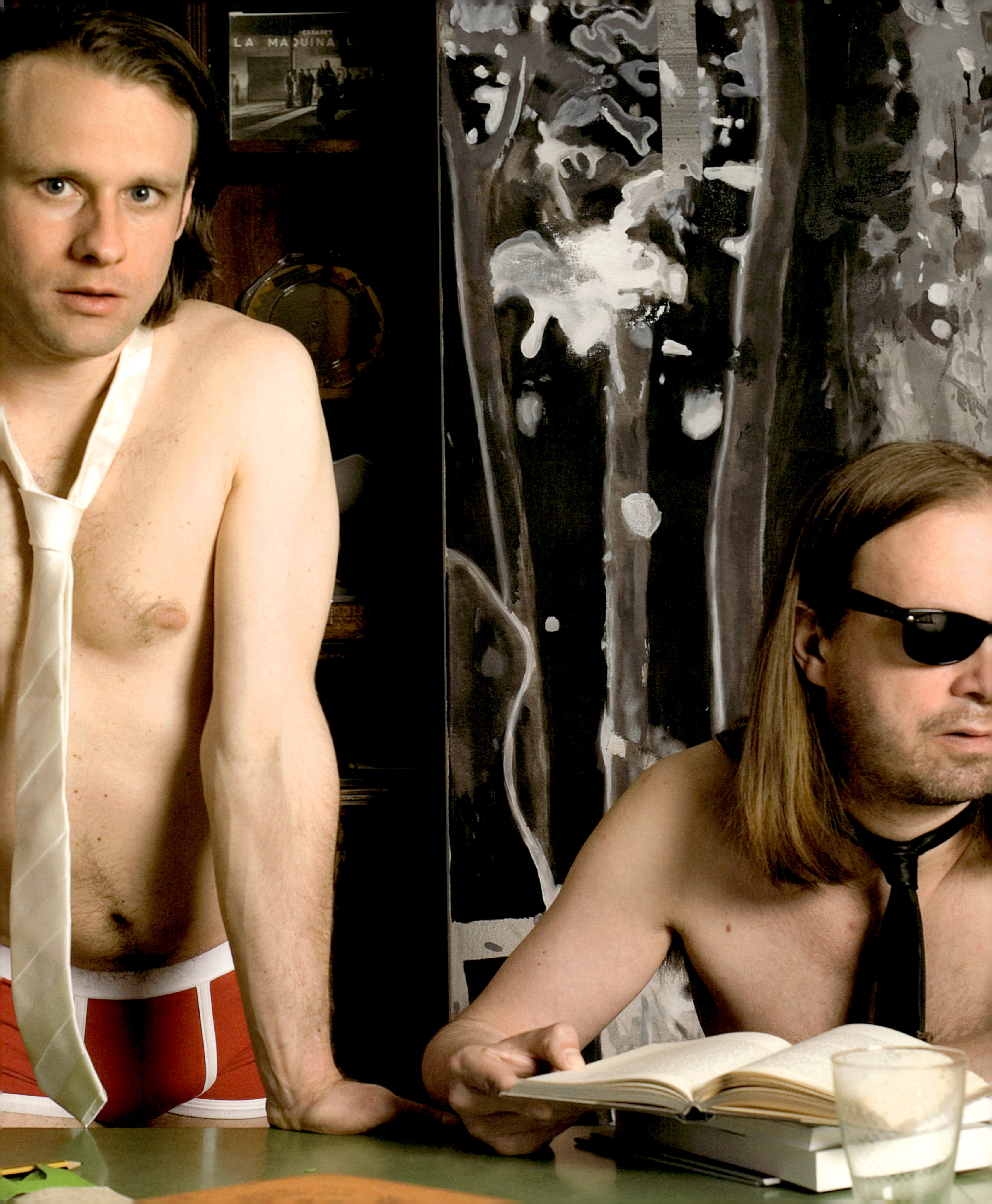

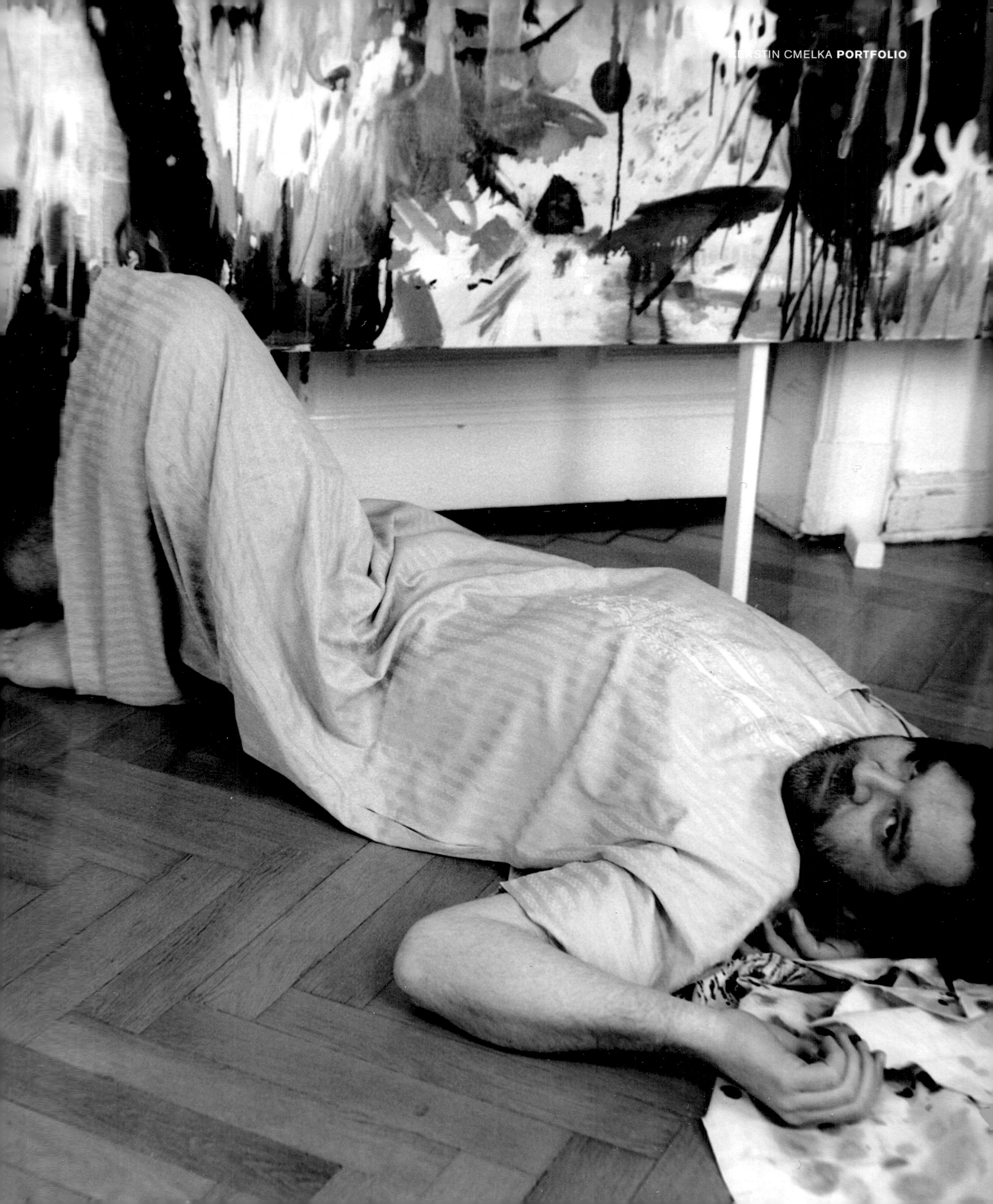

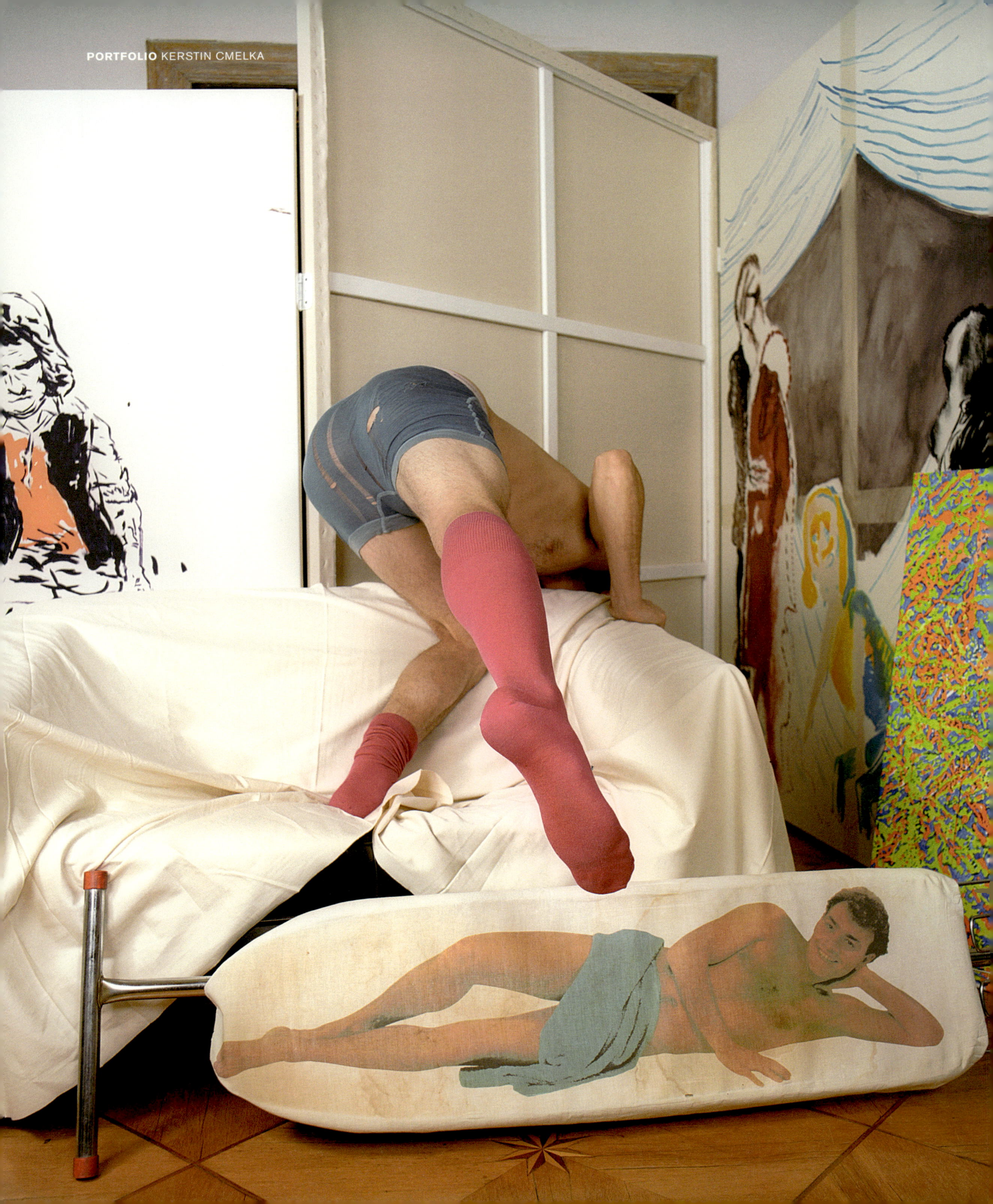

JOHN OPERA is the protagonist of this issue's Pop Up section. Opera's series *Anthotypes* harkens back to the seminal moments of photography's prehistory. During the mid 18th century, it was discovered that pigmented solutions derived from various flower and fruit extracts are light sensitive enough to be used as rudimentary print emulsions. This process takes up to three weeks of exposure in direct sunlight to render an image. Opera uses the Anthotype process to emphasize the dialectic between photography's surface qualities and its qualities as illusionistic and indexical space. These works also make reference to the inherent relationship between liquid chemical reactions inside the natural world and their connected activity that brings a traditional photographic image into being. The *Anthotypes* are object-images that are allegories of the alchemical qualities of photographic image formation and its complex relationship with the physical experience of seeing. Opera is an artist and educator based in Chicago. In 2009, he had a solo exhibition at the Museum of Contemporary Photography, Chicago; a catalog accompanying the exhibition has been published by Aperture. *johnopera.com*

AMY MACKIE is the Director of Visual Arts at the Contemporary Arts Center in New Orleans. She was previously a Curatorial Associate at the New Museum in New York. Mackie was the recipient of a 2009 CEC Artslink Grant to organize a project in Sofia, Bulgaria and completed a fellowship in 2010 at the Henry Moore Institute in Leeds, UK, where she researched the work of Helen Chadwick.

ANDRÉ PRÍNCIPE Porto, Portugal, 1976, works with photography, film and video. He has exhibited solo shows extensively in Portugal and in many international group shows. He published *Tunnels* in 2005 with Booth-Clibborn Editions, and *Master and Everyone, and I Thought You Knew Where All of the Elephants Lie Down* with his own Pierre von Kleist Editions in 2010. *Smell of Tiger precedes Tiger* will be published in 2011. He co-directed *Traces of a Diary* with Marco Martins, a 16mm film shot in Japan. Currently he's working on *Before the Ghost House* and *Flamingo Field Without Flamingos*, a road movie to be shot in Portugal. He lives in Lisbon. *pierrevonkleist.com*

BENJAMIN GODSILL is a curator based in New York. Projects he has orchestrated have taken place in locations as bizarre and beautiful as Tbilisi, Republic of Georgia and Città della Pieve, Italy, as well as at the New Museum in New York. He plays well with others.

CAROLINA FUENTES Saltillo, Mexico, 1977, studied graphic design and photography. She works as a freelance photographer and opened her own studio in 2007, focusing on advertising, industrial and portrait photography. Her artistic projects are primarily centered on land and cityscape imagery, a result of her love for travel. She has participated in solo and group exhibitions internationally, and was selected to attend the Lens Culture FotoFest Paris 2010. *carolinafuentesphoto.com*

DEVIKA DAULET-SINGH is the director of Photoink, a New Delhi-based photo agency, publisher and gallery. She was the associate curator of the Indian photography presented at Les Rencontres d'Arles 2007. In 2009, she co-curated *The Self and The Other - Portraiture in Contemporary Indian Photography* at the Palau de la Virreina and Artium in Spain. *photoink.net*

EMMA REEVES a freelance creative consultant working in a broad field from curation to photographic commissioning for brands. Former photographic director at London-based *Dazed & Confused*, *Another Magazine* and *Another Man*, she currently lives in New York and is on the board of the Swiss Institute.

FRANCESCA TAROCCO is a scholar and critic based between Shanghai and London. She received her M.A. and Ph.D. from SOAS, University of London. Her research focuses on pivotal moments in the history of modern Chinese culture, ranging from the cultural practices of early 20th century Shanghai, to the emergence of globalization and new media over the past decade. She contributes to many international journals and magazines and is the author of *The Cultural Practices of Modern Chinese Buddhism: Attuning the Dharma*, Routledge, 2007; *Karaoke: the Global Phenomenon*, Reaktion Books and Chicago University Press, 2007; and *New Chinese Writers*, Mondadori, 2008.

GERRY BADGER is a photographer, architect, and photography critic born in Northampton, England, in 1946. Among his books are *The Genius of Photography*, 2007; *The Pleasures of Good Photographs*, Aperture, 2010, winner of the ICP Infinity Writer's Award, 2011. He published *The Photobook: A History*, 2 vols., 2004 and 2006, with Martin Parr, which won the Kraszna Krausz Prize in 2007.

KATIA FIORENTINO was born in Ischia and moved to London in 1994 to study art direction and costuming. She lives and works in London as an illustrator and costume designer.

WALTER GUADAGNINI was born in Italy in 1961. He currently lives and works in Bologna where, since 1992, has held a professorship in History of Contemporary Art at the Academy of Fine Arts. He has curated numerous international exhibitions, including *Pop Art! 1956 – 1968* at the Scuderie del Quirinale in Rome, and was Commissaire Unique for the Italian section of Paris Photo in 2007. Between 1995 and 2005, he was head of the Galleria Civica in Modena. Since 2004 he is the Chair of the Scientific Committee of the UniCredit & Art Project, and the head of photography section of *Il Giornale dell'Arte*.

SHELLEY FOX AARONS is a board certified psychiatrist who maintained a private practice in NYC for many years, before retiring to spend more time looking at, reading about, and collecting contemporary art, primarily the work of living artists. With her husband, Philip E. Aarons, she has provided support for many not for profit arts institutions, exhibitions, and artist publications. She is a trustee of The New Museum in NYC.

TIM MILLS Born 1981 in Swindon, UK, is an independent photographic facilitator and lecturer who works as an associate with Fotonow, a community interest company that develops lens based practice and research in the southwest of England. *fotonow.org*

COLOPHON

EDITORS
Cay Sophie Rabinowitz, Selva Barni
editorial@fantomeditions.com

ASSOCIATE EDITOR
Francesco Zanot
francesco@fantomeditions.com

CONTRIBUTING EDITOR
Emma Reeves
emma@fantomeditions.com

ART DIRECTOR
Giorgio Di Salvo
giorgiodisalvo.com

EDITORIAL OFFICE
Didier Falzone
didier@fantomeditions.com

EDITORIAL ASSISTANT
Arianne Di Nardo
arianne@fantomeditions.com

EDITORIAL INTERN (NEW YORK)
Carmen Rosenberg Miller

EDITOR-AT-LARGE
Massimo Torrigiani

TRANSLATIONS
Judith Mundell

DESIGN ASSISTANT
Daniel Sansavini

THANKS TO
Agnese Bossi, Christian Rattemeyer, Davies Costacurta, Luca Cipelletti,
Luca Martinazzoli, Martina Scapinello, Mary Skinner, Massimo Mezzavilla,
Pasquale Marini, Pino Pipoli, Roberto Rossi Gandolfi, Skype, Sofia Sizzi and
Iacopo Falai, Stefano Pitigliani.

WWW.FANTOMEDITIONS.COM

FANTOM OFFICE MILANO
Via Lanzone 22, 20123 Milano, Italy

FANTOM OFFICE NEW YORK
137 Grand Street, 10013 New York, NY, USA

ADVERTISING ENQUIRIES
info@fantomeditions.com

SUBSCRIPTIONS
Bruil & van de Staaij
PO Box 75, 7940 AB Meppel, The Netherlands
T +31 522 261303 - F +31 522 257827
www.bruil.info

DISTRIBUTION
Italia and International: S.I.E.S. S.r.l.
Via Bettola 18, 20092 Cinisello Balsamo (MI), Italy
T +39 02 66030400 - F +39 02 66030269
sies@siesnet.it - www.siesnet.it

North America: D.A.P./Distributed Art Publishers
155 Sixth Avenue, 2nd Floor, 10013 New York, NY, USA
T +1 212 627 1999 – F +1 212 627 9484
www.artbook.com

PUBLISHED BY
Boiler Corporation Srl
Piazza Castello 19, 20121 Milano, Italy
Numero di Iscrizione al R.O.C. 19.061 del 12/10/2009

PUBLISHERS
Ivan Maria Vele, Massimo Torrigiani, Susanna Cucco

PROJECT MANAGER
Pier Mario Simula
p.simula@boilercorporation.com

ASSISTANT
Simone Castelli
s.castelli@boilercorporation.com

Printed in Italy by Grafiche Antiga, Via delle Industrie 1
31035 Crocetta del Montello (TV), Italy
www.graficheantiga.it

Periodico registrato presso il Tribunale di Milano
N° 436 del 07/10/2009
Direttore Responsabile: Selva Barni

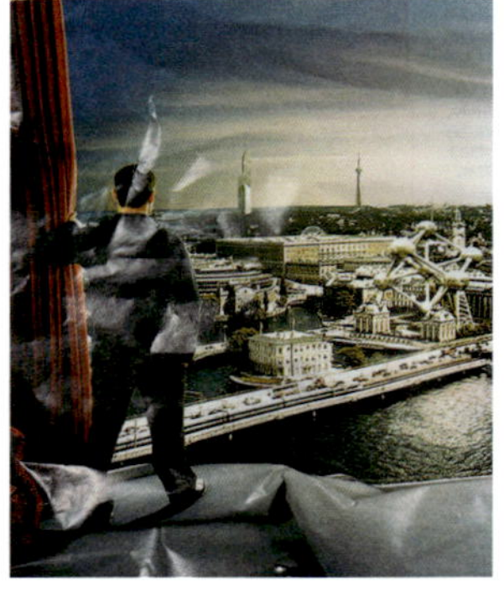

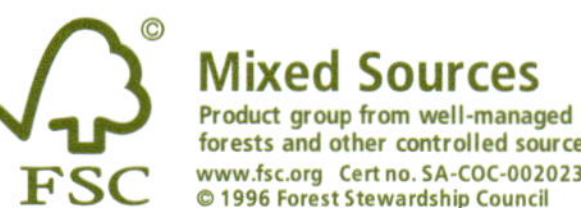

Fantom cover artist Liu Gang will be featured in our next issue, out in
Autumn 2011. On this cover: Paper Dream N.06, 2008, C-print.
Image © the artist, courtesy C-Space, Beijing

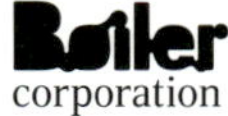

FANTOM

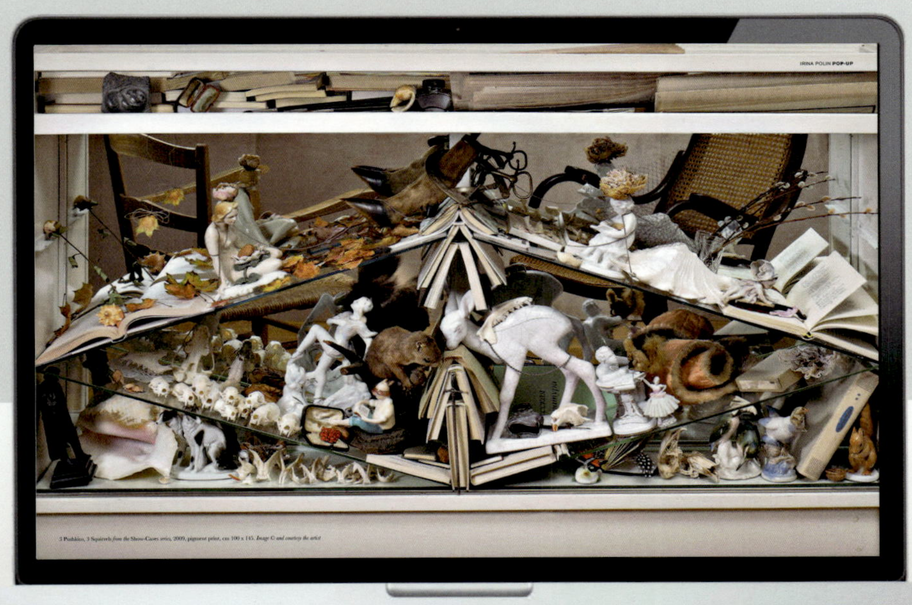

NOW ANYTIME,
ANYWHERE.

Other Edition.com

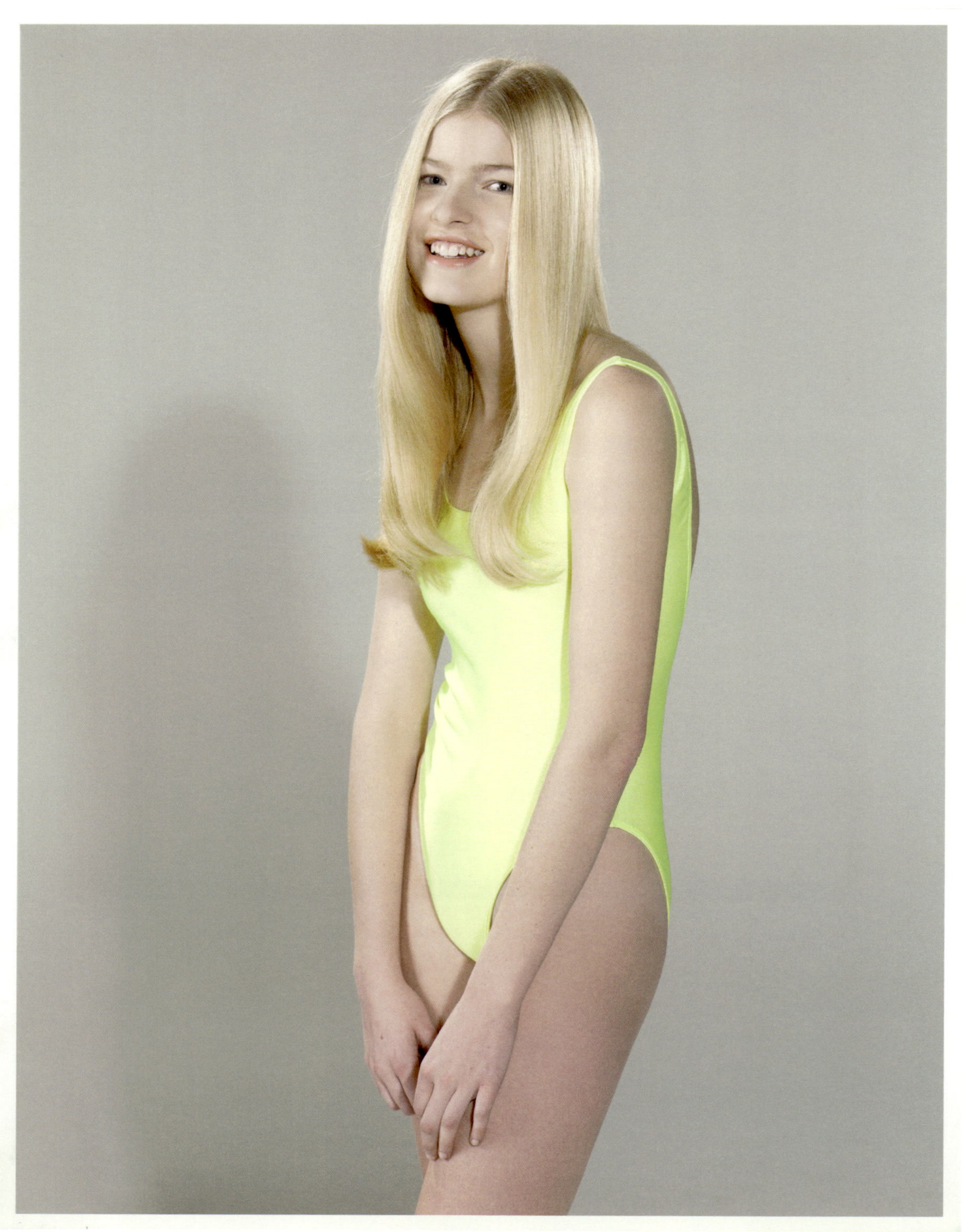

Roe Ethridge Le Luxe

Published by MACK mackbooks.co.uk

Art | 42 | Basel | 15–19 | 6 | 11

Vernissage | giugno 14, 2011 | unicamente su invito
Art Basel Conversations | dal 15 al 19 giugno 2011 | dalle ore 10 alle 11
Ordinazione del catalogo | Tel. +49 711 4405204, Fax +49 711 4405220, www.hatjecantz.de

Follow us on Facebook and Twitter | www.facebook.com/artbasel | www.twitter.com/artbasel

The International Art Show – La Mostra Internazionale d'Arte
Art 42 Basel, MCH Fiera Svizzera (Basilea) SA, CH-4005 Basel
Tel. +41 58 206 26 86, info@artbasel.com, www.artbasel.com

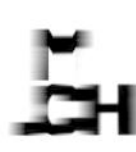

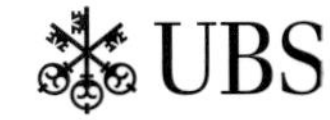

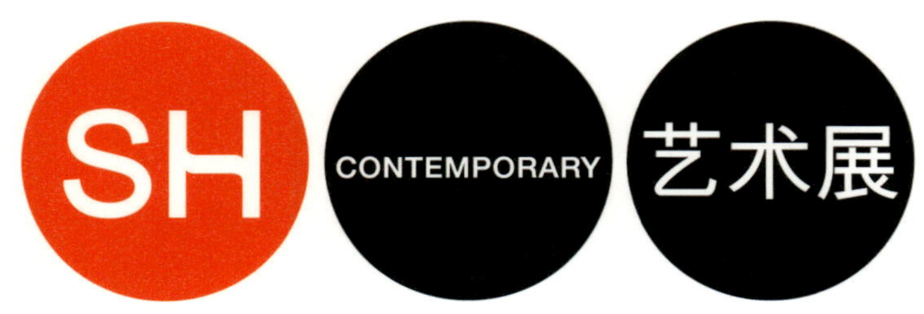

SH CONTEMPORARY 艺术展
THE ASIA PACIFIC
CONTEMPORARY ART FAIR
SHANGHAI, CHINA
上海艺术博览会 国际当代艺术展
2011.09.08-10
SHANGHAI EXHIBITION CENTER
上海展览中心
www.shcontemporary.info
ALL THAT IS NEW IN SHANGHAI
Organizers:
主办方：
上海国际文化传播协会

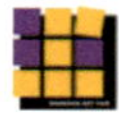

BolognaFiere GROUP
BF INTERNATIONAL FAIRS S.R.L.

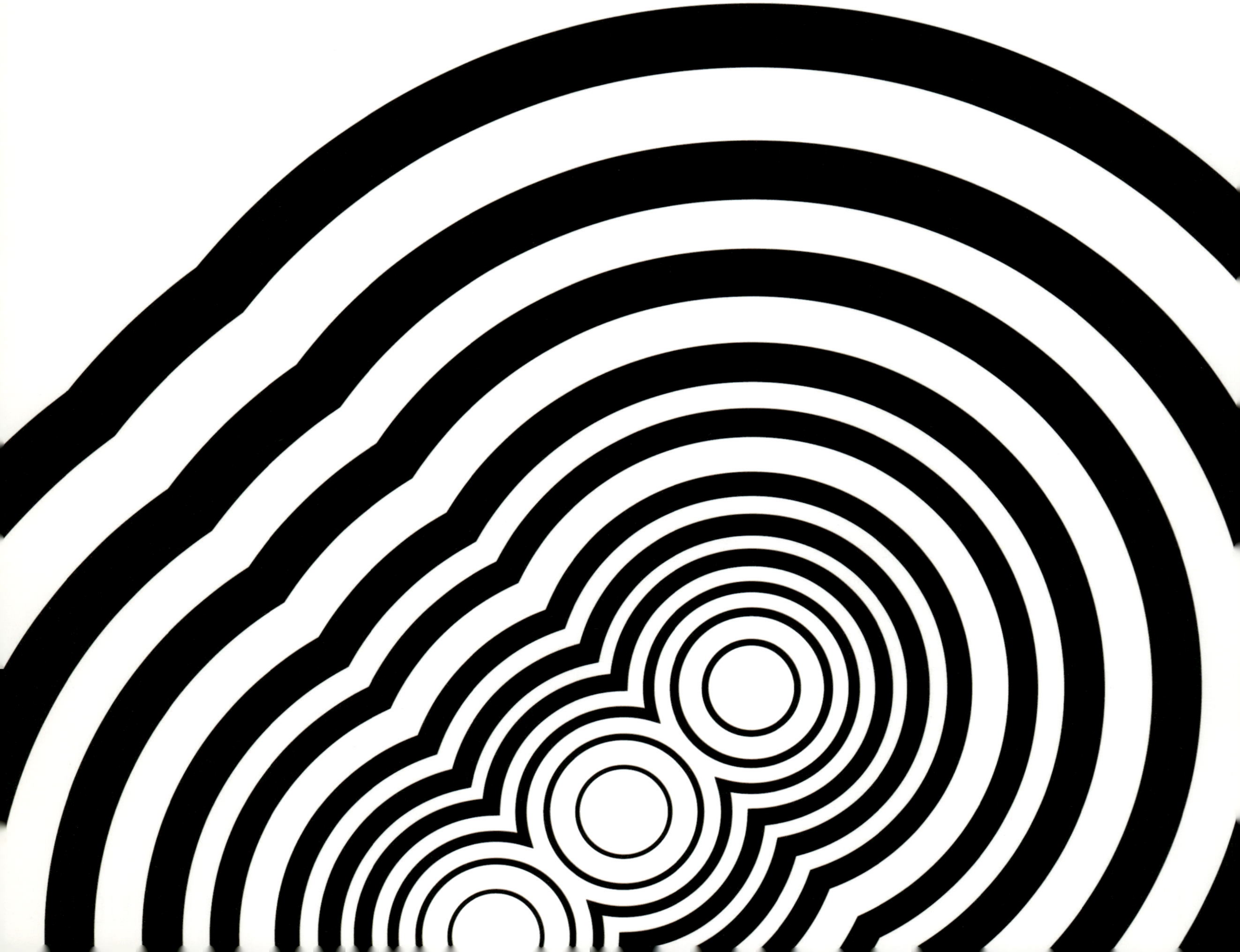

Printed Matter, Inc. presents

THE NY ART BOOK FAIR 2011

30 SEPTEMBER – 2 OCTOBER

AT MoMA PS1

PREVIEW 29 SEPTEMBER

WWW.NYARTBOOKFAIR.COM

Art | Basel | Miami Beach

1–4 | Dec | 11

Vernissage | November 30, 2011 | by invitation only
Catalog order | Tel. +1 212 627 1999, www.artbook.com

Follow us on Facebook and Twitter | www.facebook.com/artbaselmiamibeach | www.twitter.com/abmb

The International Art Show – La Exposición Internacional de Arte
Art Basel Miami Beach, MCH Swiss Exhibition (Basel) Ltd., CH-4005 Basel
Fax +41 58 206 31 32, miamibeach@artbasel.com, www.artbasel.com

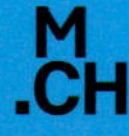

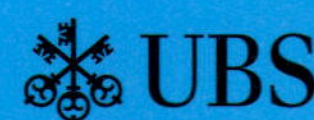

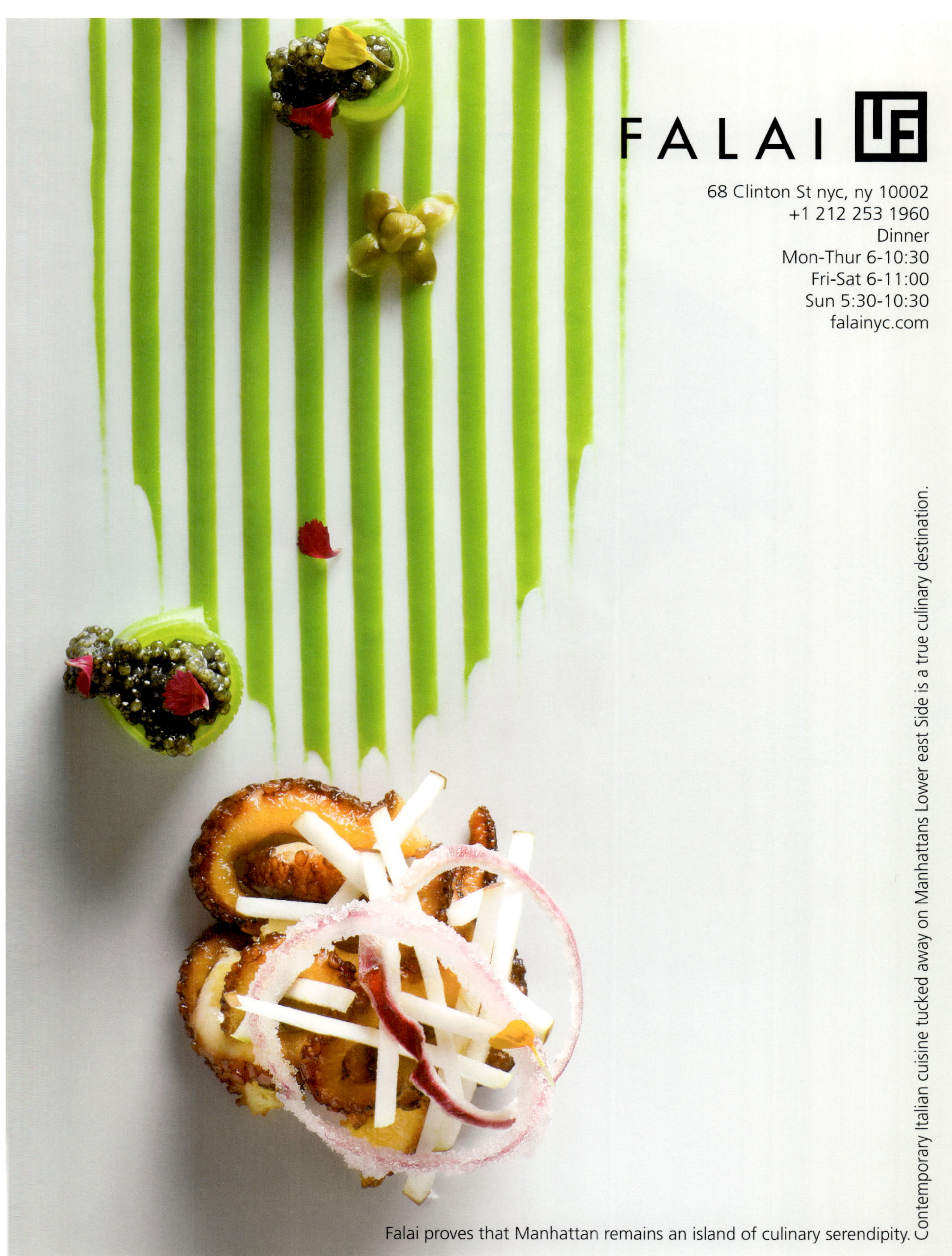

FALAI

68 Clinton St nyc, ny 10002
+1 212 253 1960
Dinner
Mon-Thur 6-10:30
Fri-Sat 6-11:00
Sun 5:30-10:30
falainyc.com

Contemporary Italian cuisine tucked away on Manhattans Lower east Side is a true culinary destination.

Falai proves that Manhattan remains an island of culinary serendipity.

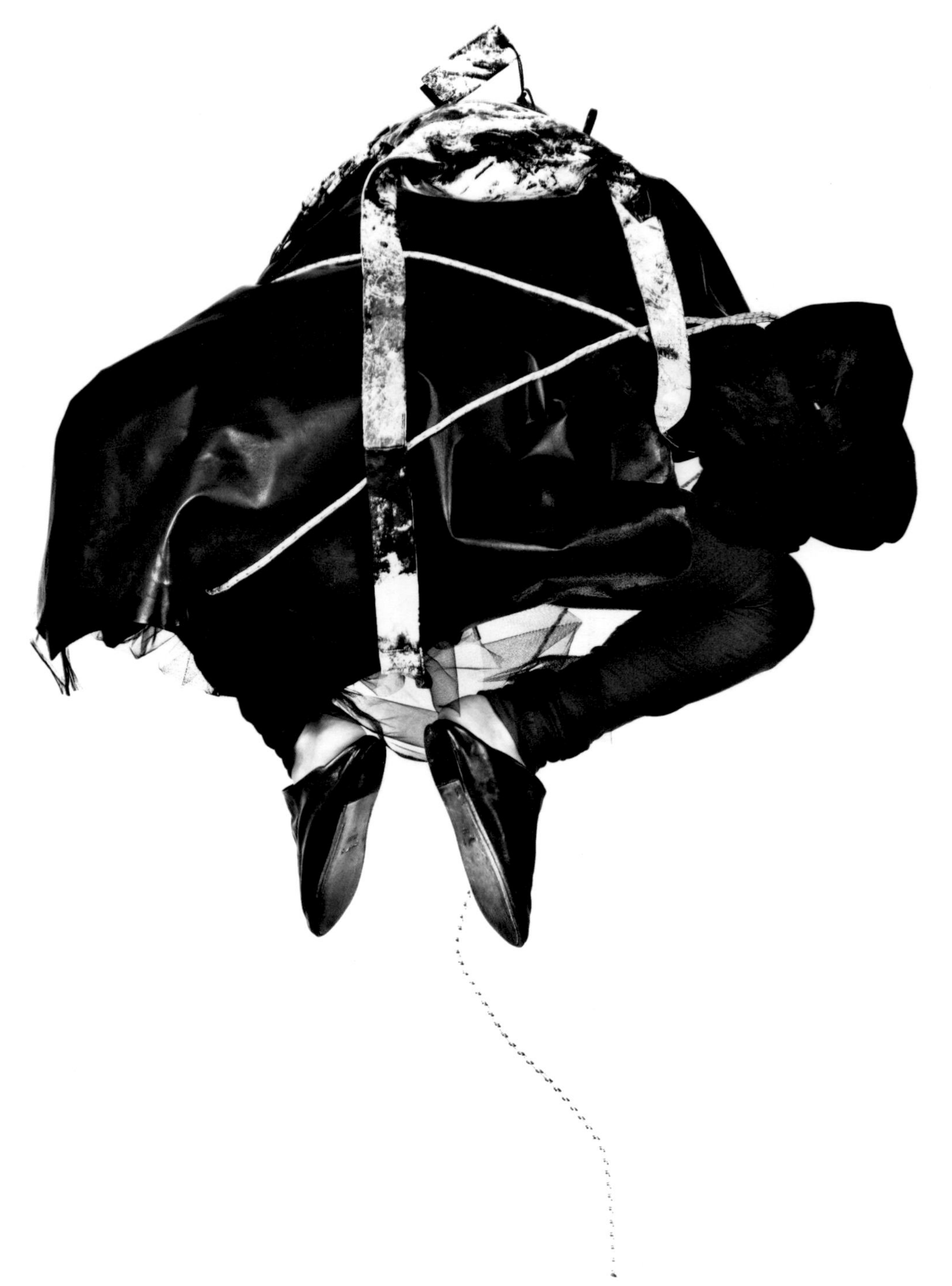